Popular Culture and the Intellectual
Media Trends and Social Change

Edited by

William P. Huddy and Andrea Marshall

WH
WATERHILL
PUBLISHING

ISBN 978-1-7753096-1-1

Contents

ii

List of Contributors

Colin Ackerman is a PhD candidate in Media Studies at the University of Colorado, Boulder. He is a former kindergarten teacher who explores the ways in which the use of digital media and technology transforms the nature of teaching and learning.

Camila Cornutti Barbosa earned a PhD in Communication and Information (UFRGS, 2015) focusing on the study of cyberculture, celebrities and humor. She did a Post-Doctorate at UNISINOS (2015) and a doctoral internship at New University of Lisbon, Portugal - FCSH/NOVA (2014/1). She presently is the coordinator of Photography and Advertisement for undergraduate programs at Centro Universitário da Serra Gaúcha – FSG.

Leocadia Diaz Romero is a tenured Professor in Political Communication and Public Opinion at the University of Murcia. Her research interests are Campaigns and Elections, Political Marketing, Political Movements, Media and Democracy, European Union (Political Integration, EU Democracy, EU Elections), International Relations, and Comparative Politics.

Ian Dixon completed his PhD on John Cassavetes at The University of Melbourne in 2011 and works as Assoc. Professor at Nanyang Technological University, Singapore. Ian delivers academic addresses internationally including a plenary speech for CEA in USA and a keynote for Scopus in India. Recently, he won the best paper award through CMCS conference at University of Southern California. He also acts, writes and directs for film and television.

Jenny Hauser is a PhD candidate at the Dublin Institute of Technology researching network journalism among elite news media. She is also a news editor with ten years experience in digital journalism and social media newsgathering. Currently, she works at the European Broadcasting Union in Geneva and previously worked for the social media news agency Storyful in Dublin.

William P. Huddy (Ph.D., University of Denver) is a Lecturer in the Department of Communication Arts and Sciences at Metropolitan State University of Denver. After a 20-year career in television news, his turn to academic interests include Celebrity and Media Studies, Political Communication, and Communication Activism/Social Justice.

Aleksandra Krstić is the Assistant Professor of TV journalism at the Faculty of Political Sciences, University of Belgrade. Her research interests are in television and journalism studies, media ethics, mediatization of politics, EU-media relations, media democratization and visual communication.

Susan Liesenberg is a journalist with a Master in Communication and Information (UFRGS, 2012), focusing on social networks and new technologies. She is presently finishing her Doctorate on Communication and Consumers Practices at ESPM, São Paulo. Ms. Liesenberg is dedicated to studying celebrity-making on the Internet and the processes of communication energization (linked to buzz and affection agency of web media consumption).

Andrea R. Marshall is a PhD candidate at Drexel University's College of Computing and Informatics. She is a digital anthropologist who applies critical pedagogic approaches to STEM learning and studies feminist sociotechnical identity formation within digital geek cultures and modern maker cultures. Her fields of interest include accessibility within design thinking and gendered learning practices in STEM education.

Kerry McElroy is a cultural historian of women, film, and performance, currently completing her doctoral thesis on women in Hollywood as classed subjects at Concordia University, Montreal. She is also a freelance writer and author of the Independent magazine series "Bette, Marilyn, and #MeToo: What Studio-Era Actresses Can Teach Us About Economics and Resistance Post-Weinstein." She holds master's degrees from Columbia and Carnegie Mellon Universities.

Walter Metz is a Professor in the Department of Cinema and Photography at Southern Illinois University, where he teaches film and television studies. He is the author of three books: *Engaging Film Criticism* (2004), *Bewitched* (2007), and *Gilligan's Island* (2012). His film criticism website can be found at: http://waltermetz.com.

Belinda Middleweek is a Senior Lecturer at the University of Technology Sydney, Australia. Her research focuses on gender and journalism as well as mediations and technologies of intimacy. She is the co-author of *Real Sex Films: The New Intimacy and Risk in Cinema* (2017).

Bernardo Palau Cabrera is a Chilean filmmaker and creative producer with a MA in Media, Television and Cross-media Culture from the University of Amsterdam. He directed a feature film called "Salvarte" ("Saving you"), along with several short films and web-series for different brands. In recent years he has specialized in online video and branded content.

MJ Robinson is an Assistant Professor of convergent journalism and media studies and the Bernard H. Stern Professor of Humor at Brooklyn College/CUNY. She is the author of *Television on Demand: Curatorial Culture and the Transformation of Television* (2017). Her current research examines the historical role and effectiveness of televised political satire on political culture and debate.

Janne Salminen is a doctoral student at the University of Helsinki. He is currently writing his dissertation on the gender narratives of serialized blockbuster films. While most of his research revolves around gender, his other interests include diversity, popular culture, queer narratives, US politics, technology, and fandom.

John Tulloch is Professor Emeritus in Media at Charles Sturt University, Australia and Adjunct Professor in Communication at Newcastle University, Australia. He has a BA in History from Cambridge University, England, an interdisciplinary Masters in the Sociology of Art and Literature and PhD in the Sociology of Theatre at Sussex University, England. His recent books are *Risk and Hypeconnectivity: Media and Memories of Neoliberalism* (2017) and *Real Sex Films: The New Intimacy and Risk in Cinema* (2017).

Introduction

William P. Huddy and Andrea Marshall

The tensions and oppositions – real or imagined – between 'high-art' and 'popular art' have been described and analyzed by scholars, intellectuals, and critics for years. Of course, cinema and television productions have not escaped this scrutiny, and more recently, new media as well.

In this edited volume, authors discuss the ever-changing contours of this often-binary debate about the value of mass-market media productions. They also delve into the radical transformations, both in the media industry and in society, that popular culture, critics, industry practitioners, and scholars both study and enable.

Should popular culture be seen in opposition or in complementarity to the progress of a more informed and engaged citizen? Is popular culture intellectual and pedagogical, or pure entertainment? What is its value to society? What is the role of journalists, critics, industry practitioners, and scholars in these endeavors? How has popular culture – manifested in cinema, television, and online – evolved in recent years with a rapidly changing society and technological environment? By asking these questions, the authors of this volume, who are themselves involved in popular culture – as scholars, journalists, critics, etc. – are positioned both as investigators and objects of their investigation.

The book charts a warped course to explore the fluid tensions and pressures, collisions even, between what is popular (hence mere entertainment to keep the masses attention away from key sociopolitical issues) and what is intellectual (and therefore, perhaps, useful to social progress) in television, films, and new media.

The authors of this volume provide both answers and pose new questions, investigating filmmaking, television, journalism and new media through the evolution of their work and the examination of never-ending societal changes.

The book first chapters investigate the current state of filmmaking which continues to reflect the strange contradictions present within the reality of modernity, whilst applying conventional narrational tropes to construct imaginaria that disrupt societal protocols as well as support them. The authors of these chapters apply interdisciplinary approaches to questions of audience participation, film criticism, Hollywood conventionality, iconoclastic characters, gendered critiques, societal change, and most importantly the opportunities for activism at all levels of filmmaking, film critiques, and film studies. These scholars ask crucial questions about how film can function as a reflexive medium, sentimental propaganda, one extended view of an artist's vision, and finally, a catalyst for sociopolitical change.

Walter Metz's paper *Northrop Frye in Reel Time: Reinventing American Film Criticism* proposes that popular media discussions of films, subject to the whims of the film industry, and academic film criticism, constrained by the disciplinary conventions of Film Studies, have between them an analytical schism. Metz's critical deconstruction of films demonstrates how bridging this gap through the generation of a new type of analysis might find common ground within such discrete domains. To create symbiotic interactions between those who make films and those who write about film and formulate new ways of understanding reflexive perspectives therein, it is crucial for discussions of filmmakers and critics within scholarly and popular domains to occupy the same analytical terrain.

Camila Cornutti Barbosa and Susan Liesenberg seek to extrapolate the messy and multiple narrative contexts that emerge within modern Brazilian film in their paper *Refuse, resist: 'Aquarius' and the cinema of resistance in Brazil*. Filmmaking as critique and commentary are two core themes explored by the authors as they investigate the blurred lines between contemporary Brazil and its cinematic representation in the movie "Aquarius." The authors examine the uproar created by the film's release during the zenith of the political coup d'état in Brazil at the time, and desire to understand how filmmakers, critics, and audiences can converge as "agents articulated with activism." In this instance, the act of viewing the film continues the narrative as a declaration of social activism; depictions of gender, media, economics, politics, and culture exist in a simulacrum that reflects both the civil unrest within Brazil during the film's release and how the film itself contributed to the uproar, refusing and resisting to be silent.

Ian Dixon's *Twisting Fate in Rosemary's Baby: Cassavetes/Polanski Interface as Hollywood Influence* uses John Cassavetes' film "Rosemary's Baby" to demonstrate how his oeuvre defies classification solely as a herald of independent cinematic tropes that include improvisation and cinema verité. Dixon's analysis uses Braudy's open/closed axiom to highlight the conflict Cassavetes had with Roman Polanski and how, throughout his career, Cassavetes subverted the Hollywood system to create cinematic masterpieces that explored the human condition. Dixon illustrates the opportunity for celebrity and film scholars to apply Cassavetes' revolutionary approach to narratives as an activist strategy to create new conversations and support dynamic critical perspectives.

Kerry McElroy's *The Actress as Activist: Subversion of a Century of Hollywood Misogyny in Five Modes* inquires how social justice activism in film studies can function as a gendered critique of Hollywood as a patriarchal-capitalist apparatus. McElroy employs the methodological approach of social justice historiography to present women's and actresses' authentic experiences within the Hollywood misogynist machine through their own voices. McElroy reveals how women's writings on the gendered discrimination of Hollywood can function as social justice texts, and indeed, how dismantling misconceptions of gendered exploitations within Hollywood is scholarly activism.

Janne Salminen's *Another Day of Sun: The Conservative Gender Politics of Damien Chazelle's Whiplash and La La Land* investigates how heteronormative gender politics within two of Damien Chazelle's films promotes androcentric ideals of white masculinity. Salminen's gendered analyses identify idealized protagonists that are dedicated to the traditional artistic notion of genius as male as well as the narrative journeys of heteronormative white men as characters who are social successes. Salminen's critique situates these ideological constraints to reveal an insistence on rigid and asymmetrical gender roles within these two movies, as well as an emphasis on the white straight male as Everyman trope that is both troubling and reductive. Bridging the gap between heteronormative patriarchal practices and alternative masculinities that are possible within scholarly conversations about modern cinema, Salminen uses feminist approaches to cinematic critique as a frame within which to better understand the conservative sentimentality present within Chazelle's work.

Next, the book moves into the realm of television and new media. The rapid and transformational way we obtain and generate news and other information has had profound sociopolitical impacts. Indeed, the democratization of information dissemination, the rise of reality television, and the shifting boundaries between news and spectacle have created questions about the credibility of information and the value of intellectuals. As a consequence of the transformed citizen participation and media landscape, the prominent role of politicians, scholars, and journalists has been altered.

In that respect, the first chapter of that series by Leocadia Diaz Romero explores the "intertwining of politics and entertainment" in an examination of the *Implications of Political Entertainment Today*. Diaz Romero asks the question: does political entertainment on television enhance or hinder citizens' political involvement and engagement? Moreover, regarding the issue of public trust, she questions whether this new genre is a reliable source of political information. These questions are central, according to many scholars, to the efficacy of working democracies.

Collin Ackerman then critically examines the television series *Teen Mom (MTV)* in his paper *Learning from Young Mothers and Dr. Drew: MTV's Teen Mom as Public Pedagogy*. Ackerman investigates whether the show's cast members could be considered intellectuals, and to what degree the show meets the requirements of public pedagogy. The author points out the "dichotomy between traditional and organic intellectuals" and provides an interesting point-of-view on the impact of popular culture on society.

John Tulloch and Belinda Middleweek examine the role of celebrities and public intellectuals in television coverage. Their paper *Talking of Terror: British Television Intellectuals and Bridging the Gap between Celebrity and Intellectual Culture* brings forth a contrasting public discourse and analysis emanating from the British television series Atheism, the documentary series "I Survived," and television news reports produced by British and Dutch journalists. Contained in their research, Tulloch and Middleweek illuminate "institutional constraints" imposed on the media when reporting on terrorist attacks. Their research also relies on the real-world narrative of Professor Tulloch, a survivor of the horrific 7 July 2005 terrorist attacks in London which killed 52 people and injured more than 700.

Aleksandra Krstić brings attention to the role of academics in society and their relationship with television journalists in Serbia. *Expert Crisis or Journalistic Laziness: Bridging the Gaps between Academics and TV Journalists in Serbia* examines key aspects of the gap between academics and journalists, with each group having expectations and perceptions of the other that differ. Furthermore, Krstić points out that academics who 'go public' are criticized by their peers for "betraying their discipline." Yet, many academics think of reaching out to the population through media as their civic duty, but they fail to understand mainstream media requirements. On the other hand, television journalists also do not understand academics. Krstić's research, however, identifies a commonality between academics and journalists: both desire contributions based on knowledge.

The next chapter by MJ Robinson, *Curatorial Culture's Challenge to the Television Critic as Public Intellectual* continues on the topic of television and the rapidly changing media landscape. MJ Robinson's paper suggests this change includes a new power for consumers of information – one highlighting the consumer/critic as "driver" of this media vehicle in a new landscape highway referred to as a "curatorial culture." Robinson contends this new landscape has created a "media environment in which academics, public scholars and intellectuals can create and distribute television programming that makes important and crucial interventions in our polis." The author argues that accomplished television critics wedded to traditional forms of media have suffered a "loss of gravitas, authority and audience" due to a "demassified and vastly fragmented audience" caused in large part by this new curatorial culture. This research portends major changes in traditional media in the years to come.

The final two chapters delve into the impact of technologies. First, Bernardo Palau Cabrera maintains that there is a "new visual language" being offered to all purveyors of film – largely the result of a new aesthetic brought to the public through online video. In *Towards an aesthetic of amateur online video*, Palau claims that this new recording format has brought forth the birth of a new visual language that breaks through the barriers of established video formats. He suggests that online video provides a path to the future of film and television production, "especially considering that the millennial generation, which is the main consumer of this kind of content, will lead the development of television and film in years to come."

Finally, Jenny Hauser critically analyzes the role of the professional journalist in the digital age in her chapter, *Guarding the Gates in Interactive Newsgathering*. Hauser observes that social media have become "an integral part of many journalists' toolkits, offering both opportunities and posing risks for the profession." Hauser says that journalists find themselves in a constant position of "negotiating" their role in an increasingly online world. The paper investigates how journalists maintain "their roles as 'gatekeepers' and professionals" in a news environment that has become "open, de-professionalized and inherently participatory."

As Co-Editors of this volume, we would like to thank Dr. Samita Nandy (Director, Centre for Media and Celebrity Studies), Dr. Andrew Mendelson (Assoc. Dean and Conference Host, Craig Newmark School of Journalism, CUNY), and the WaterHill Publishing team for their input and guidance throughout this project.

Northrop Frye in Reel Time: Reinventing American Film Criticism

Walter Metz

Abstract. Between the invention of cinema in the 1890s and the present, little has changed to bridge the gap between an intelligent writing about film, and the popular publicity apparatus attendant to actual filmmaking. For example, the people making films in Los Angeles' classical Hollywood (1917-1960) did not know or care that Harvard applied psychologist Hugo Munsterberg was inventing film theory on the other coast of the same nation. In this essay, I perform critical readings of films to demonstrate the utility of a middle ground between popular, journalistic writing about movies (sycophantic to the film industry) and academic film criticism (beholden to the discipline of Film Studies). The resultant criticism could help bridge the gap between filmmakers and those who write informedly about films.

Keywords: Academia, Anti-intellectualism, Criticism, Film, Popular Culture

Introduction

Shortly after starting my first academic job as an Assistant Professor of Film Studies at Montana State University in 1998, the editor of the Bozeman arts monthly, *The Tributary* asked me to write a weekly column of film criticism. As I learned to edit my bloated 5,000-word academic essays into terse 750-word reviews, I became convinced that the gulf between popular and academic film criticism was completely unnecessary. Journalists falsely believe they should write short reviews of films to tell people whether they should spend their hard-earned money. For our part, academics believe they need thousands of words to develop methods for theorizing about the cinema.

I have spent the better part of the last two decades attempting to demonstrate that neither of these modes is inevitable, and that imagined institutional boundaries demand to be jumped. Both sectors should require that our criticism find a middle ground, one which both forces journalists to say something new and interesting about the cinema and its relationship to the world, yet also presses academic approaches to be less filled with jargon and obfuscation. When I write a review of a film for my website (http://waltermetz.com), I am producing the same critical interventions as I am in my refereed books and journal articles, removing the footnotes and translating the theoretical methods into more readable prose.

Such an intervention would have a corollary benefit, a bridge between the creative artists in Hollywood who make our audio-visual entertainment and the academics who study it. This divide is not inevitable either, as various filmmaker-theorists can attest. One of the most useful essays on video surveillance I teach was penned by queer Canadian filmmaker John Greyson, whose film, *Urinal* (1989) envisions what he theorizes. Similar examples can be found from Sergei Eisenstein to Wim Wenders.

However, my project today is not to scold Hollywood filmmakers for anti-intellectualism, but instead to focus our gaze on what we as academic critics can do to make our interventions more useful to the filmmaking community more generally. I suggest four interventions: 1) highlighting the fact that a connection between a world of ideas and audio-visual entertainment was already a feature of Weimar Germany, and is fully available to us today; 2) demonstrating that the historical and theoretical methods of academic film criticism are just as useful for analyzing popular, Hollywood genre cinema as they are for international art cinema; 3) conversely making sure North Americans preserve their formerly strong engagement (particularly in the 1960s) with the continuingly vibrant international art cinema tradition; and 4) ensuring that our interventions into audio-visual culture happen in the present, before the culture around us moves on to considering newer objects. In short, I imagine a culture that: cares about ideas, considers what is popular just as carefully as what is more obviously compelling, attends to cinema as a global phenomenon, and is delivered in real time.

Toward an Intellectual Climate for Effective Criticism

In Christopher Nolan's *The Prestige* (2006), a magician seeks out the mystery of a rival's teleportation trick at visionary scientist Nikola Tesla's laboratory. The scientist (David Bowie) demonstrates his electrical device, intended to make objects disappear. As Angier the magician (Hugh Jackman) leaves the grounds, thinking the machine a failure because it has no effect on the top hats and cats Tesla uses as samples, he stumbles upon a huge pile of such hats swarming with cats out in the woods, indicating that the machine, in fact, creates clones of the original objects. In short, the device mechanically reproduces both inanimate and living matter. The film thus exemplifies the central obsession of one of the most important acts of criticism of the 20th century, Walter Benjamin's "The Work of Art in the Age of Mechanical Reproduction" (1936).

Virtually ubiquitous in academic cultural theory, Benjamin's essay argues that traditional artworks lose their 'aura' when they can be so easily reproduced, not by human hands, but instead by machines such as still photographic and cinematic cameras. Benjamin studies the late 19th century, the moment when the era of the stage magician gave way to the filmmaker. Like Benjamin, Nolan's film equivocates about the implications of this development. On the one hand, the loss of traditional magic at the hands of ever increasingly scientific gadgetry on the stage leads to horrific death and destruction. The resultant magic trick, "The New Transported Man" requires a clone to be murdered each time the act is performed. On the other hand, *The Prestige* is an exquisite example of technological wizardry, using the full array of techniques of 21st century filmmaking (lighting, sound reproduction, computer effects, and the like) to tell its story.

Benjamin celebrated the democratization of mechanically reproduced art in the guise of Charlie Chaplin comedies while at the same time expressing his outrage at Nazi Germany's use of mass art to aestheticize politics. For Benjamin, the Nuremberg rallies wherein masses of people were reduced to geometric arrays relate directly to the cinema's construction of passive spectators overwhelmed by easily reproducible images. *The Prestige* provides a startling opportunity to pose Benjamin's questions again. Does mechanically reproduced art render us more human because it is democratically available to all, or does it strip away our humanity in denying us access to the unique accomplishments of the artisan's hands?

The Prestige is caught in the crosshairs of Benjamin's essay, a populist film that laments the death of magic, and yet a masterful achievement of mechanical reproduction, a film whose aura-less top hats and cats would have fascinated the German critic. Our 21st century North American civilization, baffled by the contradiction between the benefits and horrors of technological modernity, is in desperate need of both popular art such as *The Prestige* and the thoughtful criticism that Benjamin provided in Weimar Germany, writing for popular German newspapers, such as the *Frankfurter Zeitung*.

If one reads today's popular journalistic reviews of Nolan's film, there is no trace of such engagement. We need a re-invented film criticism, imbued with historical and theoretical ideas, housed in comprehensible prose. It is time we start training journalists to write with greater theoretical and critical rigor, and academics to write with comprehensibility as a central goal. If we accomplish both tasks, it will become clear that they are one and the same.

Amber Ways of Gain, or Why Popular Cinema?

In his excellent film production textbook, *Film Production Theory*, film scholar Jean-Pierre Geuens laments a Hollywood film industry in which many creative artists work so hard on films that they care about nothing beyond their small craft contributions, such that they will never even bother to watch the final version of their work in its entirety in a movie theater. Using the Frankfurt School, and the Marxism that underlies it, Geuens posits that this is a classic case of the alienation of labor common to modernity. My intervention is to create a criticism that demands thoughtful and provocative analysis of films in current release that slip through the cracks of academic analysis, to demonstrate to such craftspeople the overall utility of their work.

Consider the case of the James Franco freak-out comedy, *Why Him?* (2016), a standard Christmas season Hollywood film released to poor reviews and consequently relatively weak performance at the box office (the $50 million budgeted project produced $100 million in receipts). In *Anatomy of Criticism*, literary critic Northrop Frye argues that the conflict between civilization and nature lies at the center of the Shakespearean comedy. Youngsters must enter what Frye calls the "green world" to work out various disconnects from civilization before returning to take over political power from their elders.

For example, in *A Midsummer Night's Dream* (1596), youngsters enter the forest and engage with magical fairies to sort out their gender and sexual identity before returning to marriage in Athens at the end of the play. Shakespeare's play has served as the source for many films, ranging from Peter Brooks' 1968 production, influenced by the flower power movement of the late 1960s, through to Woody Allen's *A Midsummer Night's Sex Comedy* (1982), which grapples with the onset of modernity.

Frye's concept of the green world illuminates director John Hamburg's *Why Him?*, a seemingly formulaic Hollywood romantic comedy in ways that suggest the film is far more interesting than it at first seems. The film concerns the love affair of Stanford undergraduate Stephanie (Zoey Deutsch) and Silicon Valley billionaire, Laird Mayhew (James Franco), much to the consternation of Stephanie's father, Grand Rapids, Michigan businessman, Ned Fleming (Bryan Cranston).

The film begins with a party celebrating Ned's birthday, but a bittersweet one, as his printing business is slowly being strangled by the dominance of e-commerce. The opening of the film is bathed in the glaring white snow of a northern Midwest winter. As in Shakespeare's plays, the world of adults is entombed in social ice.

When Ned learns of his daughter's romance with the Internet tycoon in mid-December, he and his wife, Barb (Megan Mullaly) hop on a plane to San Jose. Upon landing, the color design of the film changes radically, now bathed in the burnt-out grass of desiccated California. Given Laird's spending excess, let's call these beautiful images the film's celebration of 'amber ways of gain.' However, when the family arrives at Laird's compound, they discover Frye's green world. Flush with capital, Laird has the magical ability to transform lifeless Silicon Valley into a lush world of green grass, and free-range animals.

Like the realm of the fairies in *A Midsummer Night's Dream*, something is not quite right in this green world. Laird's house is filled with absurd James Franco paintings representing animals of all sorts fornicating. The tycoon's company is built upon perversions of nature: video gamers must help gorillas surf.

The climax of the film occurs when Ned confronts Laird as a terrible choice for his daughter, punching the libidinal billionaire in the face. To escape Ned's wrath, Laird uses his parkour training to climb atop his mansion's central sculpture, a moose entombed in a glass case filled with urine. The glass shatters, bathing everyone in the family in yellow urea. Let's call this the return of the repressed of California amber, a transformation that propels the film into its third act, out of the green world and back to the snow.

Stephanie is horrified, banishing her father to his home in Michigan. However, desperate for familial harmony, Laird flies Stephanie to her parents' house in his helicopter. There, amidst the snow-covered streets, he reunites the family. Stephanie declines Laird's marriage proposal and agrees to continue her education; in exchange, Ned accepts his daughter's romantic relationship with his new found 'bromance' partner. The ending highlights the remarkable transformations of the Shakespearean comedy. No longer does the elder generation sit on the sidelines, only to appear at the beginning of Act I and the end of Act V but impinges upon the plot in all three Hollywood scriptwriting acts.

Ned undergoes a parallel transformation to his daughter, enraptured by the magic of Laird' green world, a realm of the future in which high technology transforms basic human function. Laird helps Ned rescue his failing printing company by retrofitting his factory to make smart toilets, the misuse of which earlier in the film being its funniest scene. The film's magical Puck, Laird Mayhew escapes his artificial green world, finding in the snowy Midwest the family he never had. Why him? I think because the film beautifully demonstrates the power of Shakespearean comedy in the contemporary Hollywood romantic comedy. *Why Him?* is a compelling film, far more of interest to our culture than indicated by the say nothing nature of popular criticism, and the complete ignoring of the film in academic circles. In short, we can demonstrate with the power of our criticism that creative artists who toiled on such films not despair because of weak financial returns on investment or negative criticism from populist reviewers. Rather than obsessing on whether films are 'good' or not, successful or not, we can guide the society toward considering what films do sociologically, and why they perform this work, for good or for ill.

Whither International Cinema in the Age of Hollywood Globalization?

Contrastingly, the past fifty years has seen a remarkable decline in North American distribution of, and enthusiasm for, films from around the world, particularly those of the European art cinema. Take, for example, the career of Dutch filmmaker, Paul Verhoeven. He is mostly known for hyper-violent Hollywood films like *Robocop* (1987) and *Starship Troopers* (1997). The Fascist nature of the violence in these films is so graphically drawn that it begins to seem as if the special effects and their subsequent visceral effects in the audience encourage violence rather than critique it. This, of course, cannot be Verhoeven's intention, raised under the Nazi occupation in Holland, and as a Dutch filmmaker, in the 1970s, having made a sparkling film about the Dutch resistance, *Soldier of Orange* (1977).

Recently, Verhoeven has returned to his origins, the international art cinema. In his latest film, *Elle* (2016), Verhoeven does not retreat from the ambiguities of the violence in his big budget American films, but instead doubles down on them. The French-language film stars Isabelle Huppert as Michele, the adult daughter of an unstable father jailed long ago for a crime spree in which he killed dozens of people. As a result, Michele has grown up to become someone cold and indifferent to the suffering of others. When she learns that her son's pregnant girlfriend has gone into labor prematurely, and is in intense pain, she barely responds, instead turning away from her family members to go find a cup of coffee.

In the first sequence of the film, we witness the aftermath of Michele getting raped in her home by a masked burglar. After the assailant leaves, Michele under-reacts, calmly sweeping up the shards of china that have fallen to the floor during the assault. Shortly thereafter, we see Michele at work. She and her friend, Anna run a successful video game company. The entirely male staff of computer programmers have designed a viciously sexist and violent game. In the test screening room, the workers watch a scene from the game in which a gigantic orc sprouts tentacles and impales a young woman in the head, all while bending the young woman over a table. After the screening is over, Michele berates her workers, not for their excess, but because the "orgasmic convulsions" are not exciting enough.

One of the computer programmers, Kurt similarly responds not by berating the game's violence and sexism, but complaining about the poor quality of the controller. He argues that until they fix that hardware, this fretting about the content is pointless. Kurt blames Michele's background in literature (her ex-husband is a literary critic), not appearing to notice that no contemporary literary scholar would ignore the game's horrifying sexism. The fact that Michele, immediately after the brutal sexual attack on her person, does not retreat from the representation of sexual violence, but intensifies it, is the film's central challenge to its viewers, territory that a Hollywood film would traverse at its own financial and critical peril.

Furthermore, this proves Verhoeven's most canny intervention into the criticism of his own Hollywood films, a stance that insists on a difference between reality and representation, cutting against academic feminist dogma which often conflates the two. At a later point in the film, Michele worries that her ex-husband's new girlfriend has pegged her as Medea, the scorned ex-wife who plots the death of all around her in vengeance, ultimately murdering her two children to punish her philandering husband, Jason. Of course, at the end of Euripides' play, the Gods favor the violent murderer, and in the *deus ex machina* ending most critiqued by Aristotle in *The Poetics*, sweep her off the stage to safety.

The scorned woman's hyper-violence does not result in retribution by the gods, but instead support. Academic feminists have similarly rescued Medea as a resistance fighter against patriarchal control and violence (Kerrigan, "Medea Variations"). Verhoeven thus places the criticism of his films within a literary context, demonstrating that the critique of violence and sexism in ancient Greece was no less fraught than in our present, and that representing horrific violence is not the same as endorsing it.

Indeed, in *Elle*, Verhoeven has produced one of the strangest rape-revenge films in history. This sub-genre of horror film was most prominent in North American film history in the wake of the women's liberation movement. Films such as *I Spit on Your Grave* (Meir Zarchi, 1978) and *Ms. 45* (Abel Ferrara, 1981) featured first acts of vicious sexual violence against women, saving their second two acts for the woman's triumphant, brutal revenge killings against her attackers.

There is no such easy resolution in *Elle*. As in a rape-revenge film, Michele refuses to call the police, knowing that they can do nothing to help her. She begins following the clues, searching for her assailant. She dreams of him attacking her again so that she might smash his brains out. Instead, Michele discovers the identity of her attacker, and begins a sado-masochistic relationship with him.

Elle resonates not with Verhoeven's forays into big budget Hollywood, nor American exploitation films, but with the international art cinema. In Liliana Cavani's infamous *The Night Porter* (1974), a former female inmate of a Nazi concentration camp meets her former captor after the war, now working at a hotel. She resumes their sexual relationship, in which he transforms from abuser to victim. In the film's most visceral moment, after they've had sex, she breaks a glass in the bathroom and lies in wait for him to cut his bare foot. As he enters the bathroom, she grabs his foot, but he deliberately steps down onto the glass.

The second half of *Elle* interrogates Michele's psychological complexities in the aftermath of her traumatic life, both her father's murder spree and the rape. After her son murders the rapist, Michele goes to talk with the man's wife as she moves out of her home. The wife, a devout Catholic, states blankly that her husband was a good man, but troubled. Huppert as Michele stares at her, indicating not just contempt, but her character's own equivocations, as this is exactly what her mother argued about her father.

Verhoeven ends the film with no certainties about what we have just witnessed. Like his American science-fiction films, which hover between fascist aesthetics and the critique of totalitarian violence, *Elle* swirls around a woman emotionally crippled by patriarchal violence, yet continuing to exist amid a world of cruel and sexist video games, from which she seemingly gladly profits. When Michele produces the video games, she replicates Verhoeven's American films, the legacy of which brutally ensnares her, not even seeming to acknowledge the connection to her lived experience. In its slippage across the genders of character and director, *Elle* represents the autobiographical impulse in cinema in a surprising, yet powerful way, a method so common to international art cinema, but virtually non-existent within the Hollywood comic book machine.

Clinton's Daisy Chain

As my most pressing plea, we must redesign academic publishing such that it engages with audio-visual objects in real time, as they matter to the culture around us. I can't imagine anything more pressing in my own life right now as reeling from the election of Donald Trump as President of the United States in late 2016.

As Eric Barnouw taught us long ago in his television history, *Tube of Plenty*, one astonishing thing about the 1964 Doyle Dane Bernbach ad campaign featuring "the daisy girl" is that it was produced when Lyndon

Johnson was planning the escalation of U.S. fighting in Vietnam. In the one-minute spot, a young girl picks leaves off a daisy. Her counting is replaced by preparations for a missile launch. Johnson's voice states menacingly, "These are the stakes. To make a world in which all God's children can live, or go into the dark. We must either love each other, or we must die."

By refusing to depict in any way its intended target, Barry Goldwater, the rhetoric made him seem more frightening. However, the minimalist images carry very little weight: there is a push into the girl's eye, after which we see a mushroom cloud. But otherwise, the force of the ad is purely aural. The girl's hesitant counting, the mechanistic countdown, and then the sound of the atomic blast is replaced by Johnson's calm, reasonable, and humanistic voice. A deep-voiced man then tells us to go to vote on in early November: "The stakes are too high for you to stay home."

For the 2016 presidential campaign, Hilary Clinton's team ran a thirty-second ad haunted by the 'daisy' spot. Speaking from the Ellsworth Missile Site in South Dakota, a former nuclear launch officer tells us about the military responsibility to fire when the president orders them to do so. At first, a soft, understated piano score gives the spot a restrained feel. However, when Bruce Blair tells us "self-control may be all that keeps these missiles from firing," the political commercial exponentially increases its rhetorical aggressiveness.

As a launch alarm sounds, three clips of Donald Trump spouting vitriol—"I would bomb the [bleep] out of them...I want to be unpredictable...I love war" cause Blair to state: "The thought of Donald Trump with nuclear weapons scares me to death. It should scare everyone." A snare drum increases the pace of the music, competing with and then overwhelming the piano. A final stinger from the drum ends the music and introduces Hilary Clinton in profile, looking upward presidentially; she declares in voice-off: "I'm Hilary Clinton, and I approved this message." Her logo, "Strong Together" ends the spot.

The Clinton spot transforms 'daisy' profoundly. While by no means subtle, the earlier TV ad was aesthetically constrained, refusing music, and most importantly the need to dignify Barry Goldwater with an appearance. Conversely, Clinton's pulls out all of the stops: like a classical documentary from the 1930s, its music is emotionally programmatic in its functioning. The trio of Donald Trump snippets places his dangerous bluster square in the middle of the ad. What does it mean that Clinton has returned to 'daisy' in the first place?

Is the rhetorical maneuver—Donald Trump is worse than Barry Goldwater—the sole message? He certainly makes Mitt Romney and John McCain seem reasonable in comparison. But if Trump is indeed worse, why is the return to 1930s documentary techniques (evocative music and script, elegant images, telegraphed emotional content) so necessary? Does the callback to 'daisy' signal that, like Johnson before her, Clinton too would have escalated, a hawkish Democratic proclivity since the Kennedy administration? Even if our vitriolic rhetoric makes us deserve the utter abjection of Trump, why does the American public not also merit a candidate of *de-escalation*?

It is clear my worries about the election of Donald Trump, on a wave of anti-intellectualism, cut against my first two interventions, far more optimistic about the potential of aligning academic writing, popular criticism, and Hollywood filmmakers. But it seems this is precisely why we need to make such interventions. Traditional academic work has been kept on the margins of social life for decades, at least since the Kennedy administration. Making tactical interventions, such as intervening in real time, with a spirit of building bridges, should be our mission as we attempt to navigate 2017 and beyond.

Cinema as Salvation: On the Perils of Not Heeding Jimmy Carter's Warning

I conclude with a recent example of a film that responds more effectively to the malaise of 2016 than did Clinton's shockingly unsuccessful 'daisy" rehash. *20th Century Women* is an ambitious character study that uses American history to explore the relationship between a Depression-era mother, Dorothea (Annette Bening) and her son, Jamie. Director Mike Mills' film is set in 1979 (on the threshold of a similar neo-conservative revolution), but it uses the traditions of film, music, literature, and sociology to explore the nature of American subjectivity, particularly that of women, as it was constructed by forty years of social transformation.

Dorothea and Jamie befriend Abbie (Greta Gerwig), a photographer with cervical cancer who rents a room in Dorothea's house, and Julie (Elle Fanning), a sexually troubled seventeen-year-old girl. Yet the plot swirls around Dorothea, one of the most profoundly engaging adult women characters in recent memory.

Twentieth Century Women is a visual critical essay, replete with footnotes, in the guise of subtitles informing us of texts important to understanding America in the 1970s. Abbie gives Jamie the book, *Sisterhood is Powerful*, edited by Robin Morgan, an anthology of feminist criticism. Jamie reads aloud to his mother Zoe Moss' 1970 essay, "It Hurts to Be Alive and Obsolete: The Ageing Woman."

When Dorothea responds with anger and defensiveness to Moss' lament at middle-age women being discarded by patriarchal culture, Mills steers his film from didacticism to emotional resonance. Dorothea scolds her son, "I don't need a book to know about myself." Mills' characters may be too pained to interrogate themselves and the social order which has devastated them, but his film demonstrates how important such knowledge is for understanding why people suffer.

Mills' references to the 20th century history of cinema structure the film. As Dorothea describes Jamie's birth, Mills inserts a shot of an elephant from an early Edison film made at the turn of the 19th to 20th centuries. Shortly thereafter, Dorothea watches *Casablanca* (1942) with Jamie, snuggling on the couch together. Later in the film, Dorothea tells us that after watching Nicholas Roeg's *The Man Who Fell to Earth* (1976), featuring David Bowie as a beleaguered space alien, Abbie dyed her hair red. Mills proposes that 20th century women developed across the century in the gravitational field that is the cinema.

In the film's most compelling scene, and the one with which I will conclude this essay about how the cinema and its criticism helps us fight anti-intellectualism, the adoptive clan gather to watch Jimmy Carter's 1979 "crisis of confidence" speech. On July 15, 1979, the President delivered what is now derisively referred to as "the malaise speech." Yet in retrospect, living under the neo-Fascism of Donald Trump, the speech sounds shockingly prescient: "There is a growing disrespect for government, for schools, the news media, and other institutions. This is not a message of happiness, or reassurance. But it is the truth. And it is a warning."

After the speech is over, the guests reflect that Carter is "so screwed. It's over for him." Dorothy alone is deeply moved: "Wow. That was so beautiful." In his book, *What the Heck are You Up To, Mr. President?: Jimmy Carter, America's 'Malaise,' and the Speech That Should Have Changed the Country* (2009), Kevin Mattson indicates, however right Dorothea is, the crowd around her produces the reaction that would allow for the neo-conservative destruction of our nation's long-term well-being, with the election of Ronald Reagan in November 1980.

Carter's speech was a warning that the values of consumerism and materialism would overwhelm America's traditional greatness, its people's commitment to the transformative values of justice and freedom. Mills reinforces this message not with politics, but with cinema. He accompanies the audio of the speech to visual images from Godfrey Reggio's celebrated experimental documentary, *Koyaanisqatsi* (1982).

The subtitle informs us that director Godfrey Reggio's footage was shot in the years 1975-1979, not only the exact years of the Carter Administration, but also the setting of *Twentieth Century Women*. *Koyaanisqatsi*, famous for its time-lapse footage of white America's technological civilization intercut with Native American mythological reflections on nature, is subtitled, "life out of balance." *Twentieth Century Women* thus sociologically positions *Koyaanisqatsi* as the filmic fellow traveler of Carter's speech. It is an astonishing act of cinematic criticism.

Mills takes the premise of my film criticism project one step further. While I lament the fact that contemporary criticism is not equipped to extract the complex artistic and sociological meaning out of a vast range of cinemas we consume, Mills demonstrates that a different form of visual art could function itself as criticism. If such a cinema would arise at this historical moment, not only could we correct the nation's course away from the Scylla and Charybdis of which Carter so desperately warned, but film criticism itself could evolve into something much more profound, developing new paths toward greater human liberation.

Conclusion

Between the invention of cinema in the 1890s and the present, little has changed to bridge the gap between an intelligent writing about film, and the popular publicity apparatus attendant to actual filmmaking. The people making films in Los Angeles' classical Hollywood (1917-1960) did not know or care that Harvard applied psychologist Hugo Munsterberg was inventing film theory across the country on the other coast of the same nation (Langdale, 2001). The above critical readings of a range of films demonstrate the utility of a middle ground between popular, journalistic writing about movies (sycophantic to the film industry) and academic film criticism (beholden to the discipline of Film Studies). It is my profound hope that the resultant criticism could help bridge the gap between filmmakers and those who write informedly about film.

References

Aristotle. *The Poetics*. http://classics.mit.edu/Aristotle/poetics.html

Barnouw, E. (1990). *Tube of Plenty: The Evolution of American Television*. 2nd Revised Ed., New York: Oxford University Press.

Benjamin, W. (1969). The Work of Art in the Age of Mechanical Reproduction. *Illuminations: Essays and Reflections*. Ed. Hannah Arendt. NY: Schocken.

Frye, N. (2000). *Anatomy of Criticism: Four Essays*. Revised ed., Princeton: Princeton University Press.

Geuens, J-P. (2000). *Film Production Theory*. Albany: SUNY Press.

Greyson, J. (1993). Security Blankets: Sex, Video and the Police. *Queer Looks: Perspectives on Lesian and Gay Film and Video*. Eds. Martha Gever, *et. al.* New York and London: Routledge.

Kerrigan, J. (2017, April 26). Medea Variations: Feminism and Revenge. *Revenge Tragedy: Aeschylus to Armageddon*. Oxford Scholarship Online, 1997. http://www.oxfordscholarship.com/view/10.1093/acprof:oso/9780198184515.001.0001/acprof-9780198184515-chapter-13.

Langdale, A. (2001) *Hugo Munsterberg on Film: The Photoplay, A Psychological Study and Other Writings*. New York: Routledge.

Mattson, K. (2009) *What the Heck are You Up To, Mr. President?: Jimmy Carter, America's 'Malaise,' and the Speech That Should Have Changed the Country*. New York: Bloomsbury.

Morgan, R. (1970) *Sisterhood is Powerful: An Anthology of Writings from the Women's Liberation Movement*. New York: Vintage.

Moss, Z. (1970) "It Hurts to Be Alive and Obsolete: The Ageing Woman." In Robin Morgan (Ed.) *Sisterhood is Powerful*.

Refuse, Resist: "Aquarius" and the Cinema of Resistance in Brazil

Camila Cornutti Barbosa and Susan Liesenberg

Abstract. The article reflects on the context of reception to the film "Aquarius." The script presents a female lead, from the middle class, who is an independent woman, idiosyncratic and who is resisting the *status quo* when she fights to preserve her "vertical island" (her apartment in an old building, "Aquarius," by the seashore in the Brazilian northeast). She is trying to prevent the expropriation of the building which is facing real estate speculation. The focus of the discussion falls on a narrative that points to several tension sources in contemporary Brazil such as: a) the political context (the impeachment of the then president Dilma Rousseff, led by political maneuverings and influenced by the media, and considered to be a coup d'état); b) the social context (a woman as head of the household, the role of ageing, the condemnation of values such as owning property and obtaining profit); c) the economic context (showing the corruption and dishonesty in a violent and unequal country); and d) the media context (showing all the camaraderie and protectionism in the domain of information, as well as the repercussions of the movie both locally and internationally). The film converged to the neuralgic point of a historical moment when it was released. All of the elements here cited are understood as agents articulated with activism – both in film production and in the criticism arising from "Aquarius" – by its meaning, its social representations and self-reflexive provocation, above all, of the Brazilian middle class.

Keywords: "Aquarius", Cinema, Resistance, Brazil.

Introduction

"'Aquarius' *is* Brazil," answers, vehemently, Brazilian actress Sônia Braga, when questioned during an interview about the similarities and the relations between this 2016 movie and the obvious aspects of current Brazilian reality pictured on it. Just as she emphasizes in her answer, "it *is* Brazil," and from the movie's plot, different elements emerge, showing sometimes discreet and sometimes blatant similarities between fiction and reality concerning social, political, economic and media aspects. This is not a unique point of view of the actress, confused and identifying with Clara, her character on the movie, as Sônia had previously said she felt. "Aquarius," one of the most awarded and talked about Brazilian movies, has become more than an entertainment product intended for consumption between a theater screen and a bucket of popcorn in a leisurely time. This investigative and exploratory study seeks to reflect about the movie "Aquarius[1]" from the point of view of the social tensions that the production created, shattering and resizing the different contexts that compose the panorama and the circumstances around its release. Contrary to theories that state that audiovisual products tend to be a digression, a departure from reality – for they are associated with the relaxing and the turning away from reality (as cited by Citelli, 2000) – this essay intends to highlight the potential of a film production to evoke reality articulated into its plot, contributing, by its artistic concept, to a consumption that provides an insight on what is lived in the flesh in daily life (Matterlart & Neveu, 2003).

We have identified four analysis axis or 'transversal contexts' to study the film narrative in connection with the situation in contemporary Brazil: the political, the social, the economic, and the media context in which the picture is screened, consumed and resignified by the spectators (including those who have not seen it in a movie theater, but have "watched" it through its ostensive repercussion and production of significations in other media, beyond the movie theater). We are interested in analyzing these contexts as vertices from a network point of view, in which we see the film as a product and a narrative interwoven with the reality of contemporary Brazil in the year of its exhibition. The conceptual idea of observation of heterogeneous materials which cross each other (the so-called 'transversal contexts') is based in the idea of a network here seen as a methodology. According to Virgínia Kastrup (2004, p. 80), a network is "not defined by its shape, by its limits and frontiers, but by its connections. This is why a network should be understood based on a connections logic," just as we have analytically designed here, observing the above mentioned transversal contexts which have had an impact on the reception of "Aquarius." These contexts have much to say, in a great arc, about the composition of the film landscape in "Aquarius." That is to say, they are transversal contexts which show the film landscape, the social landscape it is inserted in (or from which it emerges) and which is integrated as a production in the midst of society by the consumption of the work of art. The concept of landscape is important in itself, for it can be understood not only as physical territory but also as the social and psychological panorama. Indeed, the film landscape is designed as scenery filled with conflict and tension – which *is*, as Sônia Braga has stated, contemporary Brazil itself.

---

[1] "Aquarius" (Brazil/France) is the second feature film by Brazilian director Kleber Mendonça Filho. The filming took place from August to September 2015. The film's world premiere was on May 17th 2016 – at the 69th Cannes Festival – where it was nominated for the *Palme d'Or*.

Synopsis – The Story Inside of History

"Aquarius" follows three decades in the life of the main character, Clara, played by Sônia Braga – a retired journalist, specialist in Brazilian music. In 2016, the year in which the main story develops, she is a widow, living in a modest building called Aquarius for more than 30 years (and where she raised her three children who are now adults). There she keeps objects, feelings and memories, and becomes the last person living in the building located in a valuable plot of land by the sea in Recife, the capital city of Brazil's northeastern state of Pernambuco, and surrounded by several other buildings, mainly newly-built ones. All the other apartments in her building were bought by a real estate developing company, which has a real urgency in bringing down the old building in order to build a modern one by the seashore. Clara loves her apartment and has no intention of moving out – which she promptly told the investors from the beginning.

The story develops, portraying the routine of an independent woman, head of the family, with financial stability (unlike most women in Brazil), and very critical of the world she lives in. Clara swims in the shark-infested ocean, she goes to laugh-therapy, makes friends, listens to her vinyls, drinks her bottles of wine, smokes her weed, walks at the beach anytime she likes, reads her books, goes out dancing and has some love affairs, not limiting her sexuality because of her mastectomy after she had breast cancer. Clara is her own woman. Because of her insistence in remaining in the building, she starts to be harassed, the building gets invaded and sabotaged, and she starts to receive threats in order to sell and leave. The pressure comes from neighbors, who have already signed contracts with the developer, and also from her family, who worry about her safety living in an old building lacking some comforts, and who are very surprised by her refusal to accept a seven-digit proposal, without even wanting to know the actual amount offered. The conflict in the movie starts when Diego (Humberto Carrão), a young engineer who has recently come back from a course in real estate business in the USA, and who is the grandson of one of the investors in the deal, says to Clara that he has "blood in his eyes" and wants to "attack" and build something new and modern where "the building used to be" to which Clara replies "It is still here. You are standing on it". She keeps her ground and resists his threats.

Political Context

From Clara's decision to stand by her convictions and to firmly stay in the apartment where she built her family and where she has lived most of her life, "Aquarius" aims at a double perspective: to resist and to exist. The movie gives the spectator the opportunity to reflect about matters beyond the movie itself, an awakening of insights into the country's reality. The time when the movie is released, a delicate period for the democratic regime, with the imminent impeachment of the then president Dilma Rousseff and at a high risk of a coup d'état at that time (May 2016), makes it evident that there seems to be a kind of dictatorship going on (economic and political, but not military). And in the film – with the image of the real estate developers – now the coercion and social violence come in suits, with polite words (an analogy to the right-wing conservative government that took power after Dilma Rousseff was impeached), with a new kind of language and a new dress code, but with the same danger and violent coercion. In movie theaters across the country, there were manifestations with people shouting "Out with Temer" during the exhibition of the film, a reference to the newly sworn-in president, Michel Temer, former vice-president, who took power after Ms. Rousseff was impeached, and who is highly criticized for the policies he started to implement.

Mendonça Filho, director of "Aquarius," when talking about the movie's core ideas, commented on the political crisis and the imminent coup in May 2016 when in Cannes, and associating it with the mood of "Aquarius". The cast protested on the red carpet, which deflagrated as much support as contempt in social media, mostly due to the increasing ideological polarization between both right-wing [coxinhas] and left-wing [petralhas] activists[2]. Later on, the Ministry of Justice, who is responsible for the age classification of movies in Brazil, moved to rate the film "+18" (restricted for audiences under 18 years of age) which was interpreted as retaliation on the part of the government by the critics – with the justification that the movie contained explicit sex scenes and consumption of illegal drugs. The producers appealed, defending that a +16 classification would be more suitable to a movie with great cultural relevance (for it had already been distributed to over 60 countries), and also because the sex and nudity scenes were not explicit. Some critics pointed out that this government's decision had been an attempt to hurt box office numbers. Mendonça Filho has also been the target of a frustrated

---

[2] Starting in 2016, there has been an increasing ideological polarization in the political manifestations in Brazil: on one side there are the right-wing protesters [coxinhas] who supported actions to take the Workers' Party (PT) from power and who incite hatred against anything relating to the party or to left-wing policies; on the other side there are the left-wing protesters [petralhas] who defended the government programs instituted by former president Lula and by president Dilma Rousseff, who had social programs at their core principles, such as income distribution programs, and the inclusion of the poorest in health programs, education and the incentive of consumption.

investigation on the funding of the movie, which only worsened the criticism and accusations of government persecution of the producers.

These episodes show that "Aquarius" has become political resistant cinema, and highlighted the capacity of the movie to show the reality of the new government on screen (such as had happened to "Elite Squad" [Tropa de Elite, 2007] by José Padilha, which showed blatant police corruption throughout its plot, "Aquarius" is in synergy with contemporary Brazilian news). Dilma's impeachment was underway during the filming and was festering during the film's release. It was an ongoing narrative, which influenced the context of the movie's reception (which premiered amidst an effervescent news festival of corruption denunciations involving construction companies, businessmen and politicians, the same themes pictured in the script of "Aquarius"). There are those who see the reflection of Dilma Rousseff in Clara (because of the persecution, coercion and resistance shown in the movie). If we think about the pressure both of these women have endured, we may say that there is a shadow of Dilma on the character, and this fact was widely talked about in the media and also social media by the public. In these terms, "Aquarius" confuses itself with the current political context in Brazil.

Another relevant aspect of the political context in the narrative of "Aquarius" is the soundtrack. The songs are not just musical support that brings out messages from the recent political past in Brazil, but they are effectively a part of the story told in the movie. This is true from the start – the movie opens with "Today" ["Hoje"] a hit by Taiguara (who got censored by the Military Regime in Brazil[3]). The 1969 song is romantic and feisty, just like Clara – a music critic who collects vinyls. The opening line from the song says "Today I bring on my body the scars of my time" and it is the musical background for the scene that presents the main character – we see her without a breast, a scar from breast cancer surgery (curiously, Taiguara also had cancer, but did not survive it). "Aquarius" goes through important times in the history of Brazilian popular music [*"MPB"*] and this is evident through the choice of songs for the soundtrack. According to Betton (1987):

> Music has a considerable psychological function in cinema, already recognized during the silent movies era: to give the spectator the feeling of a duration effectively lived, and "to free them from the terrible weight of silence". It also has an aesthetic and psychological function of the highest degree, creating an oneiric state, and atmosphere, affective shocks to exalt emotion (p. 47).

---

[3] Military Regime in Brazil took place from 1964 until 1985.

That is to say that the movie's atmosphere is also built by the songs – mainly fragments of MPB (with compositions by Alcione, Roberto Carlos with "My neighbor's backyard", Gilberto Gil with "Every girl from Bahia", Reginaldo Rossi with "Recife, my city", Altemar Dutra with "Overly Sentimental", Maria Bethânia with "A stupid way to love you" and so on) and international pop songs (mainly by rock group Queen in two moments: with 1980's "Another one bites the dust", and 1978's "Fat bottomed girls"), many of them are emblematic songs, linked to movements of criticism to the military regime, and women's emancipation movements. As Rodrigues stated (2004, p. 15), "music has a role in underlining the emotion in the pictures. The sound impression reinforces the visual one". To this we can link the idea of the high power of suggestion inherent to music as stated by Sekeff (1998):

> Music is a system of signs which promotes communication and expression. It is a syntactic system of autonomous semantics, it is a language with qualities, an iconic language, which only talks about itself, and because of that, it has a highly suggestive power. With a corpus of rules, principles, laws and theories that guarantee its legitimacy and its identity, its genre, style and form, music is a language based on systems grounded in a culture (...) (p. 36).

If we understand music as a language that systematizes cultural repertoire, we have to mention how MPB – Brazilian Popular Music – had (and still has) a prominent role in the understanding of an idea of resistance, serving as a political instrument against authoritarian and anti-democratic manifestations that have been intermittently taking place in the history of Brazil. The soundtrack for "Aquarius", in this light, sounds current, when faced to the political landscape in Brazil, and it inserts criticism into the plot, such as the songs featured in the film did at the time of their original release.

Social Context

Specifically relating to social context, the movie touches, in a very subtle and implicit way, grave and latent matters in Brazil. Among the several delicate features of Brazilian culture pictured in it, and the social reality of the country, gender conflict is one of the most evident: Clara is a free woman, strong, who steered her family after the death of her husband. In the country, there is a direct association with the fact that almost 40% of families are headed by women[4]—and this happens because of several factors, such as male abandonment and domestic violence. This also makes evident a tension about

---

[4] Data from the Brazilian Institute of Applied Economic Research (Ipea).

what is expected of women and their imposed social roles. Contrary to what a male dominant culture would expect, she grows old healthily, she is open to life, love, pleasure, sex (even being rejected by a man at a party when he realizes Clara does not have one of her breasts anymore – which is a way to show the difficulty of accepting someone else's body when it does not conform to the expected beauty standard), she leads an independent life in the city, and she exercises her civic rights and duties.

The character Clara personifies a real possibility for a contemporary woman, and brings into light the difficult conditions faced by women in Brazil. Also, the narrative also brings criticism into matters of racial prejudice and urban violence[5]. Black people, in the plot, appear as some kind of threat – or in the role of those who steal and cheat. We can see a conditioning (a pedagogy or a previously established grammar) about "what to expect", when a group of black children appear and the "expectation" in their view presumes that there will be a robbery or some violent act, and the exact opposite happens: they get together to have laughter therapy. Here the film has a role of breaking with the spectator's expectations, who gets surprised – by their own and other people's preconceptions – when they feel trapped by a narrative that breaks down their certainties (because deep down, their common sense predicted that a certain thing would happen). This is a moment when the movie says more about who is watching it than about what is effectively shown on screen (almost as the line that says "a text says more about the person writing it than about its actual subject"). But, in this case, the spectators see themselves getting into conclusions based on their preconceptions. The breaking of expectations is one of the main narrative lines. Along the story, more than real estate speculation, it is this break in expectations that attracts the spectator and builds up the narrative.

We may infer that in "Aquarius" what is at stake is not quite the physical space (the building, the apartment, the real estate opportunity) but the ways of life, the freedom, the non-conformism. This makes us reflect upon the time and space we live in, as well as upon new ways of communicating, thinking and feeling: what kinds of attachments are we creating in a time when we see and hear things we cannot touch? Even with the presence of these panoramas of violence in the social context – of standards, of experiences, of freedom and of circulation, we see that the movie is not about being pamphletary. It purports a message, of the vital need for democracy and respect in a time when such

---

[5] Data from the report "Index of Juvenile Vulnerability to Violence and Racial Imbalance" (2014) show that the black population between the ages 12 and 29 in Brazil are the main victims of violence. The same study reveals that young black males are 2.5 times more victimized by murder than their white counterparts.

things seem to be cut down by the State, by the media and by a section of Brazilian society who behave in a very contained and standardized way.

Economic Context

The main point of the plot: the harassing propositions made by a big developer to make Clara give up her apartment, to make her sell it and move out, to keep out of their way. A series of menacing acts take place: contractors hire people to hold noisy religious ceremonies in the building, they put drug users and orgy participants right above her ceiling, they promote parties with very loud music, all in an attempt to get her angry and make her move out, and they even sabotage the structure of the building, planting a termite colony into it. By sheer pressure of economic power – and also by a notion of an ever-expanding city that runs over and dehumanizes its inhabitants – the plot brings scenes of corruption, dishonesty and inequality. A system of living that has as its main values "how much you earn or profit" is seen in Clara's children, when they try to convince their mother to sell the place – a form of abandoning family memories for the opportunity to profit a great amount in the sale.

These scenes show the *modus operandi* of real estate speculation by developers in Brazil – in a political context of daily news of corruption scandals, political crisis and police investigations relating to this industry. We may even see correlations between the movie and recent real cases that happened in Brazil. Among them, there is the recent and polemic "revitalization" of Hotel Nacional (designed by the renowned architect Oscar Niemeyer) proposed by a group of investors who wish to build two 13-stories towers, with room for about a thousand people to live in, and inflate a noble region that does not have the structure to hold such an extra influx of people, not to mention the environmental impact[6].

The power of the story and the questions brought about by the movie were such that, by the end of 2016, newspapers ran the story of another scandal surrounding Temer's government, pictured as "Aquarius from Bahia." The president himself put pressure on the then minister of culture, Marcelo Calero, to grant a license by the National Institute of Artistic and Historical Heritage

---

[6] Other cases similar to the plot of "Aquarius": the movement "Occupy Estelita" – a mobilization in the city of Recife against construction companies intended to show the scandalous contrast between capitalist development and democracy; the project of revitalization of the Guaíba lake shore in Porto Alegre, another Brazilian state capital – the town hall did not even hold a public contest for choosing a project (they have paid a great amount of money to a private architectural office belonging to a politician). The project suffered great criticism by the population because it planned to turn a public square into parking space and to remove all of the riparian area.

[IPHAN] that allowed the construction of a tower of luxury apartments near the historic center of Salvador, capital of Bahia, known for its rich architectural history. The *El País* newspaper was categorical in the correlation between fact and fiction: "It is as president Michel Temer, in this never ending 2016, the year of 'alternative-facts,' ended up in the movie 'Aquarius,' by director Mendonça Filho." With this particular episode, we can see how concrete and real the situations pictured in the movie are. Acts of conspiracy and corruption – mostly involving favor-exchanging with politicians and the incessant need for profit by the construction companies, real estate market and developers. "Aquarius" seems to have voiced a recurring conflict in modern big cities in Brazil: the conflict among economic power, heritage conservation, environment preservation and standards of living. It seems to be as if the movie is continuously brought to life in new situations exposing harassment, corruption and other "arrangements" involving politicians, business people and construction companies, in Brazil and also in other Latin American countries.

Media Context

"Aquarius" exposes another critical situation in Brazil: media power relations institutionalized and dominated by camaraderie, protectionism and information domination. According to data from 2015 on Forbes magazine, Brazilian media is the 8th most representative in a ranking of 13 industries led by manufacturing, banking and food. According to the National Forum for Communications Democratization, only 11 families control the main communication outlets in Brazil. Also, 25% of Republic Senators and 10% of Legislative Representatives own radio and television concessions, besides major printed newspapers. There is data pointing to the concentration of power in media – which is also reflected on the movie, when Clara seeks out a journalist friend to denounce the harassment she has been suffering and finds out that the family that owns the newspaper is linked, by money and corruption, to the construction company that has been harassing her. "It's only natural," the journalist tells Clara, that there is a close relationship between political and economic power and the media. "Of course," Clara says. Beyond exposing a reality reflected in Brazilian journalism, we must also consider the impact and repercussion of the movie in the press (nationally and also internationally). French press, for example, praised the movie. Newspaper *Aujourd'hui en France* said that the movie "is a unique film by its theme, a testimony of the perverse methods of capitalist society."

"Few movies have touched a nerve in Brazil in recent years like "Aquarius,"" said The New York Times (Romero, 2017), with special emphasis to the revival of resistance cinema in Brazil, its connection with a more political past in the movie industry, because it produced a movie with no polite and politically opportunistic interpretations and "unleashing a fierce debate over the dividing line between art and politics", because of all the pressure, censorship and persecution that the film and its director have suffered. In a long article, the newspaper says that "Aquarius", "which explores class and racial tension in northeast Brazil, does not explicitly delve into Brazil's recent political turmoil, in which the former president, Dilma Rousseff, was ousted in a contentious impeachment trial." The piece goes deeper into the problems arising from the movie premiere, also saying that "in theaters across Brazil, audiences have been shouting, "Out with Temer," at the culmination of "Aquarius," which is emerging as a box-office hit":

> In an intense way, all the retaliation against 'Aquarius' is backfiring," said Mr. Mendonça Filho, the director. He compared the passions around "Aquarius" to those involving "Network," the 1976 film about broadcast news in the era of Watergate, in which an anchor persuades his viewers to shout out their windows, "I'm as mad as hell and I'm not going to take this anymore!" (...) Suddenly "Aquarius" has also become a catalyst for expressing outrage in a recession-weary country troubled by corruption scandals. (...) The committee's choice had nothing to do with the film's artistic merits, critics contend. To the contrary, they condemn the decision as a form of political retaliation, made solely because of the cast and crew's public distaste for Brazil's new president, Michel Temer (Romero, 2017).

In the national and international press coverage, and also social media impact, we can see how movies have a strong symbolic capital in a culture of consumption of images and representations, one of their most potent and notable vocations. For example, in 2008, Oscar winner for best movie, "The Hurt Locker" defeated the favorite "Avatar" and also stirred debate in American society about war and its impacts, as well as some other transversal themes that went beyond the scope of the film, such as women's presence in movies, with the award for best director being won, for the first time, by a woman, Kathryn Bigelow. "The time has come," praised Barbra Streisand when announcing the winner at this historical moment for the movie industry.

Transmethodology – Crossings and Analytical Context

Just as in digital ambiance, we think on terms of multifocal ethnography, considering a world system composed by the juxtaposition and circulation of meaning, objects, identities and cultural expressions in a diffuse space-time, here we can understand the social landscape in "Aquarius" as part of a contextual architecture (Marcus, 2001, p. 111). When someone watches a movie and sees the contextual transversalities that crosses it, such as the ones listed previously, we can observe in that work what Herwitz (2008) categorizes as an intermediate aura between the production's content and the daily life of the audience, according to the tone of the country's political, social and media discourses.

> An aura emerges through a perceptual transaction between the properties of the thing/person and someone viewing it or taking it. An aura is a way of seeing, hearing, feeling a thing, an intersubjective image of it, a way of imagining and responding to a thing. Things or persons are invested with auras through direct experience of them and also through representations that lend them special signs or transfiguring moods (Herwitz, 2008, p. 59).

About this *Zeitgeist* and the transversality of impacting elements perceived in the aura of "Aquarius" as a methodology here designed upon the meaning of the work of art, Citelli (2000, p. 71) brings us an important perspective when it states that we should "consider less of the problem of the means themselves as sources capable of exerting social control and more of the social and cultural mediation around the experiences of the recipient of those messages" in the process of consumption of a product, a work of art, a movie. When we take into consideration the experience of the audience, because here we did not apply a study of reception (with focus groups, surveys or any other methodology directly applied to the public) but instead we drafted an exploratory investigation around the context of that reception, i.e. the social landscape of the film, Martín-Barbero (2004) said that "thinking communication in Latin America is more and more an anthropological task" (Martín-Barbero, 2004, p. 209), and he complements the idea:

> (...) as scandalous as it may seem, it is a fact that the masses in Latin America are incorporating themselves into modern times not through books, or by an illustrated project, but by the formats and genres of the cultural audiovisual industry. And this change in sensibilities, not by an educated culture, but by audiovisual culture presents us some grave challenges. Beginning with the fact that the majority of people may appropriate modern times without giving up their oral culture, transforming it into a secondary oral culture, i.e., with an imposed grammar stemming from dispositives and syntax from radio, cinema and television (Martín-Barbero, 2004, p. 210).

Continuing his train of thought, Martín-Barbero said that in communication research, "it will be very difficult to keep calling uncultured a sensibility that defies our notion of culture and modernity, and from which people are transforming their views, imagination, narratives, feelings and thoughts" (2004, p. 210). About this complex and delicate mixture of elements to be identified and analyzed in a process of reception, the author talks about a "new map of problems" in which it is pertinent to analyze the matter of subjects and social timing, i.e. the weave of modernity, discontinuities and transformations of the *sensorium* which gravitate around the processes of constitution of discourses and genres of collective communication" (Martín-Barbero, 2004, p. 212-213), such as cinema and what we have proposed here as a methodology, by the analysis of several contexts together. According to Martín-Barbero & Rey (2004):

> Audiovisual media (Hollywood-type movies, television and most of video) are, at the same time, a discourse of antonomasia and bricolage of times – which effortlessly makes it familiar to us, extracting it from the complexities and ambiguities of its time, with any past fact – and the discourse that better expresses the *compression* of the present, the transformation of the extended time of history into the intensive *instant* picture. Intensity of a time that reaches its pinnacle in the simultaneity that the direct take inserts between the fact and its image (p. 35).

Thinking about material ontology with a foundation in psychology, Dunker (2015) says that "if there is homology between symptom and work of art we then must consider each new suffering as an invention and a response to the transformations in the horizon of a period of time" (Dunker, 2015, p. 22). This argument is indissociably linked to the analysis of the impact of "Aquarius" and the context of its reception, thus the necessity to carve apart this contextual architecture. Jaguaribe (2007, p. 11) says that "aesthetic realism in photography, cinema literature and media contribute to shape our perception of reality", highlighting that the codes of aesthetic realism have the pedagogical power to weave the portraits of reality: "it is as if only they have the weight of the legitimacy of consensus, although, at the same time, these same realistic codes coexist with the charming practices of the cultural daily life" (Jaguaribe, 2007, p. 11), as a globalized discourse of the advertisement narratives, virtual reality and other cultural products, such as films. We are not talking about an aesthetics solely based on visual language, but an aesthetic of realism that portraits facts, and takes from life the building materials for art. If "the paradox of realism is to invent fiction that looks like reality" (Jaguaribe, 2007, p. 16), in "Aquarius", reality sprays, pours from the fictional screen, touching a public already inundated by it in their daily lives.

For Harvey (2008), the production of a visual society, where merchandise – such as audiovisual productions and cinema, the author exemplifies – act on symbolic systems to build the representations of the world, fictionally and realistically, build social significance, turning the merchandise into an anchoring spot for social imagination, in which the means of communication (newspapers, magazines, television, movies, and so on) have an integrating role on cultural practices, and on the life of a society and public opinion, such as "Aquarius" showed in its plot, in an honest dialogue about the difficult times Brazil is going through. Keeping "true to the principles surrounding the arising of critical reflections about media universes and the cultural ambiance they are into" (Baitello, 2010, p. 9), Baitello evokes a perspective of Media Theory that has been trying to "exorcize product fetishism, which isolates it, and the fetishism of technical language, which keeps it apart from the environment they were born into, and may provoke deep and wide transformations". For this reason, it changes the focus of attention on the information to the "generation of attachment and attachment environments, more complex entities, which require a multidisciplinary confluence and a prospective view" he emphasizes, "concerning the impacts and unfolding of contemporary media practices". In this sense, Cogo (2009) talks about the mediation, understood as a cultural instance from which the recipients produce and appropriate the meanings and significations, thinking about the complex process of interaction between audiences and information consumption. The author says that mediation "does not come exclusively from the means, genre, programs and messages but from diverse sources – both internal and external – previous and post reception", from individual experiences and collective experiences by the audience (Cogo, 2009, p. 5) through to daily life elements which permeate the process of information consumption (of a newspaper, text, movie).

Mediation may be individual (considering the experiences of every individual subject), situational (where consumption happens) and/or institutional (derived from the bond with the spectators and how they act on the means of communication in this relationship). Cogo (2009) adds that "institutional mediation are constituted by the sceneries where the processes of reception happen, and where the multiple appropriations by television happen, at the moment or right after the moment of perception" (Cogo, 2009, p. 5). Because of that, we may notice and conceive the multiple sources of mediation present at the process of reception, configured by the historical social, political, cultural elements present in the movie.

Conclusion

Inconvenient proposals, insisting and imposing invasive offers by credit card companies, cable TV, internet providers and the relations of marketing and political systems that force people to buy or opt-in to things they neither need nor agree with, are the background to "Aquarius." The film addresses critical points of Brazilian reality – the limiting of freedom of choice, and the respect for citizenship, individuality and civil rights. In this exploratory investigation, we chose to build and analyze a multifaceted panorama of elements that compose the contextual architecture surrounding "Aquarius," starting from the transversality of themes interwoven in its plot, and the reality in which the production is inserted and finds its meaning. Just as queer, feminist and resistance cinemas, which play a strong part in the democratization of the new identity narratives, alterity and the representation of diversity[7], "Aquarius" points to a political and artistic past. Political because of the memories of authoritarian regimes Brazil has endured – and still does. And artistic because it embodies social criticism, built into its script, and because the film has a resonance among its audiences and other repercussion spaces (the media coverage, the political turmoil it caused, and the social conscience it awakens) such as the movies from the 1960's through the 1970's, a period when movie producers and social thinkers joined forces, intersecting themes of social relevance with the production of films.

When we proposed an analysis/essay on the four transversalities that weave the film and are perceived and reflected on Brazilian daily life, the political, social, economic and the media context, we tried to expose the communication potential of "Aquarius" by its film landscape and its direct reflection on latent issues in the country today. By this reflection, we also tried to expose how it is possible to produce movie narratives that can evoke a discourse and an attitude of resistance facing a rising wave of conservatism (in politics and even in aesthetics) and antidemocratic manifestations. Finally, we would like to stress that art, through filmic productions, is not only the forefront in the search for the new (and for the debate on art and its practices), but it also "allows the new to be an update of the past" (Cornutti & Liesenberg, 2013, p. 6). What we see in "Aquarius" and its mosaic of references (musical, political, economic, social, media) indicates that contemporary cinema in Brazil can also make way for a constant and provoking flux of reflections on the present and memory that allows us to think about the country in which we wish to live and collectively build.

---

[7] Research published by the Group of Multidisciplinary Studies of Affirmative Action [Gemma] at the Rio de Janeiro State University [UERJ], revealed that, from 2002 to 2014, 84% of filmmakers in Brazil were white males, 14% were white women and only 2% were black males, with no black women.

Acknowledgments

We are grateful to our long-time collaborator Raquel Nunes Ebert for translating this paper to English.

References

Baitello, N. (2010). *A Serpente, a Maçã e o Holograma*. São Paulo: Paulus.

Betton, G. (1987). *Estética do cinema*. São Paulo: Martins Fontes.

Braga, S. (n.d.). AQUARIUS - Sonia Braga e diretor falam sobre censura, golpe e muito mais! (2016, September 09) [Interview]. Retrieved December 2, 2018, from https://www.youtube.com/watch?v=bWhEXMM6uSM

Citelli, A. (2004). *Comunicação e educação. A linguagem em movimento*. SP: Senac.

Cornutti, C. & Liesenberg, S. (2013). *Aproximações com o conceito de apropriação: uma associação com as imagens de celebridades no blog "Te Dou Um Dado"*, from http://compos.org.br/data/biblioteca_1977.pdf

Cogo, D. (2009). *Los Estudios de Recepción en America Latina: perspectivas teórico-metodológicas*. Barcelona: Instituto de la Comunicación (InCOM) de la UAB (Universidad Autónoma de Barcelona).

Folha. (2016, September 28). Jornais franceses repercutem estreia de 'Aquarius' na França nesta quarta. Retrieved December 2, 2018, from https://www1.folha.uol.com.br/ilustrada/2016/09/1817591-jornais-franceses-repercutem-estreia-de-aquarius-na-franca-nesta-quarta.shtml

France Presse. Equipe de 'Aquarius' protesta em Cannes contra impeachment de Dilma. (2016, May 17). Retrieved December 2, 2018, from http://g1.globo.com/pop-arte/cinema/noticia/2016/05/equipe-de-aquarius-protesta-em-cannes-contra-impeachment-de-dilma.html

Harvey, D. (2008). *A Condição Pós-Moderna*. São Paulo: Edições Loyola.

Kastrup, V. (2004). *A rede: uma figura empírica da ontologia do presente*. In: Parente, A. (Org.). Tramas da rede – novas dimensões filosóficas, estéticas e políticas da comunicação. Porto Alegre: Sulina.

Martín-Barbero, J. (2004). *Ofício de Cartógrafo – Travessias latino-americanas da comunicação na cultura*. São Paulo: Edições Loyola.

Martín-Barbero, J. & Rey, G (2004). *Os exercícios do ver: hegemonia audiovisual e ficção televisiva*. São Paulo: Senac.

Mattelart, A. & Neveu, É. (2003). *Introdução aos Estudos Culturais*. SP: Parábola.

Nogueira, A. & Pessoa, G. S. (n.d.). Em nova polêmica, 'Aquarius' recebe classificação indicativa de 18 anos. Retrieved December 2, 2018, from https://www1.folha.uol.com.br/ilustrada/2016/08/1806117-em-nova-polemica-aquarius-recebe-classificacao-indicativa-de-18-anos.shtml

Rincón, O. (2006). *Narrativas mediáticas*. Barcelona: Editorial Gedisa.

Rodrigues, C. R. M. (2004). "Pipoca com Guaraná": A música como instrumento de *recall na criação publicitária*. Monografia. Pato Branco: FADEP – PR.

Romero, S. (2017, December 21). Brazilian Politics Smother a Film's Oscar Ambitions. Retrieved December 2, 2018, from https://www.nytimes.com/2016/09/28/world/americas/brazilian-politics-smother-a-films-oscar-ambitions.html?_r=0

Sá, X. & Alves, J. (2016, November 25). Geddel e Temer na versão baiana de 'Aquarius'. Retrieved December 2, 2018, from https://brasil.elpais.com/brasil/2016/11/25/opinion/1480073195_307146.html

Sekeff, M. L. (1998). *Música e Semiótica*. In: Tomás, L. (org). De sons e signos: música, mídia e contemporaneidade. São Paulo: EDUC.

Twisting Fate in *Rosemary's Baby*: Cassavetes/Polanski Interface as Hollywood Influence

Ian Dixon

Abstract. From the 1950s to the 1980s, John Cassavetes was a Hollywood actor with a mission: to challenge cinematic art by generating enduring performance authenticity for the ("accidental") advancement of film art by dramatizing the human dilemma (Fine, 2006). By exemplifying the actor-director's legendary clash with auteur Roman Polanski on *Rosemary's Baby* (1968), through Leo Braudy's (1977) axiom for "Open" and "Closed" filmmaking, Cassavetes can be seen to operate within the Hollywood system to subvert it in the way he understood human experience – from within. Cassavetes resisted the "destiny-locked" plot of the thriller-horror form by contributing to one of Hollywood's most enduring classics: *Rosemary's Baby*. The paper demonstrates how Cassavetes changed Hollywood through 'accidental' activism and how celebrity scholars might utilize the history of Cassavetes' cinema (Fine, 2006).

Keywords: John Cassavetes, Celebrity, Film, Roman Polanski, Hollywood.

Introduction[1]

Between 1950s Hollywood classicism and the reinventions of New Hollywood (post-9/11), *Rosemary's Baby* (1968) exemplifies the shifting ground of studio and independent filmmaking. At the creative epicenter of this seminal Paramount/Castle Hill production stand two masters of cinema: Roman Polanski and John Cassavetes, both actor-directors representing opposite poles of Leo Braudy's (1977) axiom for 'closed' and 'open' filmmaking. The former a virtuoso of super-uncanny suspense, the latter a pragmatist who declared: "I hate that spooky-dooky stuff" (Carney, 2001, p. 410). As Raymond Carney expounds: "Their shouting matches became the stuff of Hollywood legend" (2001, p. 182).

By investigating the on-set conflict between these two Hollywood icons (Carney, 2001), their methodologies and influences, this paper analyses, questions and problematizes Braudy's binary division. In particular, and in contrast to Polanski's horror, Cassavetes champions women's rights and protests against the objectification of women; supports the mentally ill and

---

[1] Disclaimer: This paper analyses the craft of Polanski and does not condone his actions taken outside the film *Rosemary's Baby*.

spectrum disorder children; and argues for animal rights – using his celebrity influence to advocate for change. This study begins with Braudy's (1977) axiom for open and closed filmmaking, which forms the basis for investigating the Cassavetes/Polanski interface with particular emphasis on the filmmakers' influences and performance codes.

Braudy's Open/Closed Axiom

Braudy illustrates his open/closed dialectic in cinema contemporaneous to Cassavetes and Polanski's oeuvre. In closed film, the narrative is destiny-locked and manipulative of the actor trapped within its fixed cinematic space. Open film, on the other hand, incorporates the artistic input of the actor, thus influencing the plot (1977, p. 219). The closed film deals with themes of determinism and directors such as Hitchcock and Polanski disorientate their characters within oppressive worlds to accommodate this. Actors in such films may be treated as 'cattle' or physical signifiers, rather than living beings with agency. Conversely, for open filmmakers such as Cassavetes or Renoir, "characters often talk, think, or act solely for themselves, enhancing our sense of their separate existence, rather than re-affirming their place in a pre-ordained scheme of theme and story" (Braudy, 1977, 219-220). As a maverick filmmaker, Cassavetes realizes Braudy's standard of the open film in which: "collusion between actor and director becomes, in the 1960s, much more prevalent a mode than the manipulation of actor by director" (1977, p. 252).

Examining screen performance, as impacted by this open/closed binary, Braudy expresses another fundamental determinant of cinema in his adage, "Mystery replaces articulation" (1977, p. 184). To explain this, Braudy states: "No matter how much we [the audience] know, there is always something more, something analysis can never quite totally encompass" (1977, p. 184). Braudy suggests that the cinema audience interprets this mystery in a manner resembling visual art (rather than theater or prose) by emphasizing the gap between the seen and the surmised. For Braudy, the elusive nature of character in film and painting depends upon an assumed "core," which is effectively "hidden within the visible body" (1977, pp. 184-186).

Braudy insists that cinema engages its audience in a pseudo-analytical guessing game to ascertain character motivation (1977, p. 187). Despite the internality of Cassavetes' Stanislavskian training, he codifies his own performances to suggest interpretation of such a mystery. When directing, Cassavetes ensures his actors' invisible agendas convey a "sense of extension beyond the film" and an ability to reinvent the diegetic world around them instead of being yet another object in the imposed interpretation of the director

(Braudy 1977, p. 184). For open filmmaker, John Cassavetes, this is achieved through performance "authenticity" as opposed to the manipulated significations of "visionary/symbolic" directors such as Fritz Lang, Hitchcock or Polanski (Carney, 1994, p. 13; Clurman in Counsell, 1996, p. 54). For example, in Cassavetes' *Woman under the Influence* (1974), the pensive confusion of Gena Rowlands' character (Cassavetes' wife), Mabel Longhetti, suggests a further life off-screen, uncontrolled by the manipulative hand of an external director. In this way, Cassavetes' mission to reinvent Hollywood performance standards exacerbates the gap between Polanski and himself and eventually succeeds in transforming mainstream cinema. This is poignant as contemporary scholarship acknowledges kinaesthetic and sensorial approaches to film analysis, which supersede the "ocular-centric model that dominated film theory in the 1970s and 80s" (Ndalianis, 2012, p. 4). Despite such developments, Polanski represents the opposite pole: closed filmmaking.

Polanski, *Rosemary's Baby* and Horror of the Demonic

Rosemary's Baby demonstrates Polanski's masterful control of closed film in the subgenre known as "horror of the demonic" (Derry, 2009). Producer, Robert Evans (2014), claims *Rosemary's Baby* as "the beginning of a new genre," but the subgenre is actually based on precedents from as early as D.W. Griffiths' *The Sorrows of Satan* (1925) (Newman, 2011, p. 57). Horror of the demonic flourishes after the demise of classic horror with Hitchcock's *Psycho* in 1960 – a film contemporary to both Polanski's *Knife in the Water* (1962) and Cassavetes' debut feature *Shadows* (1959).

Eschewing the "mad scientists and remote islands" of classic horror, modern horror (from *Psycho* to 9/11) foregrounds psychoanalysis, sexuality, death, "the social function of the family, patriarchy and money" (Humphries, 2002, p. 85). Derry, acknowledges horror of the demonic as the third great subgenre of the 1960s attributing its popularity to the longstanding tradition of eastern American Puritanism, "with its emphasis on damnation and antichrists" (2009, p. 90): a phenomenon climaxing in the 1692/1693 witch burnings in Salem, Massachusetts. According to Derry, horror of the demonic owes much to the emergence of "liberal dissent" (2009, p. 90) in the 1960s as exemplified by *Time* Magazine's infamous 1966 cover article, *Is God Dead?* Indeed, Derry describes witchcraft as the "inversion" (2009, p. 90) of Roman Catholic ritual claiming that, in the 1960s, it was convenient to blame the devil rather than embrace the politico-sexual "social strife" (2009, p. 90) at the root of this popular discourse, yet social strife is a source Cassavetean authenticity acknowledges.

In *Rosemary's Baby* – contrary to producer Robert Evans' (2014) claim to a new genre – Derry (2009) denotes two Scandinavian films as significant forerunners to Polanski's definitive version. Firstly, one of Cassavetes' favored directors, Carl Theodore Dreyer's *Day of Wrath* (1943) and secondly, Ingmar Bergman's *The Devil's Wanton* (also known as *Prison*) (1949) (Derry, 2009, p. 89/90; Carney, 2001).

Polanski's 1968 film *Rosemary's Baby* is cited as the definitive Hollywood exemplar of this subgenre (Derry 2009; Humphries, 2002). It synthesizes Derry's four tenets for defining the subgenre: vengeance (as shown in the devil's "mythically rooted revenge against God for the birth of Christ"); corruption of innocence (as Rosemary accepts motherhood to the devil – an example dramatizing the social fear of youth protesting on the streets); mystic phenomena (especially possession); and an emphasis on Christian symbology (such as the appearance of the Pope and Rosemary's "Madonna blue" costume design by Anthea Sylbert) (Derry, 2009, p. 91; Vice, 2014). All four themes are in keeping with the tyrannical world of Braudy's (1977) closed film principles. Indeed, Polanski's genius for turning mundane banality into destiny-locked horror leaves no apparent room for improvisation within its tightly scripted, closed film scenario.

In the manner of the closed film and despite Newman's labeling the film as "a feminist rethinking of the traditionally vulnerable heroine role" (2011, p. 58), *Rosemary's Baby* enacts the reactionary politics of late 1960s paranoia. Humphries illustrates that Rosemary submits to the same ideology as Marion Crane, best exemplified in the line from head witch, Roman Castevet (Sidney Blackmer), "He has his father's eyes," which implies that dutiful mothers must submit to the dominant order (Humphries, 2002, p. 89). As such, the fear of Satan enacts patriarchy's hidden agenda; a notion rejected by Cassavetes' open filmmaking.

As a performer himself, Polanski indicated that the actor as signifier should forget their "outside world" (thus placing themselves at the mercy of the director's "tyrannical" form). In *Rosemary's Baby,* Polanski also used his performance skills to demonstrate how the actors should play their parts – an imitative, result-driven process redolent with closed film practices (Weston, 1996). Although amenable to Farrow, the method proved arduous for Cassavetes. Footage from *The Criterion Collection* of Polanski leading the two stars along preconceived markings on the floor during rehearsal shows a compliant Farrow and, a few paces behind, a palpably recalcitrant Cassavetes silently protesting the strictures of Polanski's closed film methodology. While describing Cassavetes as a "terribly talented man with his own interpretation,"

Polanski denigrates Cassavetes' rebelliousness by commenting: "If you took off his sneakers, he had problems with his acting" (Vice, 2014).

Like *Knife in the Water*, *Rosemary's Baby* reflects Polanski's painstaking attention to design, of which the actors are a component. The overhead shot of the protagonist (Zygmunt Malanowicz) in *Knife* assuming crucifixion pose on a yacht testifies to this. In such a design, the actor's entrapment in the plot renders their efforts destiny-locked by manipulative directors (Braudy, 1977; McKee, 1999). Indeed, Robert McKee analyzes *Rosemary's Baby*'s "Negation of the Negation" as "plights in which death would be a mercy and we'd beg for it" (1999, p. 324), which circumscribes closed film sensibilities. A psychological thriller such as Polanski's film, with its overbearing themes of fate and claustrophobic evil, proved anathema to Cassavetes (Carney, 2001).

Cassavetes' Influences and Open Direction

If there is subversion present in *Rosemary's Baby* it lies with the "Accidental Genius" of John Cassavetes (Fine, 2006). Although Farrow reports Polanski and Cassavetes bonding superbly during rehearsals, Polanski, Farrow continues, is "opposite" to Cassavetes, given that Polanski's actors and camera are placed with exactitude. "John wished to improvise," Farrow asserts, indicating that Cassavetes films were "freewheeling and improvised" (Vice, 2014), which, according to Cassavetes experts, is not correct (Carney, 2001; Fine, 2006).

Cassavetes enacted Orson Welles' assertion that actors (not directors) are central to film art (Rosenbaum, 1995, p. 161), which opposes Polanski's belief in the subservience of actors. By contrast to Polanski, Cassavetes' filmmaking was influenced by: *Cinéma Vérité*; Italian Neo-Realism; and, Lionel Rogosin's genre-defying open film *On the Bowery* (1956) (Carney, 2001). Rogosin's *Bowery* combined documentary and drama, splicing real events into contrived interplay between actual persons (Cassavetes in Gelmis, 1971). Inspired by *Bowery*, according to Comolli and Pierre (1986), films such as Cassavetes' *Faces* synthesized narrative writing and documentary form. Cassavetes also cast unemployed actors on the fringe of Hollywood and championed the subversive in mainstream movie making: the disenfranchised; the victims of poor race relations; women's issues; and gender politics (Carney, 1994). In this way, Cassavetes contributed to the evolution of *Cinéma Vérité*, thus adding to the canon of open filmmaking.

Despite Carney's claims to Cassavetes' separation from Hollywood, Cassavetes operated close to Hollywood and was sustained by the economic power of the studio system in varying ways (Carney, 1994; 2001; Kouvaros,

2004). Father of independent cinema though he may be (Carney, 2001), financing, such as his ruse to raise funds for *Shadows* via Jean Shepherd's New York radio program rested upon Cassavetes' notoriety from the television series *Johnny Staccato* (1959). Funds were therefore accessible for Cassavetes via the cultural capital his Hollywood star status provided.

Indeed, as a television star, Cassavetes pushed beyond Francesco Alberoni's notion of "The Powerless Elite" using his celebrity influence to advocate for change within industry and morality (as cited in Dyer, 1986, p. 7). *Shadows* saw the casting of three African American leads in a film dramatizing race relations early in the civil rights movement. The filmmaker also advocated for animal rights in his eccentric depiction of sibling relationships in *Love Streams*. His films embraced women's rights and ethical positioning on the objectification of women (*Faces* (1968); *A Woman under the Influence* (1974); *Opening Night* (1977)). His cinematic treatment of otherwise functional 'weepy' themes, such as mental illness in *Woman* or the trauma of institutionalizing spectrum disorder children in *A Child is Waiting* (1963) defied format-written screenplays and activated authentic issue-based cinema.

Similarly audacious, Cassavetes' rehearsals were reputedly ebullient, a "playground," where acting became silly and elemental and ultimately transferred to the filmed image (Carney 2001, p. 53). For example, while rehearsing a serious domestic dispute between Hollywood heavyweights Jon Voigt and Gena Rowlands in 1980, Cassavetes climbed on the dinner table declaring: "I'll play the chicken." Cassavetes proceeded to lie on his back with feet and imaginary wings trussed up and comatose to effect authenticity in the scene (Kiselyak, 2000). He believed in the "validity of a person's inner desires" (Cassavetes in Gelmis, 1971, p. 81), which challenges Braudy's notion of the cinema's "right and proper inability to explain the inner world" (1986, p. 324). Cassavetes was also acutely aware of the ways a director could "unconsciously intimidate the performer" (Carney, 2001, p. 157). Sometimes, his actors were refused any direction whatsoever, but never forced into a "pre-ordained scheme," which leaves the performer no room to extemporize (Carney, 2001, p. 330).

By contrast, Sylvie Pierre suggests Cassavetes was a filmmaker rare in the 1960s who could envision scenes from a kinaesthetic position, which challenges the formal boundaries of Hollywood classicism such as *Rosemary's Baby* exploits. As Braudy indicates, such formalism conceals cinema's "inability to explain the inner world" by presenting only external signs of "inner turmoil" (1986, p. 324). Indeed, Cassavetes' hidden agendas are skillfully displayed by his actors in a more 'authentic' manner than standard "visionary/symbolic" or closed filmmakers such as Polanski (Carney, 1994, p. 13; Braudy, 1977, p. 220).

Closed Film/Open Film Interface in *Rosemary's Baby*

Given the extremities of the closed film/open film interface, Braudy's theory proves effective for studying the hiatus between Polanski and Cassavetes. The binary also provides insight into Hollywood's commercial forms such as horror and thriller, with their demonstrable success rate. For Cassavetes, a director enamored with performance 'authenticity,' the constrictions of *Rosemary's Baby* become palpable on screen. Having encouraged "emotional improvisation" in his own actors and employed non-interventional direction, which in Braudy's sense "incorporates the artistic input of the actor" (1977, p. 219), Cassavetes' rebellious behavior on set indicates an open resistance to the constraint of Polanski's closed technique (Carney, 2001).

In an interview with Anthony Loeb (1982), Cassavetes cautioned against the anti-art pretensions of closed filmmaking that *Rosemary's Baby* exemplified, accusing the film's auteur of pandering to the "dictated design" of studio practice and formulaic writing. Cassavetes opines:

> Take a guy like Polanski who did pictures in Poland: *Knife in the Water* and later *Repulsion*. You could see in those works a pulse that was meaningful and creative and intense. You can't dispute the fact that he's an artist, but yet you have to say that *Rosemary's Baby* is not art. It is a dictated design – boom, boom, boom. People are used within that design to make a commercial product to sell to people. I'm not saying that is bad. I was in it. I'm fine. I'm happy. But it isn't art (as cited in Loeb, 1982, p. 3).

Cassavetes' comment conveys his open filmmaking bias and ostensible opposition to Hollywood mainstream in contrast to genre films like *Rosemary's Baby*. For Cassavetes, actor/director "collusion" resulting in character surprises was fundamental to his art (Braudy, 1977, p. 252). In *Rosemary's Baby* the audience may be confused and paranoid, but this becomes "another element in the visual pattern" of Polanski's dictated design: disciplined, streamlined and destiny-locked (Braudy, 1977, p. 219).

Polanski's Dictated Design

In *Rosemary's Baby*, Polanski's plot is organized around novelist Ira Levin's two opposing possibilities: Rosemary's fevered imagination versus the machinations of the devil. The polemic realizes Braudy's estimation of closed characters under "limitation and repression." As mentioned, Polanski appears in his own films as Cassavetes does. However, Polanski's personal performances indicate a self-conscious player in a masterful, often surreal environment influenced by theater of the absurd such as *The Tenant* (1976) displays within the thriller form. However, where *The Tenant* is scathing in its subversion of capitalist banality, *Rosemary's Baby* remains a conservative ideological vehicle despite its complexity. The non-decidability of Levin's plot encourages a plural reading: is Rosemary paranoid or haunted? Producer William Castle describes Polanski's clever juxtaposition of witchcraft and mental instability as: "you see nothing: it's as scary as hell" (Vice, 2014). Humphries opines that in this film there is, "not a shred of evidence that Rosemary was impregnated by the Devil and that the child should not be the fruit of her union with Guy [John Cassavetes]" (2002, p. 86-87).

Polanski is keenly aware of Cassavetes' profile as actor-director and his pluralistic screen signification, which exploits Braudy's determinant in complex manner. Indeed, in *Rosemary's Baby,* the steely gaze of Cassavetes leaves much "Mystery" for the pseudo-analyst to unravel (Braudy, 1977, p. 184/187); the star's psychological complexity pinioned between Cassavetes' "long, intense look" and confident, "closed-mouth grin" (Gelmis, 1971, p. 76) – the two signifiers in combination connoting a palpable duplicitousness. In combination with Cassavetes' open capacity for naturalizing the formulaic, Polanski exploits the actor-appearing-as-actor in a closed sense to sign the machinations of the devil. Cassavetes' visage alone connotes three of Derry's principles for identifying the sub-genre: vengeance, corruption and mystic phenomena - leaving the fourth, Christian symbology, to Polanski's closed *mise-en-scène* (Derry, 2009).

To problematize the open/closed polarity, however, it should be noted that Polanski's direction is not entirely autocratic. Polanski claims that he never tells actors where to go or what to do, but rather allows them to find their spatialized blocking. In this way, the line between open and closed filmmaking blurs as Polanski allows them to "interpret the world" (Braudy 1977, p. 220; Vice, 2014). However, the "trickery" of Polanski to elicit performance cannot emulate that of Cassavetes. Polanski may draw upon improvisation, but nevertheless simulates a tyrannical world where the actor is trapped (Braudy 1977), yet Cassavetes' presence in the production challenges that form.

Cassavetes Disrupts Polanski's Dictated Design

For Polanski, Cassavetes was "a pain in the ass" who retarded the shooting schedule and threatened the hegemony of the auteur (Vice, 2014). However, Polanski's dismissal of Cassavetes as an actor who could not act without his sneakers betrays an approach to performance, which should not be treated glibly. Under the influence of the Stanislavskian (1980) system, Cassavetes was trained that costume – especially shoes – were vital to characterization, which counteracts Polanski's claim. Cassavetes' desire to "talk, think, or act solely for [himself]" was no trivial addition as the diegetic suspense was reinforced by the quality of realism that Cassavetes brought to Polanski's masterpiece (Braudy, 1977, 219-220). In order to illustrate Cassavetes' agency from within and without Hollywood as a director with rare sensitivity to the craft of acting (Jousse as cited in Kouvaros, 2004), I cite six ways with which Cassavetes challenged mainstream normativity to disrupt *Rosemary's Baby's* dictated design. Beginning with funding processes for his own films, I illustrate how Cassavetes exploits open film principles for diversity in casting and subject matter; allows gestural performance and 'authenticity' to manifest in unique ways (which ultimately affects the direction New Hollywood eventually took); facilitates agency for women and accordingly the depiction of sex on film.

Cassavetes' agency as indie filmmaker eschewing Hollywood norms begins with his casting process. Jettisoning power-based Hollywood auditioning conventions, Cassavetes would simply speak with his actors, engage them and explore how he might express elements of their personality and personal contribution within his production (Carney, 2001). According to Judith Weston (1996), Cassavetes negates the lackadaisical casting system prevalent in Hollywood, where directors expect the perfect candidate to suit their vision. By contrast, Cassavetes grew emotionally close to his actors, talking to them and trusting his filmmaker's eye to recognize their "invisible mind" in Braudy's sense (1977, p. 184). *Faces* star, Lynn Carlin was Robert Altman's secretary who had no previous acting experience before Cassavetes cast her opposite veteran actor John Marley. Contributing to film form in Braudy's sense, Carlin suggested the title, *Faces*, after an initial screening, superseding the working title, *Dinosaurs* (Carney, 2001). These are encouragements to performers' agency Polanski might never abide, but Cassavetes suggests: "A filmmaker has to trust himself and his actors. You have to trust your own feelings and the belief that audiences want what you want, that you're no different" (Cassavetes in Carney, 2001, p. 264).

This is a principle ignored by Polanski in *Rosemary's Baby*. When Robert Redford proved unavailable, Polanski cast Cassavetes as Rosemary's "struggling actor" husband Guy Woodhouse primarily on his signification, thus enacting the Hollywood casting phenomenon (Weston, 1996). "I needed someone who looked like an actor...like a New York actor," Polanski reflects, "Cassavetes fitted the part wonderfully" (Evans & Polanski, 1968). Cassavetes' casting along with Hollywood's growing adherence to method acting principles is churlishly mocked in Polanski's text through Roman Castevets' statement: "You have a most interesting inner quality, Guy" (Levin & Polanski, 1967, p. 42). Nonetheless lampooned, Cassavetes' gestural performance authenticates the text of *Rosemary's Baby* in ways Redford might never have achieved.

Rosemary's Baby's dictated design is also partly undermined by the gestural language of Cassavetes' performance. As Carney illustrates: "Cassavetes the actor was identical to Cassavetes the director" (2001, p. 182). As director, Cassavetes' 'Non-style' (Carney, 1994), his *Vérité* leanings and insistence on emotional-based pacing influence his performance in Polanski's film. As an actor, Cassavetes' long pauses accompanied by repetitive stuttering and the gestural hallmarks of Stanislavskian acting take precedence over the formulaic pacing of *Rosemary's Baby* (Carney, 2001; Counsell, 1996). This includes Cassavetes' capacity for emotional improvisation to qualify the tight scripting of dialogue (Braudy, 1977, p. 219-220; Carney, 2001). As Carney suggests, dramatic language: "inevitably tames, systematizes and abstracts the surging fluidity of our feelings" but Cassavetes resists such strictures (Carney, 1994, p. 149). Cassavetes "freed [the actor] of resultant self-consciousness," which is evident in his own performance subverting *Rosemary's Baby*. For example, Cassavetes' mockery of the porter (Elisha Cooke Jr.) at the beginning of the film displays Cassavetes' naturalization of the dialogue, but nevertheless entraps Cassavetes in plot, space, language and camera movement. For Cassavetes, his 'fake' laughter is interspersed with an authentic portrayal of a narcissistic husband whose right of ownership of his wife's body causes him grief only when he is exposed as a conspirator. Nevertheless, self-consciousness entraps all the actors in Polanski's film – especially Ruth Gordon's vaudevillian villainess – but, by striving for a "present tense" illusion, Cassavetes enacts his 'soft' subversion within the design (Naremore, 1988). The falsifications within his performance are indicative of result-driven direction on the part of the closed film director who, as Judith Weston points out, violates the "actor's delicate emotional mechanisms" (Weston, 1996, p. 18). Indeed, Cassavetes' mundane interpretation render's Guy's monstrosity more heinous than a 'functional' actor might, which brings the argument to a consideration of authenticity.

Cassavetes' authenticity and its signage for Hollywood mainstream can be traced through Cassavetes' gestural performance in *Rosemary's Baby*.

Cassavetes maintains a genuinely guilty "internality" under Guy's "controlled mask" (Counsell, 1996, p. 69), resulting in a "sense of extension beyond the film" achieved through Stanislavskian principles (Braudy, 1977, pp. 184-220). Polanski, however, gauges the extent to which the audience are allowed to interpret the signs elicited in performance. An example of differing open/closed performance codes can be detected in the 'deep-two' shot of Cassavetes and Dr Sapirstein (Ralph Bellamy) 'rescuing' Rosemary from Dr Hill. As a functional aspect of the 'tyrannical' plot, Bellamy urges Rosemary to "come quietly" while the authenticity is carried by Cassavetes in the background. As Braudy suggests, the elusive nature of his character depends upon an assumed 'core,' which is effectively "hidden within the visible body" as Cassavetes' idiosyncratic intensity contrasts with the uncanny stillness of his body. Polanski provides the exterior signs of husband squirming in emotional turmoil: Cassavetes' hand covering his low-lit face (melodramatic code for shame) and emphasizes his inability to face his wife Rosemary. However, as Carney illustrates, a lesser actor than Cassavetes might merely "sleepwalk" through the part (1994, p. 101).[2] Instead, Cassavetes' dedication to open film authenticity is palpable even within the closed form encasing him. Cassavetes' line: "we wanna take you home" is brimming with subtext – demonstrating his trademark duplicity as he smiles through widened eyes – a gesture which imitates Derry's hallmark horror of the demonic trait: the "innocence" of an infant while communicating its diametrical opposite: corruption. The contrast between Cassavetes and Bellamy reflects the formal division between the actors: the former rendering an open quality of "potential and variety," the latter presenting a closed film character as "limitation and repression" (Braudy, 1977, p. 219). Having said that, Guy's hand-biting is an externalized addition in the closed film sense rather than an organic choice for Cassavetes. Where every other sign in this scene is portrayed as per the screenplay: "Guy starts to rise but sits down again"; "Guy - whose eyes are hidden behind a hand"; "Guy looks out at Rosemary from under his hand" (Levin & Polanski, 1967, p. 161-163); there is no evidence that states: "Guy bites his hand." This suggests the gesture arrives through Guy's "given circumstances" much as Dreyer or Rogosin's characters might discover. In this way, Cassavetes' Guy returns to subversive filmmaking traits in antipathy to Polanski's dictated commercial design (yet ironically supports it).

Also functional in *Rosemary's Baby* closed form is Cassavetes' open filmmaking politic for non-exploitative depictions of women. Regarding soft-core pornification in mainstream cinema, Cassavetes states:

---

[2] Carney claims James Stewart 'sleepwalk[s]' through *Rear Window* (1954) (1994, p. 101).

I'm very concerned about the depiction of women on the screen. It's related to their being either high- or low-class concubines, and the only question is when or where, and with whom or how many. There's nothing to do with the dreams of women (2001 p. 35).

Ironically, after feminist criticism's contempt for Polanski's *Repulsion* (1965), the director references the (second wave) women's movement to make the *Rosemary's Baby* narrative possible, as Newman (2011) intimates. However, Polanski's reactionary position in *Rosemary's Baby* contrasts to Cassavetes' celebrated pro-feminism in *Woman under the Influence*. A poignant example of the open film actor's subversion within closed form is Cassavetes' refusal to pander to Hollywood standards of sensuality in Guy and Rosemary's lovemaking scene. Engaging his personal politic, Cassavetes demurs the scene's nudity and objectification of Farrow as: "phony exploitative and commercial. It's cheap voyeurism" (Carney, 2001, pp. 182/296).

Given his concerns, Cassavetes' invents comic business to subvert the dictated design in which Farrow is frequently disrobed. When preparing for lovemaking, Cassavetes struggles on the floor in distinctly non-Hollywood fashion, gyrating about with the attention-seeking gestures of a histrionic actor (like a trussed chicken), but right down to his underpants, he avoids what Naremore refers to as the mainstream convention of "frontality" from David Bordwell's "geocities" (Naremore, 1988, p. 41). The moment is simple, non-clichéd and poignant in its honesty, escaping Hollywood prefabrication of connubial bliss. The male gazing audience is still afforded voyeuristic advantage over the shy nudity of Farrow, but Cassavetes' wriggling chicken distances the cheap eroticism of the scene through comic foil.

Further, Cassavetes' depiction of husband-as-necrophile relies on his authenticating portrayal of self-serving evil: a lesser actor might not have achieved this. Guy's banal monstrosity highlights the insecurities of patriarchy, which further subverts the conservative form of *Rosemary's Baby* because the monstrous is palpable in Cassavetes' prosaic embodiment. In this way, Newman's interpretation of the film as, "feminist rethinking of the traditionally vulnerable heroine role" is at least given a chance to surface (2011, p. 58), but ultimately collapses under 1960s reactionary politics to assume, "unconsciously the ideology of patriarchy" (Humphries, 2002, p. 86). Nevertheless, Cassavetes remains an iconoclastic presence within the film.

In his own filmmaking, the open hysteria of *Woman* portrays the politico-sexual horror lurking under the surface of domesticity, earning Rowland's an Oscar nomination and highlighting the politic. Similarly, the unglamorous portrayal of women in *Chinese Bookie* or the non-clichéd evocation of prostitution in *Faces* points to the inner lives of women while emphasizing their protest against the follies of men (Carney, 2001). Cassavetes' presence in *Rosemary's Baby* can only attempt such subversion and does so as internal disruption.

Cassavetes authentic performance highlights his character's narcissistic banality in Derry's sense: becoming a tool within the devil's vengeful plan; opposing and corrupting the innocence of Rosemary; relying on mystic phenomena such as his agency in Baumgart's (Tony Curtis) blindness and abetting Rosemary's possession; within the tyrannical oppression of Polanski's Christian symbology (2009, p. 91). Even the naked vengeance of his own real-life mother, Katherine Cassavetes, against the innocence of Mabel and her children in *Woman* outshines the genre-based authenticity of Polanski. Cassavetes' *Opening Night* dramatizes mystic possession as the ghost of the dead girl haunts Rowlands' character, Myrtle Gordon. However, Cassavetes films are closer in ethos to raw street protesting than obscured in Christian symbology. In this way, Cassavetes filmmaking and his presence in Polanski's contrived plot reveals the politico-sexual "social strife" the horror genre attempts to obfuscate (Derry, 2009, p. 90-91): and remains a further source of Cassavetean authenticity. Cassavetes ameliorates the genre through his open technique to question the "tyrannical" worlds of closed film principles, which further problematizes Braudy's division (Braudy, 1977, p. 219-220). The affective tenor of Cassavetes' 'soft' rebellion can be detected in open filmmaking contemporaneously.

Conclusion

With *Rosemary's Baby,* the commercial product Cassavetes so despised is one result of Hollywood's careful attention to audience reception of genre since the 1930s. However, contrary to Alberoni's depiction of celebrity as a "Powerless Elite" (as cited in Dyer, 1986, p. 7), once he had become jaded with his own celebrity, Cassavetes used his influence to effect change. If Cassavetes' agency as a filmmaker is a byproduct of his close Hollywood proximity, then his subversion of Hollywood text such as Polanski's *Rosemary's Baby* may be as accidental as his genius. Nevertheless, Cassavetes influences industry standards for the casting process, women's issues, gender politics and performance conventions indirectly inherited from Stanislavskian 'authenticity.'

As with *Rosemary's Baby*, New Hollywood directors influenced by Polanski invest years in their dictated design, yet concede to open film techniques in Cassavetean fashion: present tense action, authenticity and spontaneity (Naremore, 1988). In this way, genre filmmaking "incorporates the artistic input of the actor" significantly more than *Rosemary's Baby* demonstrates in 1968 (Braudy, 1977, p. 219). In such a genre film, Polanski becomes a director under the influence of his recalcitrant actor, John Cassavetes. Similarly, Cassavetes demonstrable resistance creates activism from within Hollywood: a convention reaching into contemporary cinema almost half a century later.

References

Braudy, L. (1977). *The world in a frame: What we see in films*. Garden City, New York: Anchor Press & Doubleday.

Braunsberg, A. (Producer), & Polanski, R. (Director). (1976). *The Tenant* [Motion picture]. France: Marianne Productions.

Carney, R. (1994). *The films of John Cassavetes: Pragmatism, modernism and the movies*. United States of America: Cambridge University Press.

Carney, R. (2001). *Cassavetes on Cassavetes*. R. Carney (Ed.). New York: Faber & Faber Inc.

Comolli, J. (1986). Back to back: Two faces of Faces. Cahiers du Cinéma Volume 2: New wave, new cinema, re-evaluating Hollywood: An anthology from Cahiers du Cinéma nos 103-207: January 1960 – December 1968, *2*(205), 325-327, London: Routledge & Kegan Paul.

Counsell, C. (1996). *Signs of performance: An introduction to twentieth-century theatre*. London & New York: Routledge.

Derry, C. (2009). *Dark dreams 2.0: A psychological history of the modern horror film from the 1950s to the 21st century*. Jefferson, North Carolina & London: McFarland & Company, Inc.

Dreyer, C. Th. (Producer), & Dreyer, C. Th. (Director). (1943). *Day of wrath*. [Motion picture]. Paris: Palladium Productions.

Evans, R. (Producer), & Polanski, R. (Director). (1968). *Rosemary's baby*. [Motion picture] United States of America: William Castle Enterprises.

Fine, M. (2006). *Accidental genius: How John Cassavetes invented the independent film* (1st ed.). United States of America: Miramax.

Gelmis, J. (1971). John Cassavetes. In J. Gelmis, (Ed.), *The film director as superstar* (pp. 75-87). London: Secker & Warburg.

Globus, Y. & Golan, M. (Producers), & Cassavetes, J. (Director). (1984). *Love streams* [Motion picture]. United States of America: Cannon Films.

Gutowski, G. (Producer), & Polanski, R. (Director). (1965). *Repulsion* [Motion picture]. United Kingdon: Compton Films.

Hayden, J. (Director). (1960). Swinging long hair. In *Johnny Staccato* [Television series]. United States of America: Revue Studios.

Humphries, R. (2002). *The American horror film: An introduction.* Edinburgh: Edinburgh University Press.

Hitchcock, A. (Producer), & Hitchcock, A. (Director). (1960). *Psycho* [Motion picture]. United States of America: Shamley Productions.

Kiselyak, C. (Producer), & Kiselyak, C. (Director), (2000). *A constant forge: The life and art of John Cassavetes* [Motion picture]. United States of America: Castle Hill Productions & The Criterion Collection.

Kouvaros, G. (2004). *Where does it happen? John Cassavetes and cinema at the breaking point.* Minneapolis: University of Minnesota Press.

Kramer, S. (Producer), & Cassavetes, J. (Director). (1963). *A child is waiting* [Motion picture]. United States of America: Stanley Kramer Productions.

Levin, I. & Polanski, R. (Writers). (1967) *Rosemary's Baby: Original version.* USA: William Castle Enterprises.

Loeb, A. (1982). *Filmmakers in conversation.* Columbia: The Film Department, Columbia College.

Marmstedt, L. (Producer), & Bergman, I. (Director). (1949). *The devil's wanton* [Motion picture]. Sweden: Terrafilm.

McEndree, M. & Papatakis, N. (Producers), & Cassavetes, J. (Director/Writer). (1959). *Shadows* [Motion picture]. United States of America: Gena Productions & Lion International.

McEndree, M. (Producer), & Cassavetes, J. (Director). (1968). *Faces* [Motion picture]. United States of America: Faces International Films, Inc.

McKee, R. (1999). *Story: Substance, structure, style and the principles of screenwriting.* Great Britain: Methuen Publishing Limited.

Naremore, J. (1988). *Acting in the cinema.* Berkeley and Los Angeles: University of California Press.

Ndalianis, A. (2012). *The horror sensorium: Media and the senses.* North Carolina: McFarland & Company, Inc.

Pierre, S. (1986). Around the void: Two faces of Faces. *Cahiers du Cinéma* Volume 2: New wave, new cinema, re-evaluating Hollywood: An anthology from Cahiers du Cinéma nos 103-207: January 1960 – December 1968, *2*(205), 324-325, London: Routledge & Kegan Paul.

Rosenbaum, J. (1995). Love films: A Cassavetes retrospective. In J. Rosenbaum (Ed.), *Placing movies: The practice of film criticism* (pp. 156-162). Berkeley & Los Angeles, California: University of California Press.

Shaw, S. (Producer), & Cassavetes, J. (Director). (1974). *A woman under the influence* [Motion picture]. United States of America: Faces International Films, Inc.

Shaw, S. (Producer), & Cassavetes, J. (Director). (1977). *Opening night* [Motion picture]. United States of America: Faces International Films, Inc.

Vice (Producer). (2014, September 14). Roman Polanski on "Rosemary's Baby": Conversations inside The Criterion Collection. Podcast retrieved from https://www.youtube.com/watch?v=6q8LbUhPzLE

Weston, J. (1996). *Directing actors: Creating memorable performances for film and television*. Studio City, CA: Michael Wiese Productions.

Zylewicz, S. (Producer), & Polanski, R. (Director). (1962). *Knife in the water* [Motion picture]. Poland: Zespol Filmowy "Kamera".

The Actress as Activist: Subversion of a Century of Hollywood Misogyny in Five Modes

Kerry McElroy

Abstract. The question of how and where to situate social justice activism in film studies is a timely one, and one that is central to my methodology as feminist film historian. I have endeavored within my scholarship to do both memoir mining and oral history interviews with women in Hollywood (largely, actresses) as a type of reclamatory social justice historiography. The ethos to moving such texts in women's own words to centrality is to correct the historical record in relation to the gender imbalances and exploitations baked into patriarchal-capitalist Hollywood from its inception. Within this approach, I am able to recast the system-critical filmic industry woman as internal, subversive activist-critic – and women's writings on the exploitations of filmic systems as, themselves, social justice texts. In this chapter, I situate the actress or filmic woman as system-critical activist both in the historical and contemporary modes, through four types of texts: memoir and archive, oral history interview, metafictional interdisciplinary text, and textual-visual journalistic piece. These sections interrogate examples of actress histories as record-correcting activism from Louise Brooks to Amber Tamblyn and the Bill Cosby accusers. I conclude by suggesting that all of these modes of actress historical activism, identifiable as anomalies several years ago, can now be read as the forerunners of the #metoo/Time's Up cultural sea change that was a century in the making. What has transpired since late 2017 amounts to a penultimate fifth mode of actress activism – one of the utmost importance.

Keywords: Hollywood, Film Industry, Women, Film History, Activism.

The question of how and where to situate social justice activism in film studies has moved from a timely one to one that is absolutely pressing, in professional and academic cultures alike. This piece began as one suggesting that we as feminist film scholars and historians look to alternative modes of film history to correct the historical record, and analysed four such modes that amalgamated modern and postmodern elements. Yet this very landscape has changed in real time. What was interesting material to study in 2015 or 2016— whether actress memoirs or interviews that problematized gendered Hollywood, or the Bill Cosby scandal as cultural marker—can now instead be seen, in retrospect, as harbingers of the great Weinstein/#metoo/Time's Up cultural cataclysm of late 2017. It is nothing short of shocking that when this chapter was first conceptualized in early 2017, it was necessary to make the case for the actress as activist at all. Such a strong assertion was needed to counter an assumption that Hollywood was yet something of a pre-feminist milieu, ripe for rebellion perhaps—but with rebellions heretofore only identifiable in small fissures and with academic detective work. Now the premise that we should read the actress as a type of activist is no longer one to be identified or teased out by film scholars. Within a span of months, it has come to be an absolute truism in the public and popular culture conversations occurring daily around the world in media, on the internet, and in public demonstration.

Film systems in general are industries in which the use-value and exchange-value of women's bodies, so well theorized to date by feminist scholars like Luce Irigaray, Gayle Rubin, and Julia Kristeva, are uniquely central (Irigaray, 1985; Rubin, 2011; Kristeva, 1986). From the perspective of nationality, this highly specific economy of female flesh seems to be far more central to Hollywood than to many other global cinemas. In fact, the Hollywood film industry's reliance on the use and exploitation of women's bodies from its earliest founding to the present day is so intrinsic that it bears obvious parallels to and slippages into both trafficked sex work and coerced pornography. All three of these tracks have at times run parallel for vulnerable women in Los Angeles. They also share a central commonality in being industries in which the display and labor of women's bodies generate revenue for others behind the scenes, with the overwhelming majority of the time those reaping the benefits being older, wealthy, male capitalists.

These exploitations of women have operated in the cultural track of the everyday, but also in the form of academic and historiographic erasure. Certainly well before this conversation moved to the cultural forefront, feminist film history and alternative star studies have recognized the problem of masculinist historiography for some time. Patrice Petro (1996), speaking of postmodern historian Hayden White, makes a point that can apply to almost all mainstream film and cultural historians when she identifies him as a male historian who "never addresses the role of gender in historiography" (p. 197). In the Richard Dyer/Richard de Cordova school of star studies, as well, gender was rarely considered. The star was primarily considered as semiotic symbol—an oversight which in fact led to considerable blind spots in the conceptualisation of the star as labouring subject or human being (Dyer, 1996; Dyer, 1998; De Cordova, 1990). Finally, the Kenneth Anger school of gossip journalism meets Hollywood history betrays a great deal of misogyny and othering in creating a mythos of the doomed, tragic woman in film and Los Angeles life (Anger. 1985). In this branch of film history, morbidity and addiction are gleefully excavated, while competency, stability, and hard work are ignored.

Even though this work has not been done nearly enough to date, one finds in undertaking it that there are, happily, overlooked theoretical models that work well. 20th century American anthropologist Hortense Powdermaker went to Hollywood for fieldwork in the 1940s, came to fascinating conclusions about a system built on exploitation, and created brilliant, unprecedented scholarship that holds up seven decades later (Powdermaker, 1950/2013). Jane Gaines continued Powdermaker's conception of the Dream Factory to apply a specific and precise concept of industrial studies to performers in the Hollywood system (Gaines, 2000). Historical deconstruction of this sort that challenges the illusions of glamour and the Dream Factory structure is a necessary step if these conditions are to evolve or finally become equitable. Finally, despite being a French philosopher writing in Europe, Simone de Beauvoir picked up on this exploited and paradoxical position of the Hollywood star in *Le Deuxième Sexe* many years before any other theorists were studying these women or their cultural significance (de Beauvoir, 1949/2011). I think it goes without saying that all of these same theorists can also prove to be particularly apropos ones to augment the aims of the Time's Up revolution on the scholarly side.

Still and overall, thus far few undertaking scholarship in film, star, and celebrity studies have looked to what should be an obvious body of expert knowledge on women in the Hollywood system: narratives written by or interviews done with system-critical women themselves. In the various entertainment businesses that have for over a century painted themselves as the international standard of glamour and success, to step out of line as industry employee and critique that system as toxic or abuse-laden has required degrees of courage and non-compliance. Such an approach leads directly to affect studies in performance industries. The approach of this project in recentring the female voice in performance and cultural history elevates women's mistreatment and subsequent endurance to something worthy of comment, and something that matters.

As a feminist film historian, I feel strongly that a historiographic commitment to memoir mining and to the use of oral history interviews with women in Hollywood has always been required. The ethos to moving such texts in women's own words to centrality has been to correct the historical record of patriarchal-capitalist Hollywood, particularly in terms of the gendered abuses and exploitations baked into it from its inception. This approach resituates the actress or Hollywood woman herself as internal activist-critic, while also challenging and deconstructing the mythos of the Dream Factory. It gives voice to the actress as witness and complainant. Taking Hollywood women seriously as system-critical means that their memoirs, interviews, and other output become historical and reclamatory social justice texts.

Thus I here reaffirm the Hollywood woman as herself such a critic and activist, both historically and in the present. I then also propose that new, hybrid modes of expression should challenge or augment traditional histories, and that we as film scholars should be incorporating them into scholarship. I return to the modes of actress activism I identified just before the #metoo/Time's Up movement broke- and argue that these modes which I identified in 2016-2017 were some of the building blocks for this cultural sea change of the last months of 2017. We can now, as historians and cultural critics, identify #metoo and its subsequent aftershocks as a true breakthrough of the postmodern actress as activist mode.

First, I analyse the evolution of Louise Brooks from actress to later life critic and revelatory agent of the odious aspects of early Hollywood. The inclusion of Brooks' writings into the film history canon is certainly of note, and generally falls within traditional methods of historiography. But there are several aspects of Brooks' critical work which qualify as historiographically unorthodox (Brooks, 1958; Brooks, 1962; Brooks, 1979; Brooks, 1982). Secondly I situate my own thesis project, *Class Acts: A Socio-Cultural History of Women, Labour, and Migration in Hollywood* (McElroy, 2019). This project has brought in Hollywood women of numerous careers and decades to speak for themselves through interview. It primarily utilises traditional and academic historical methods, but also incorporates postmodern potentialities through the use of digital media. I then move to two non-traditional projects, both presented in 2015, situating them as working in wholly new modes. The first is actress-poet Amber Tamblyn's interdisciplinary book of poetry and art on the lives of actresses, 2015's *Dark Sparkler* (Tamblyn, 2015). The second is the unprecedented 2015 New York magazine photo essay and interactive article on the Bill Cosby accusers and case, entitled "I'm No Longer Afraid: 35 Women Tell Their Stories About Being Assaulted By Bill Cosby, and the Culture That Wouldn't Listen", by Noreen Malone and Amanda Demme (Malone and Demme, 2015). These works can be seen as interdisciplinary, multimedia, and creative hybrid mediums of reclamative historiography on women in Hollywood history. Both Tamblyn's poetry volume and the *New York* magazine piece in fact constitute vital new modes of incorporating truths into the Hollywood historical record, and should be treated as worthy feminist texts in line with memoir and oral history.

Louise Brooks is the first and only actress who began her own thorough film history and self-aware critique of women in the Hollywood system as early as the 1920s and then onward, through memoir, interview, critical essay, and more. In fact, her deconstruction of the entire studio system and its exploitative and entangled sexual and financial strictures moves Brooks from the category of actress to the category of film theorist. One of Brooks' key insights into the inner workings of the film industry was that power was the central commodity, at the top of a pyramid of money and sex. From a Foucauldian perspective and, indeed even from a Brooksian one, beauty or talent without power were meaningless in the context of celebrity and the market.

As early as the 1920s, rebellious and refusenik star Brooks had already ascertained the Hollywood film industry as a sort of economic system of male-female relations akin to a free-floating brothel, and lamented its anti-intellectual and exploitative qualities (Brooks, 1982). Brooks, whose candid and insightful Hollywood deconstructions were far ahead of their time, boldly told insider tales of film actresses owned by organized crime organizations, and compared all of early Hollywood to little more than one vast pimping ring (Davis, 1996, p. 134). In her memoir *Lulu in Hollywood*, Brooks detailed how studio executives whose sexual advances were refused later found ways to damage and destroy her career and the careers of peer actresses. These men also resented and punished battles for fair pay. Speaking of her long life and its many acts, Brooks definitively did not idealise her years of Hollywood stardom as glamorous. In fact, many decades before performers, academics, or feminists discussed such themes publicly, Brooks wrote that "there was no other occupation in the world that so closely resembled enslavement as the career of a film star" (Brooks, 1982, p. 58).

Brooks was a theorist of such complexity that she not only critiqued the Hollywood system historically, but historiographically. She decried the unreliability of Hollywood film history and myth as built on lies from the beginning, merely repeatedly reinforced to dogma. Brooks referred to this as "the tragedy of film history" (Brooks, 1982, in Hastie, 2007, p. 104). It is thus ironically fitting then that in the twenty-first century, masculinist film historiography is still stymying research of feminist film historian material from the source of an actress who lived through it. Brooks' complete journals of memoir and criticism, encompassing 2000 handwritten pages, were donated to Eastman House and sealed for twenty-five years. They were unsealed in 2010 but have not yet been made available to the public. From what film scholars have been able to see thus far, Brooks' marginalia offers a remarkable new type of film history to be uncovered. Her personal collection of memoirs and film histories includes hundreds of books that she corrected, complete with sarcastic commentary and crossouts reading "lies!" (Brooks, 1982, in Hastie 2007, p. 146). Brooks continues to demonstrate the need for women to be their own historians in unfriendly and power imbalanced systems. At the same time, the withholding of her writings is allegorical for the problem of who owns and controls the histories of women in film. Both this archival problem and Brooks' belief in truth-telling as a form of courage perfectly align her with the ethos of women's revisionist Hollywood history as imperative.

Moving on from Brooks, I theorise the interviews undertaken with twenty-six Hollywood women in 2014 in support of my doctoral thesis, *Class Acts: A Socio-Cultural History of Women, Labour, and Migration in Hollywood*, as another form of actress activism. In keeping with this conceptualization, such discussion is less about scholarly methodology or the activism of the academic. Rather, it is focused on the activism enacted by these women in consenting to be interviewed and in telling their own stories, giving new information of use to scholarship, and challenging mainstream Hollywood histories. These interviews saw an amalgamation of mainly traditional historical methods of reclamative history with some assets from the digital age. The choices of these women to tell their stories in 2014 can now be read as a harbinger of the massive cultural shift of women in Hollywood that arrived in 2017.

In the 2014 interviews, the pool of women was wide-ranging in terms of all categories, from age, race, and disability-identified to experience or levels of success and failure. The interviews included Academy Award-nominated woman directors, Emmy Award winning Best Actresses, ingenue actresses, and recent film school graduates. The women interviewed ranged from their twenties to their eighties. They were primarily actresses, but also directors, producers, writers, and composers. All were asked the same questions about varied aspects of life for women in Hollywood, from beauty standards and body practices to economic concerns, competition, beauty practices, the casting couch, and realities of age and race.

The ability to interrogate the histories of older women regarding the realities of past Hollywood decades was likely the most historically rich aspect of the interviews. Women who were successful as far back as the 1950s and '60s often described a pre-feminist minefield lacking both union protections and sexual harassment laws. They described the shift to unionized systems and more laws as a godsend for women. But this shift itself did not come without hard-fought battles. One of the most historically significant interviewees was a member of the "DGA Five", the group of women who sued the Directors Guild of America in the 1970s. This Emmy-nominated documentarian told me of the economic and cultural resistance she encountered in her career, including the standard refrain that "I'd never let a woman direct me" (Chaikin, 2014).

Several women shared very traumatic histories of rape and sexual harassment from these pre-feminist eras in which they had not only felt that there was no recourse for women at the time, but little interest in their lived experiences after the fact. One survivor of rape and harassment in the 1960s television studio system was gratified to share her story, saying simply, "No one has ever asked us" (Anonymous, 2014). This same woman told of a workplace environment in which a male crew member casually sexually assaulted her as she stood on a ladder, and one in which after she was raped in an entirely different incident, it was she and not the male accused who was run out of the A-list production company- "for her own good". At the same time, working as a secretary, she was cheerfully introduced on the first day with "welcome to the meat rack", and overheard the child of the studio executive she worked for ask his father if she was his servant (Anonymous, 2014). All the more notably, this treatment happened to a young woman who was connected within the system, with a father who wrote for A-list stars. One can imagine the treatment, then, for the vast majority of young women who showed up both unprotected by patronage systems and by the laws of the later twentieth century. It is obvious from a feminist point of view that to record such histories from pre-feminist Hollywood eras is vital in terms of a more accurate record of the blatant, systemic abuse that was condoned, as well as the total lack of consequence for perpetrators.

While the above oral history from a member of the '60s generation who felt pushed out of the business amid rape and sexual harassment is bleak, at the other end of the spectrum oral history provides vivid records from the privileged and the success stories as well. In this round of interviews, I was fortunate enough to interview a groundbreaking and record-breaking television actress—the first woman to, in the 1960s, win Emmys for Best Dramatic Actress for three consecutive years. Even though her recollections of her career were largely full of gratitude, her interview painted a portrait of the restricted star. She explained that, "you were sheltered back then. There were no meetings in cafes. They locked you in, picked you up in the morning, washed your hair, and gave you breakfast" (Bain, 2014). The interview was also instructive as to the levels of disrespect and intrusion that were par for the course in the business, even for an award-winning and high-profile woman. "In the old days they could ask you in an audition if your breasts were real" (Bain, 2014). For this star, it was also important to speak about her own acts of rebellion and her personal realities in terms of the casting couch, as when she recounted that though she was told not to wear her wedding ring on auditions, she refused. She added, "People probably think I was run around the couch, I wasn't" (Bain, 2014).

Women of color provided another unique lens in this project. Tamika Lamison, black actress turned director and founder of the Make a Film Foundation, contextualized Hollywood for women in terms that very much echoed Louise Brooks' theorizations of nearly a century prior. Like many of the interview subjects, she had pursued a trajectory from above the line to below the line work, having determined that the position of the actress in Hollywood is one that lacks not just creativity, but bodily autonomy. As she explained, "what you need to do to your body to be a success as an actress in LA—no thanks" (Lamison, 2014). Using a colorful metaphor relating to women, she offered candidly that "the zombie apocalypse has been happening every day for one hundred years. It's the Hollywood system." One's job as a woman in this environment has always been, simply, how not to get chewed up and spit out (Lamison, 2014). In the 2014 interview and in what now reads as yet another foreshadowing of the #metoo sea change of 2017, Lamison connected this metaphor with an at-the-time oblique reference to avoiding predatory men.[1]

While the underpinnings of the *Class Acts* interviews may have come from traditional historical methodologies, the project was enhanced by new technologies and media. The call for interviews was spread on social media and industry listservs, which brought in the vast number of participants eager to talk. In fact, in addition to industry word-of-mouth, this was how so many participants were reached. Interviews were conducted in person but also by phone and by video conference. Many interviews were conducted in person in Los Angeles, but also by Skype and by phone both while still in Los Angeles and upon my return to Canada. Perhaps the most intriguing and gratifying example of new possibilities in collecting film historical scholarship was an interview able to be conducted with a Deaf actress via her video call software. This actress in her interview exhorted the industry, "Don't be afraid to ask us! Talk to us!", as to how to be more inclusive of performers with disabilities (Mackinnon, 2014). New technologies not only allow such performers to be heard, but for their voices to be included in film histories that would have previously excluded them. The incorporation of new media and technologies should continue to democratize inclusion of not only women, but people with disabilities and others traditionally left out of the film historical record.

The remaining two examples of revisionist women's Hollywood history given here share the commonalities of being very *au courant* in terms of both technology and #metoo/Time's Up, and of operating in modes of technology and interdisciplinarity not associated with traditional history.

---

[1] It should be noted that since our interview, Lamison has come forward and appeared in television interviews as a victim of Hollywood mega-manager Vincent Cirrincione, a white man who prided himself on procuring A-list success for black women stars like Halle Berry and Taraji P. Henson. The fact that Cirrincione is currently accused of sexual misconduct by nineteen women of colour, making him a Weinstein figure of black women's Hollywood, and yet the story has remained relatively small, is telling in itself.

Amber Tamblyn's 2015 volume of poetry, *Dark Sparkler*, reflects on the tragedy of actress lives and deaths from the triple perspective of poet, actress, and Hollywood insider. Tamblyn's adept reflections upon the actress experience stem in part from the fact that she has been a poet from a young age, but also one born into a dynastic Hollywood acting family. Her father was Russ Tamblyn of studio Hollywood fame, a well-known actor in films from *Seven Brides for Seven Brothers* to *West Side Story*. Tamblyn's own younger years in the 1990s and 2000s were ones in which she experienced the life of the child star, starring in many high-profile film and television projects. This unique life trajectory as Hollywood insider, teen starlet, and ultimately rejector of stardom for creative output makes Tamblyn's poetry and its multimedia accompaniments compelling. The text operates as interdisciplinary and interactive in the vein of both the analog and digital feminist zine. With Tamblyn's interdisciplinary background, she sought the multimedia artwork for her poetry volume not only from her actor-turned-artist father, but from friends Kid Koala, Marilyn Manson, and David Lynch.

The volume contains Tamblyn's poems, each a reflection on an actress given in the title. These are generally those who died in tragic circumstances, interspersed with a few that are ruminations on Tamblyn's own actress status and life in contemporary young Hollywood. Some reflect on the contemporary and the personal. Tamblyn writes evocatively about the dance of upward and downward mobility for the Hollywood actress and the feeling of being a body for sale competing against other actresses in an untitled poem in the epilogue:

> and one day all the agents sent her rare orchids/
> And licked the stiff slits of her red carpet genius/
> and poured Up and Coming/
> all over my Down and Going
>
> the auction of our bodies/
> passing each other by/
> between buyers' hands'/
> down and going/
> going/
> Gone (Tamblyn, 2015, p. 84-85)

Perhaps of even more interest for the film historian are the historical poems, ruminating on the lives and deaths of early film actresses, both superstar and obscure. Tamblyn achieves something extremely interesting in writing about tragic deaths that fall under Hollywood mythology, from the 1920s to the present decade. "Peg Entwhistle" takes as its subject the perfectly, morbidly iconic suicide of the young actress who jumped from the Hollywood sign to her death in 1932. The poem "Jean Harlow", too, speaks to some of the realities of studio stardom to be learned by combining study of biography and Hollywood culture with American history and racial politics:

> she rolled the dice of a career and saw no/
> numbers just black and white/
> what a depression-era star knows is/
> no blacks just whites (Tamblyn 2015, p. 13)

The poems about modern, twenty-first century young stars and child actresses as tragedies move in a different way, in a register of angry social critique of the system. Writing about the death of her friend and compatriot Brittany Murphy in a poem of the same name, Tamblyn excoriates tabloid culture and the culture of sexualized emaciation predominant in Hollywood not just in the last century, but in the current one. This poem includes the sarcastic lines, "The Country says good things/ about the body./ They print the best photos;/ the least bones, the most peach" (Tamblyn, 2015, p. 28). Taking the first person in "Abigail Nell," Tamblyn satirises the Hollywood obsession with thinness to the point of starvation and ultimately annihilation, writing "66.6 percent of the three pound human brain/ would be another two pounds down.... Anything gastric's elastic./ Ribs can be replaced with plastic" (Tamblyn, 2015, p. 38). The poem's protagonist imagines her idyllic future below size 0, musing, "I'll be the girl they say pink things to,/ so weightless she arrives by ghost" (Tamblyn, 2015, p. 39).

Tamblyn is similarly knowing and scornful of the sordid culture of sexual exploitation and the purportedly glamorous culture of sex, drugs, and rock and roll endemic to Hollywood. She writes that "A child-star actress is a double-edged dildo" (2015, p. 30) and of "going to floss my teeth with the pubic hair/of the Hollywood night air,/ memorize my lines before I snort them" (2015, 30-31)." Many of the poems have a knowing, *party's over* mood, which also touches on the problem of aging past the ingenue for the woman in Hollywood. In "Jennifer Davis," the narrator meets a boozy, has-been actress in a Manhattan bar, who quips, "Do you think you'll find me famous/ when I tell you I'm broke?/ When I tell you this drink is what keeps me going?/ When I can't remember either what I was famous for" (Tamblyn, 2015, p. 49) "Laurel Gene" sees an over-the-hill actress who has not descended into addiction, but into another life of banal domesticity and housework. This actress remembers her triumphs as the "dark sparkler" (2015, p. 68) and contemplates her slow suburban death with the words, "I am a distant explosion of myself/ again. A star. Remember/ being a star./ This is how to die in the arms of a suburban wind,/ learning how to be forgotten/ over and over again" (2015, p. 69). The poetry section of the volume ends on a morbid note with a *memento mori*: "Remember that you must die" (Tamblyn, 2015, p. 113). In partly concluding the volume, it reads as a *memento mori* of the actress' body itself. The common thread in all of the poems is, besides the exploration of all the forms of exploitation experienced by women in the Hollywood system, how they function as texts that allow the actress to be both artist and reporter.

Drafts with lines crossed out and journal entries about the difficulties of writing on such painful material add to the feminist zine aesthetic. The final thirty pages of the volume incorporate various mixed media metadata about the writing itself. There are letters written to the dead actresses, such as one to Martha Mansfield, a now-obscure silent film actress who died in 1923 when her antebellum-style costume caught fire. Tamblyn writes in a short essay, "I'm trying to write your poem, Martha Mansfield... You are the last on my list of actresses... Only no one remembers you, respectfully. No one will remember me, either...Let me search you on Wikipedia, see if I can find some oil for the engine" (Tamblyn, 2015, p. 92). The historical poems manage to operate very much in the creative twenty-first century register, by including web searches for obscure actresses of a century ago and emails to agents asking to interview aged actresses of the studio era. The volume finally becomes truly reader-interactive when it lists eight pages of recommended Google searches for the reader on the actresses discussed or cut from the volume. A nexus of the actress-as poet-as film historian is created, and then used to invite the fan or spectator into the circuit of feminist-activist film history.

In its incorporation of such new elements, I would argue that Tamblyn moves the conversation about the nature of actress life in Hollywood, past and present, to new terrain. Tamblyn forcefully identifies as a feminist and also writes explicitly feminist poetry in the volume. *Dark Sparkler* should clearly be considered a facet of Tamblyn's own activism. Tamblyn expressly said in an interview that this project was undertaken to give voice to women who had lost their own (Branch, 2015). She is thus doing the exact kind of feminist film history reclamative work described in this article in other modes, but in narrative, multimedia, postmodern form.

Feminist Beat poet Diane Di Prima's foreword to *Dark Sparkler* serves as an excellent rumination on the precise types of activism by and through actresses called for within this project. Di Prima situates Tamblyn's poems as a cartography, considering the volume a map of previously unexplored women's lives. Writing of Tamblyn's work, Di Prima states that:

> It's not 'poetic' in the foolish and flowery sense. None of it is symbolic. Amber Tamblyn is not playing with metaphor... She is gifting us with the tragedy, the power, and most of all the *truth* of these women's lives… It is also a memorial, and a magical act (Di Prima in Tamblyn, ix).

Di Prima then goes on to discuss the affective process that will take place in the reader, that connects dead actress to living actress to poet to modern cultural consumer:

> Warning: the book you are holding in your hands will break your heart… At some point you will begin to get curious. Something will start to tug at the edge of your mind/heart. At that point, go to the library or search the Internet for information about any girl/woman you find yourself thinking about (Di Prima in Tamblyn, ix).

Just as Tamblyn has utilised poetry, Di Prima is here suggesting a multimedia, postmodern mode of feminist activist reclamative film historiography.

Finally of note is the 2015 article, photoessay, and multimedia interactive online article for *New York* magazine profiling the Bill Cosby accusers. The multimedia piece, entitled "I'm No Longer Afraid: 35 Women Tell Their Stories About Being Assaulted by Bill Cosby, and the Culture That Wouldn't Listen", was written by Noreen Malone and Amanda Demme. Groundbreaking in both content and format, it presumably constitutes the first article in which all of a powerful Hollywood celebrity man's rape victims were together in one place, with their real names and faces, unashamed, celebrities and non together. In this respect, it is a necessary piece in tracing back a genealogy that led to the #metoo revolution of 2017.

There are unique multimedia and interactive features to the piece that make the case for its use-value as historical-cultural text. It is the visuality of this piece that makes it particularly striking, a sort of portraiture as interview accompanied by oral histories. The cover photo quickly became iconic, with all thirty-five women in full hair and makeup, posed in a group portrait, with one empty chair in the foreground. The individual photo portraits of each woman are equally arresting. Each portrait is in a bold, almost baroque aesthetic, with the name and year of the woman's self-reported assault underneath her. Each photo can be selected with a "read her story" icon. A click leads to an oral history vignette and mini-essay. Finally, there are six video interviews to click on at the conclusion of the piece. This amounts to a sort of profoundly new composite journalism piece.

The theme found in the section on the *Class Acts* interviews, of women not feeling able to come forward and report on an endemic culture of abuse and silence until decades later, is also inherent to the oral histories of the Cosby survivors. Just as many of the women active in 1960s Hollywood and interviewed in 2014 felt no one would listen regarding the crimes committed upon them and that nothing would change, the women of the Cosby case repeatedly described the same culturally systemic hopelessness. In this *New York* magazine piece, one of the women recounts being told, "'You do know that that's Hefner's best friend, right?' I said, 'Yes.' She says to me: 'Nobody's going to believe you. I suggest you shut your mouth'" (Malone and Demme, 2015). This constant, of not being able to come forward and report on an endemic culture of abuse and silence until the culture had finally changed, is inherent to many of the actress turned activist oral histories. Above all else, this reality can now be seen as forecasting of the Weinstein scandal and all of the cultural shift that has finally arisen from it.

At the same time, a liberatory and communal spirit of something new arises from what at first might seem to be a grim or pessimistic piece. A reclamatory women's Hollywood history has been created with the publication of this article and continued via both in-person and digital communities. As the authors wrote:

> The women have found solace in their number — discovering that
> they hadn't been alone, that there were others out there who
> believed them implicitly, with whom they didn't need to be afraid
> of sharing the darkest details of their lives. They are scattered all
> over the country — ten different states are represented — and
> most of them had no contact with their fellow accusers until
> recently. But since reading about each other's stories in the news,
> or finding one another on social media, or meeting in person at the
> photo shoots arranged by *New York,* many of the women have
> forged a bond. It is, as Tarshis calls it, "a sorrowful sisterhood"
> (Malone and Demme, 2015).

As one women recounted, "We talk, all the survivors. We just had the photo shoot. And I said it was one of the greatest experiences I ever had" (Malone and Demme, 2015).

Virginia Woolf famously said, "On or around December 1910, human character changed" (Woolf, 1924). We are living through a similar sea change regarding the revelations of the exploitation of women across all societal spheres. It will never be forgotten that this cultural shift began with women in performance industries. Since the Weinstein scandal broke, the earlier imperative for women to tell their stories as part of correcting the film historical record still remains. But the goal is now even all-encompassing, after hardly daring to be conceptualized and residing just below the surface for decades. Di Prima's conception of the cartography can serve as an excellent jumping off point for not only the contemporary, interdisciplinary film historian in light of #metoo, but the cultural and gender historian as well. The use of non-academic and non-traditional sources in tracing the history of women in Hollywood is not only a move to the socially just, but more essential than ever towards correcting inaccuracies embedded in mainstream histories.

The four different modern and postmodern modes of actress activism of recent years identified within this chapter now look, in retrospect, like precursors of the revolution that was brewing. In this light, we can read the January 2018 Time's Up manifesto as the apotheosis text of actress activism to date. Over three hundred actresses, women directors, producers, and other industry creatives, have come forward to proclaim that "we are grateful to the many individuals- survivors and allies- who are speaking out and forcing the conversation about sexual harassment, sexual assault, and gender bias out of the shadows and into the spotlight" (Time's Up, 2018). Unlike in other, earlier movements, the Time's Up organisers explicitly express solidarity and commonality with working class women in Hollywood and other industries, vowing to use their platform to help them as well. Recognising their power in sharing their stories as a form of activism, the Time's Up organisers also explicitly explained, "unlike ever before, our access to the media and to important decision makers has the potential of leading to real accountability and consequences" (Time's Up, 2018). This is, finally, a moment of real change and light, one that Louise Brooks and her compatriots might be watching with amazement as a movement whose day has finally come. Meanwhile Amber Tamblyn, the Cosby survivors, and the 2014 *Class Acts* interviewees are both taking part in and also watching with fascination as to what comes next. What could be more representative of Hollywood actress activism, a century in the making, than this?

References

Anger, K. (1986). *Hollywood Babylon*. London: Arrow.

Anonymous [Personal interview]. (2014, August 17, Los Angeles, California). [Name withheld due to inability to reach interview subject for permission].

Bain, B. [Personal interview- Phone]. (2014, September 9).

Branch, K. (2015, April 10). Amber Tamblyn Goes Dark: The Actress Opens Up About Her Poetry, Hollywood, and Lindsay Lohan. *Glamour*.

Brooks, L.

— (1958). GIsh and Garbo. *Sight and Sound, 28*(1).

— (1983). *Lulu in Hollywood*. New York: Knopf.

— (1965). Pabst and Lulu. *Sight and Sound, 34*(3).

— (1979). Why I will never write my memoirs. *Film Culture, 69*, 219-228.

Chaikin, J. [Personal interview- Phone]. (2014, August 18).

Davis, S. W. (1996). *Shrinking From Scrutiny, Seeing the Light: Advertising and the Self in American Commodity Culture, 1920-1932*. Berkeley: California.

de Beauvoir, S. (2011). *The Second Sex*. New York: Vintage.

DeCordova, R. (2001). *Picture personalities: the emergence of the star system in America*. Urbana, IL: University of Illinois Press.

Dyer, R.

— (1986). *Heavenly Bodies: Film Stars and Society*. New York: St. Martin's .

— (1998). *Stars*. London: BFI Pub.

Gaines, J. (2000). Dream/Factory. In C. Gledhill & L. Williams (Eds.), *Reinventing Film Studies*. London: Arnold.

Hastie, A. (2012). *Cupboards of Curiosity Women, Recollection, and Film History*. Durham: Duke University Press.

Irigaray, L. (1985). *The sex which is not one*. Ithaca, NY: Cornell University Press.

Kristeva, J., & Moi, T. (2002). *The Kristeva Reader*. Oxford: Blackwell.

Lamison, T. [Personal interview- Skype]. (2014, October 10).

Mackinnon, C. [Personal interview- Skype]. (2014, August 30).

Malone, N., & Demme, A. (2015, July 26). I'm No Longer Afraid: 35 Women Tell Their Stories About Being Assaulted by Bill Cosby, and the Culture That Wouldn't Listen. *New York*. https://www.thecut.com/2015/07/bill-cosbys-accusers-speak-out.html.

McElroy, K. (2019). *Class Acts: A Socio-Cultural History of Women, Labour, and Migration in Hollywood.* (Doctoral thesis, in prep). Concordia University.

Petro, P. (1996). Historical Ennui, Feminist Boredom. In V. Sobchak (Ed.), *The Persistence of History: Cinema, Television, and the Modern Event.* New York: Routledge.

Powdermaker, H. (1951). *Hollywood: the dream factory*. London: Secker & Warburg.

Rubin, G. (2011). The Traffic in Women: Notes on the Political Economy of Sex. In *Deviations: A Gayle Rubin Reader*. Durham: Duke University Press.

Tamblyn, A. (2015). *Dark sparkler*. New York: HarperPerennial.

Time's Up. (2018, January 1). Open Letter From Time's Up. *New York Times*. https://www.nytimes.com/interactive/2018/01/01/arts/02women-letter.html.

Woolf, V. (1923). Mr. Bennett and Mrs. Brown. http://www.columbia.edu/~em36/MrBennettAndMrsBrown.pdf

Another Day of Sun: The Conservative Gender Politics of Damien Chazelle's *Whiplash* and *La La Land*

Janne Salminen

Abstract. *Whiplash* (2014) and *La La Land* (2016) are Damien Chazelle's two most widely recognized films. While Chazelle is quickly becoming one of the big-name directors in Hollywood, and his movies have been extremely positively received. These two films construct a conservative narrative of gender, one that revolves around white masculinity and heteronormative gender expectations. This article examines the gender representations of *Whiplash* and *La La Land*, and how these representations connect to larger issues of gender politics. Whiplash displays its gender politics mainly through the conflict between what are acceptable modes of masculinity, while La La Land centers around a heteronormative romance and white masculinity. Both films also focus on the genius of the male lead character and how they are reclaiming their position in society.

Keywords: Gender, Films, Masculinity, Heteronormativity.

Introduction

Movies and American society have a complex relationship as films can both reflect and create gender attitudes and perceptions by portraying other representations of gender as more legitimate than others. Films can influence how everyday life is perceived, and they create representations of experience which are interpreted and acted upon by cultural members (Denzin, 1995, p. 199–200). Through repetition of certain visualized ideas, films can embed the worldview of audiences and those repeated ideas can become accepted as "reality" (Ross, 2002, p. 9). The goal of this text is not to analyze what filmmaker Damien Chazelle intended to convey with his work, but rather to understand the cultural meanings his works carry. The two films discussed in this paper, *Whiplash* (2014) and *La La Land* (2016), both have traits that are becoming trademarks for Chazelle, preoccupation with jazz, narratives centered around white men, and a rather grim portrayal of women. Both films also construe heteronormative gender narratives, while legitimizing conservative forms of masculinity. Aside from these thematic links, these films also are the two most famous building blocks of Damien Chazelle's career, who could be one of the foremost cinematic voices of our time. The critical and financial success of these two films makes them significant cultural texts, which need to be scrutinized and criticized so that we can understand what kind of reality and gender attitudes they generate.

On February 26, 2017, *La La Land* (2016) was accidentally announced as the winner of Academy Award for best picture. As the producers of the film walked on stage, it became apparent that something had gone awry. Faye Dunaway, who was announcing the best picture winner along with Warren Beatty had read contents of an envelope that had been handed to her by accident. The actual winner was *Moonlight* (2016), and for a few minutes, one of the most famous and carefully choreographed awards ceremonies viewed by hundreds of millions seemed to be falling apart at the seams. One would not expect this sort of thing to happen, even though it was not entirely without precedent. This debacle inspired some to run to their computers and other comparable devices to create memes that drew parallels between the 2016 US Presidential election, equating *La La Land* to Donald Trump and *Moonlight* to Hillary Clinton (Thorne, 2017).

In the 2010s, internet memes have become vital elements in the public discourse that minorities use to form their collective identities. Naom Gal, Limor Shifman, and Zohar Kampf argue that LGBTQ communities in particular use memes as a way to construct a collective identity that is not connected to their social or familial origins and that the relatively accessible digital media allows for the creation of narratives that deviate and challenge the dominant hegemonic narrative (Gal, Shifman & Kampf, 2016, p. 1699–1701). The memes made from the 2017 Oscars would suggest that to the people making them, *La La Land* represented the same narrative that allowed Donald Trump to win the presidency in 2016. In this context, when compared to the very queer *Moonlight*, *La La Land* does indeed appear as a conservative film that celebrates a time that has long since passed or even perhaps never existed. When compared to Damien Chazelle's previous film, *Whiplash*, *La La Land* can be viewed and contextualized as being a part of an ongoing gender narrative the writer-director is constructing and perhaps unwittingly promoting, one that presents a gender order organized around conservative masculinity and rigid heterosexuality as the norm.

Whiplash

Whiplash tells the story of Andrew Neiman (Miles Teller), who is a first-year student at a conservatory in New York and who longs to become an all-time great jazz drummer. He gains the attention of infamous instructor Terence Fletcher (J.K. Simmons), who then proceeds to tutor and torment Andrew all in the name of great art. The film establishes early on that Andrew is torn between artistic success and living an emotionally balanced, but terminally mediocre life. The film implies that a middle-ground is non-negotiable. Even when Andrew learns that Terrence's abusive teaching methods drove a former student of the conservatory to depression and eventually to suicide, Andrew's desire to impress his tutor barely diminishes.

The ideal of a strict father model is at the core of conservative thinking (Lakoff, 2002, p. 32–33), and in this model, punishment is accepted as a necessary reaction to disobedience, and that success is achieved through self-discipline and obedience (Lakoff, 2002, p. 68). Terrence demands both of these qualities to the extreme from Andrew, and the film iterates several times that this will eventually result in Andrew's personal benefit, even if it might cost him other relationships in his life. Terence might appear as a dislikable character for the majority of the film, but his methods are proven to be effective and even necessary if Andrew is to become a truly great musician.

Whiplash generates a narrative in which Terrence symbolizes a form of hegemonic masculinity. Hegemonic masculinity is a concept popularized by R.W. Connell (currently Reawyn), and it suggests that that certain forms of masculinity are seen most legitimate when trying to maintain the dominant position of men in society. This legitimacy is not established by individuals but is instead a collective product of cultural ideals reacting with institutionalized power or great wealth (Connell, 2005, p. 77), and it could be described as a canonized gender narrative for men (Connell & Pearse, 2015, p. 91–100).

The hegemonic masculinity embodied by Terrence excludes stereotypically feminine characteristics as unacceptable, subscribes to conservative notions of parenting, and while Terrence's sexuality is never explicitly discussed, he uses homophobic language that would suggest that heterosexuality is also a prerequisite for this mode of masculinity. Jim, on the other hand, represents a subaltern masculinity. Subaltern masculinities (or alternative masculinities as J. Halberstam calls them) are forms of masculinity that fail to comply with hegemonic or dominant masculinity, such as effeminate men or masculine women (Halberstam, 1998, p. 172–174). Jim's evident caring for the emotional well-being of his son is implied to have an adverse impact on Andrew's success, and Jim is also unable to understand fully what his son is trying to achieve. Terrence and Jim are also physically different, and while Terrence is continually brimming with rage, Jim rarely raises his voice.

Damien Chazelle admitted that *Whiplash* was informed by the frustrating efforts of trying to get *La La Land* made and those frustrations influenced the writing process (Hammond, 2016). This admission would suggest that these two films have a connection beyond being made one after the other and that he is aware of the aggressive themes present in *Whiplash*, both films also revolve around the genius of a noticeably masculine man, whose extraordinary vision is not given the appreciation it supposedly deserves. *La La Land* does not display these themes quite as aggressively, but whereas the romantic subplot in *Whiplash* seems almost like an afterthought to make Andrew explicitly heterosexual, in *La La Land* romance is at the front and center of the film. Perhaps the less aggressive attitudes of *La La Land* are in some way reactionary to the criticism *Whiplash* received. The gender roles and lack of empathy in *Whiplash* came under scrutiny by such critics as Richard Brody of *New Yorker* (Brody, 2014), J. Bryan Lowder of *Slate* (Lowder, 2014), and Barbara Schildkrout of *Psychology Today* (Schildkrout, 2015).

La La Land

La La Land is a musical about Mia (Emma Stone), an aspiring actress and Sebastian (Ryan Gosling), a jazz-pianist who hopes to open his own jazz club. Both live in Los Angeles and are struggling to find their big break. Mia and Sebastian run into each other a few times. Initially the two seem to despise each other, but eventually, they fall in love and have a tumultuous relationship that ends up with each of them going their separate ways.

Richard Dyer argues that postmodern audiences have been keen on reading old classic musicals as queer or camp, as Dyer (2013) puts it: "Gay sensibility holds together the intensity and irony, a fierce assertion of extreme feeling with a deprecating sense of absurdity" (p. 130). Additionally, Jane Fauer argues that the queer readings of musicals, such as *A Star is Born* (1954), or *I Could Go on Singing* (1963), displaced the heterosexual couple from the center of the genre and that Hollywood musicals have a history of being interpreted as gay male texts by and for gay men (Fauer, 1992, p. 139).

La La Land could be viewed as an homage to classic musicals, like the ones mentioned by Dyer and Fauer, but it is mostly devoid of irony or gay sensibility and features scenes that work to counter any queer readings as the film substitutes a heteronormative romance as the emotional core of the film. Scenes that are intensely lively or extremely colorful take place in the early phases of Mia and Sebastian's romance. Once the novelty of their relationship wears off, the film adopts a more realistic tone. Scenes in which Mia and Sebastian argue or struggle with mundane aspects of everyday life are visually gritty and almost depressing. Realism as a stylistic device in films has been linked with conservatism, especially when dealing with material that can be read as queer. Martin Fradley argues that the Batman films are an example of how a wildly colorful (and messy) series of films transformed into a much more realistic and strictly heterosexual series by relying on a specific mode of realism (Fradley, 2013, p. 24–27).

The queer potential of Batman could be erased or at least diminished by using an aesthetic that conveys the idea of a realistic depiction of a series of events. *La La Land* uses a similar tactic to erase or at least diminish the artificial elements of monogamous heterosexual romance. Realistic scenes reinforce the heteronormative idea of straight romance being at its core the "natural" way of things, even when it fails, and counter the potentially ironic readings of the elaborate musical numbers. Judith Butler notes that one of the ways heterosexual privilege operates is by naturalizing and rendering itself as the norm. She also adds that by deflecting homosexual elements films can maintain narrative trajectories that reinforce the boundaries of heterosexuality (Butler, 1999, p. 339).

Even though the film has two protagonists, the major events in the film are connected to Sebastian in some form or another. *La La Land* characterizes him as a person who has so much talent and vision, that he can change the direction of other people's lives, Mia's life most of all. Even if Sebastian and Mia they get approximately the same amount of screen time, they are not presented as being equal. Prior to their romance, both are agonizing to find focus and direction, but Mia lacks Sebastian's ambition and drive. Sebastian seems to find his focus once he has explained to Mia what she should be doing with her life. Sebastian is the spark that inspires Mia to pursue an acting career more seriously, and if she cannot find the projects that are suitable for her, she should write them herself. While Mia taking charge of her own career implies that she becomes independent, the subtext is that she needed someone like Sebastian to give her encouragement to follow her dreams as if on her own she could not come up with the necessary focus.

When we first see Mia and Sebastian in the film, a dichotomy is established. Sebastian drives an old-fashioned gas-guzzling convertible; she drives a Toyota Prius, which is at least perceived as an ecological choice. Julia A. Nelson writes extensively on how women are systematically linked with images and perceptions of nature. Nelson also notes that the duality of women/nature and men/culture is remarkably persistent in Western culture (Nelson, 1997, p. 157–158). Fossil fuels have been argued to be a part of the same type of toxic masculinity that views environmental issues as insignificant or at the very least not a concern for masculine men, even though environmental concerns are becoming increasingly acceptable part of contemporary masculine identity (Hultman, 2013, p. 81–89). In this early scene, Sebastian is obsessing over a piece of music, rewinding the tape in his car, but still keeping an eye on the traffic. Mia is absently going through lines for an audition and fails to notice that that the cars in front of her are moving, which is why the first interaction between these characters is Sebastian honking angrily at her for failing to move along.

Through Sebastian, the film constructs a form of hegemonic masculinity, which is comparable to the hegemonic masculinity implemented by *Whiplash*. Even if the relationship between Mia and Sebastian begins after they run into each other a few times by coincidence, it is Sebastian who initiates their courtship. In the scene when the two begin to feel attraction toward each other, Sebastian sings about Mia dismissively, echoing a misogynistic tactic of bringing down a woman's self-esteem often referred to as "negging." Ran Almog and Danny Kaplan describe "negging" as a technique that aims to undermine power than women have in the sphere of sexual relations and establish that the man who is doing the negging has control in the situation (Almog & Kaplan, 2017, 35–36). Use of this tactic places Sebastian firmly as the one in control of their relationship. This theme is revisited every time Sebastian uses his car's horn to call for Mia, which happens several times in the film. While presented as a romantic gesture, it makes Mia seem that her agency is dependent on Sebastian. He almost coerces Mia into a relationship with him, pushes her to go to auditions, and to write her one-woman play, while he begrudgingly takes a job as a touring musician.

Sebastian's "menial" job is playing keyboards in a band that aims to modernize jazz. There are some uncomfortable connotations to how the person modernizing jazz is an African American man and how the film portrays that character, Keith (played by John Legend) as a type of con-man trying to corrupt something Sebastian is trying to keep pure. This theme and its potentially racist underpinnings were noted by podcast host Jon Caramanica, who is also the pop music writer for The New York Times (Caramanica, 2017). It is almost as if Sebastian is protecting jazz form violence committed by Keith. Sebastian refers to keeping jazz alive as it is dying and the film suggests that changing it, committing violence toward it would kill it.

The interaction between Keith and Sebastian marginalizes Keith's black masculinity and places him outside of the hegemonic masculinity represented by Sebastian. R.W. Connell argues that white masculinities in the US are often constructed in relation to black men, meaning that black masculinities are sometimes marginalized in order to maintain the legitimacy of the dominant position of white masculinities, which has sometimes been utilized by right-wing politicians to maintain institutional forms of racism (Connell, 2005, p. 75–81). Keith's role in *La La Land* as a corruptor of jazz implies that a white man is more suitable to continue the traditions of the art form then an African American. Sebastian, who might have occasionally seemed in the film as an out of touch relic, now becomes the savior of a culture that is "dying" and no longer appreciated in the same manner as he appreciates it. Sebastian's frustrations with his touring job eventually cause a rift between him and Mia and the two begin drifting apart emotionally.

Once Mia and Sebastian's relationship ends, the film fast-forwards a few years into the future, showing that both of them have become successful. Mia is a prominent movie star, and Sebastian has not only opened his jazz club, but it is also a huge success. The film then re-envisions their relationship in an idealized dream sequence. In this revisionist version, the two never break up, both become hugely successful and they have a child together. In the reality of the film, Mia has found someone new, married and had a daughter. In the dream sequence, Mia and Sebastian have a son. Once the dream sequence ends, the film ends on the bittersweet note that the romance was one for the ages and audiences should see its end as a tragedy.

Jack Halberstam notes that the path of heterosexual romance is so smooth that films often generate convoluted obstacles in its way to generate drama (Halberstam, 2012, p. 115–121). While Halberstam is referring to romantic comedies, the same applies to *La La Land*; it finds sadness in a situation where two white cis-gendered straight people need to make compromises and put their dreams on hold. While this notion is heteronormative and telling of the film's gender attitudes, perhaps more revealing is how it manages to place white masculinity at the center of the narrative, even when the character most associated this masculinity is not present. Mia's decisions seem to be largely inspired by Sebastian, who is striving to recreate a past that might have been great, certainly for people like him, and the film features numerous scenes that imply that the type of masculinity that Sebastian represents is the type that aligns with attitudes which are conservative and anti-feminist.

Conclusion

Whiplash and *La La Land* both idolize and (moderately) criticize the men that the story revolves around, but they also manage to romanticize these characters and what they represent. *Whiplash* features a more obvious conservative narrative of an authoritative father being necessary when preparing a boy or a young man for greatness, while also asserting that a certain type of harsh masculinity is necessary for maintaining the dominant position of men in society. *La La Land* features similar themes but they only appear sporadically as the film's central plot does not focus on the crisis of masculinity in a similar manner as *Whiplash*. *La La Land* features scenes that point toward conservative notions on gender differences and tries to establish white masculinity as the most legitimate form of masculinity, which results in elements that could be described as racist and heteronormative.

Whiplash and *La La Land* both repeat the notion of white masculinity being in some way underappreciated in modern society and offer some half-hearted critique towards this notion, but still suggesting that things were better when straight white men were at the center of attention in society.

References

Almog, R. and Danny K. (2017). The Nerd and His Discontent: The Seduction Community and the Logic of the Game as a Geeky Solution to the Challenges of Young Masculinity. *Men and Masculinities*, *20* (1). 27-48.

Berger, F., Horowitz, J. Gilbert, G. and Platt, M. (Producers), & D. Chazelle (Director). (2016). *La La Land Land* [Motion Picture] United States: Summit Entertainment.

Blum, J, H. Estabrook, M. Litvak, D. Lancaster (Producers), & D. Chazelle (Director). (2014). *Whiplash* [Motion Picture]. United States: Sony Pictures Classics.

Brody, R. (2014). Getting Jazz Right in the Movies, *New Yorker*, October 13, 2014. Retrieved December 16, 2017 from https://www.newyorker.com/culture/richard-brody/whiplash-getting-jazz-right-movies.

Butler, J. (1999). Gender is Burning. In Feminist Film Theory (pp. 336-349). Edinburgh, UK: Edinburgh University Press.

Caramanica, J. (2017). The War Over 'La La Land': Gotta Hear Both Sides. Available at: https://www.nytimes.com/2017/01/27/arts/music/popcast-la-la-land-debate-jazz.html?_r=0. Accessed 12 Jan. 2018.

Connell, R.W. (2005). *Masculinities*. (2nd ed.). Cambridge, UK: Polity.

Connell, R.W. and Messerschmidt J. W. (2005). Hegemonic Masculinity:Rethinking the Concept. *Gender and Society*, *19* (6), 829-859.

Connell, R. W. and Pearse R. (2015). *Gender in the World Perspective*. (3rd ed.). Cambridge, UK: Polity.

Denzin, N. K. (1995). *The Cinematic Society: The Voyer's Gaze*. London: Sage Publications.

Dyer, R. (2013). *Heavenly Bodies: Film Stars and Society*. (2nd ed.). Abingdon, UK: Routledge.

Fauer, J. (1992). *The Hollywood Musical*. London, UK: The MacMillan Press.

Fradley, M. (2013) What Do You Believe In? Film Scholarship and the Cultural Politics of the *Dark Knight* Franchise. *Film Quarterly*, *66* (3), 15-27.

Gal, N., Shifman, L. and Kampf, Z. (2016). It Gets Better: Internet Memes and the Construction of Collective Identity. *New Media & Society*, *18* (8), 1668-1714.

Halberstam, J. (2012). *Gaga Feminism: Sex, Gender, and the End of Normal*. Boston, MA: Beacon Press.

Halberstam, J. (1998). *Female Masculinity*. Durham, NC: Duke University Press.

Hammond, P. (2016). Damien Chazelle's 'La La Land', An Ode To Musicals, Romance & L.A., Ready To Launch Venice And Oscar Season," *Deadline Hollywood*, August 30, 2016. Retrieved January 5, 2018 from http://deadline.com/2016/08/damien-chazelle-la-la-land-venice-film-festival-1201810810/.

Hultman, M. (2013). The Making of a Modern Environmental Hero: A History of Ecomodern Masculinity, Fuel Cells and Arnold Schwarzenegger. *Environmental Humanities*, *2* (1), 79-99.

Jeffords, S. (1994). *Hard Bodies: Hollywood Masculinity in the Reagan Era*. New Brunswick, NJ: Rutgers University Press.

Lakoff, G. (2002). *Moral Politics: How Liberals and Conservartives Think*. (2nd ed.). Chicago, IL: University of Chicago Press.

Lowder, J. B. (2014). Wailing Against the Pansies: Homophobia in *Whiplash*, *Slate*, October 22, 2014. Retrieved December 16, 2017 from http://www.slate.com/blogs/outward/2014/10/22/why_does_whiplash_damien_cha zelle_s_jazz_movie_contain_so_much_homophobia.html.

Nelson, J. A. (1997). Feminism, Ecology and the Philosophy of Economics. *Ecological Economics*, *20* (2), 155-162.

Ross, S. J. (2002). Why Movies Matter. In Steven J. Ross (Ed.), *Movies and American Society* (pp. 1-13). Malden, MA: Blackwell Publishing.

Schildkrout, B. (2015). "Witnessing an Abusive Relationship – *Whiplash*: The Movie." Psychology Today. February 22, 2015. Retrieved December 14, 2017 from https://www.psychologytoday.com/blog/the-clinical-picture/201502/witnessing-abusive-relationship-whiplash-the-movie.

Thorne, W. (2017). Oscars Best Picture Flub Gets the Meme Tratment. *Variety*, February 27, 2017. Retrieved 16.1.2018 from http://variety.com/2017/film/news/oscars-best-picture-mistake-memes-1201997840/.

Implications of Political Entertainment Today

Leocadia Díaz Romero

Abstract. This chapter explores the intertwining of politics and entertainment. We discuss this growing phenomenon, consider its origins and effects, and critically examine the normative implications for citizenship and the healthy functioning of a democracy. Is the intersection of entertainment and politics ultimately favorable or dysfunctional? Can new hybrid formats contribute to raise awareness and increase citizen knowledge on political issues? We look at the historical backgrounds and focus on the present moment, paying special attention to the 2016 U.S. Presidential Election. The extensive analysis of the literature on this topic allows us to reflect on whether popular cultural formats of everyday life can also be ways of cultivating audiences' conscious motivations for political participation; and on whether a TV show can cater to a mass audience while conveying political information and news.

Keywords: Politics, Entertainment, Democracy, Civic Engagement, Elections.

Introduction

Nowadays, we find a wide range of television programs and formats such as late-night talk shows in which satire and humor blend with political content. Additionally, contemporary election campaigns rely on television since elected officials and candidates for office use this media to reach voters, build popular support, and reinforce political messages. Certainly, "the line between news and entertainment has blurred over the last few decades" (Delli Carpini, 2012) and terms such as *Infotainment* or *Politainment* have emerged to manifest the hybrid character of these programs which have been well received by audiences since the beginning of the 21st century. They present major opportunities, not only for entertainment but also for public information, political communication and democratic discourse (Baym, 2008).

This chapter casts light on the intertwining of politics and entertainment. We discuss this growing phenomenon, consider its origins and effects, and critically examine the normative implications for citizenship and the healthy functioning of a democracy.

Clarification of Terminology

Infotainment

Scholars refer to *Infotainment* as a new genre or format where news and entertainment blend (Baym, 2008). It is useful to study this genre's impact on public information, political communication, and the democratic process. In this respect, some key aspects of this modern trend have to do with the acquisition of political knowledge, candidate examination, and political engagement. Williams and Delli Carpini (p. 8) remark on the importance to grasp in what way citizens "learn or fail to learn about politics" with these new formats. Williams and Delli Carpini (2009) are especially interested in the democratic impact and not so much on the traditional opposition or duality between news and entertainment. In previous work, they argued that entertainment plays an alternative role in political information and the democratic discourse (Delli Carpini & Williams, 1994).

The emergence of *Infotainment* is a result of the diversified, fragmented media environment characteristic of the last few decades, which favors a wider range of news forms and contents. The concurrent segmentation of the audience has played a role too. Network televisions and public broadcasting services now co-exist with other media outlets, including in particular the pervasiveness of social media. Hence, technological, economic and cultural changes have contributed to the formation of this media landscape.

These hybrids possess distinctive features. First, their themes converge on certain preferences for human-interest pieces, celebrity gossip, crime stories, and sports. Second, the style in which the information is presented includes fast-paced editing, sound and visual effects, and a tone often sensational or satirical. These are general attributes that apply to the amalgamation of news and entertainment. However, these traits vary and adapt to each particular national media system and local idiosyncrasy.

Politainment

This expression is a compound of the terms *politics* and *entertainment*. It shares many of the qualities related to *Infotainment* that we have previously mentioned. However, in this case, the integration of information and entertainment is particularly political information (political actors, subjects and processes) (Nieland, 2008). *Politainment* has found in the mediatization and professionalization of politics, inherent to modern democracies, the natural environment to grow and develop. Dörner (2001) classifies *Politainment* in two categories: entertaining politics and political entertainment. *Entertaining*

Politics alludes to the appearances of political actors in talk shows, especially during election campaigns, to appeal to voters by showing their human side and sense of humor. It can also refer to celebrities in talk shows getting involved in politics and endorsing candidates and representatives. *Political Entertainment* describes all sort of political content presented in entertaining formats (film, television). The world of politics provides good substance and inspiration—with its scandals, personalities, topics—for shows and movies. On the whole, these two approaches to *Politainment* make clear the interdependence between the world of politics and entertainment. On the one hand, political figures benefit from the entertainment industry since it is an effective channel to reach the electorate; on the other side, the showbiz recourse to political information and public content as raw material for satire and parody.

Brief History of Political Comedy

Perot announced that he would run for President in February 1992 on the *Larry King Live*. However, appearances of politicians on late night to gain the support of the electorate go back to the '60s when John F. Kennedy ran for President. In his campaign against Nixon, Kennedy attended *Tonight Starring Jack Paar*. In his intervention, he made a strong stance about the risks that the expansion of communism could pose. Nixon also appeared twice with Paar, in 1960 and in 1963. Political comedy was not so prominent during the Carter-Reagan years. Reagan only took part on *The Tonight Show With Johnny Carson* right before losing the 1976 Republican nomination against Gerald Ford. The Bush-Clinton years bring back memorable moments such as the debate when George H. W. Bush would not stop keeping an eye on his watch and could not remember the cost of a gallon of milk, or Bill Clinton playing the saxophone on *Arsenio Hall's Show*. George W. Bush appearances in the *Late Show With David Letterman* gave him some popularity since he was easygoing and approachable. Comedians Jon Stewart and Stephen Colbert were highly acclaimed during the eight years of Bush's Presidency for their spicy, satirical comments about the Republican government. During the 2008 campaign, young voters obtained considerable information in Stewart and Colbert show. Once Obama became President, he often visited the TV sets. During the 2012 campaign, Mitt Romney also made appearances on *Jimmy Fallon*. Finally, Political Entertainment in the U.S. 2016 campaign was a requirement, and both Clinton and Trump have attended the celebrated shows.

Talk Shows and Democracy

The main focus of this chapter is to study and reflect on the impact these hybrid programs have on citizen's political opinions, attitudes and behaviors (Delli Carpini, 2012). Talk shows originated in the United States in the '60s and have become highly popular in the 21st century. These shows occur during both day and evening time, but many of the theories and ideas explained in this paper refer to late night. A late-night talk show is a genre of talk show that is broadcasted in the evening, often after 10 p.m. As their name implies, entertainment talk shows are organized around conversation and integrate humorous monologues related to current news, guest interviews, comedy sketches and music performances. Through these practices, conversation is transformed into a blended form of information and entertainment. The standard format for talk shows that mix news and entertainment can range from a magazine single topic, a magazine multiple topic or a one-on-one host/guest interview.

Many shows bring to discussion relevant social and cultural topics. Therefore, some scholars recognize talk shows as "social texts": forums where society defines its values and what is to be a citizen while dealing with the various topics, issues and themes presented in the show (Timberg, 2002).

Beyond this sociological melting pot approach, we are interested in examining their political impact. Basically, following Delli Carpini (2012), we can distinguish three main positions among scholars: a) those who advocate for the "democratizing" effects of political entertainment on citizens, since political comedy expands political knowledge and awareness, especially among young people; b) those who point out the negative side of entertainment media as an element of diversion and disconnection; and, c) a middle position of those who conceive political entertainment as an alternative outlet to traditional media format for opinion formation and learning. In the following subsections, we discuss each perspective.

Democratizing effects

The first school of thought argues that political satire can reach viewers who otherwise would show little or no interest at all in news and political information, and considerably increase actual knowledge among the politically disengaged (Baum, 2003a), and foster civic engagement (Moy et al., 2005a).

This first line of research casts light as well on the repercussions humor has on political awareness. In this respect, Baum emphasizes that soft news, talk shows can increase consciousness, discernment on public affairs, especially among the electorate who does not follow mainstream news.

We can highlight the work of Gerbner, Gross, Morgan, Signorielli, and Shanahan (2002), who develop the theory of cultivation analysis and defend the role of "entertainment media as cultivator of sociopolitical worldviews" (Delli Carpini, 2012).

Ian Reilly (2011) claims that satire can be an effective mechanism for social change. In the same way, Kristy Harris (2014) outlines that talk shows illustrate and inform the audience. Jones and Baym (2010) warn about the decline of mainstream news, and praise political comedy for its trustworthiness.

Some scholars have specifically studied the impact these shows have had on public opinion during electoral campaigns. *The Jon Stewart Show* provided information for most Americans during the 2004 presidential election (Cutbirth, 2011). Waldman (2009) has even noted how *The Saturday Night Live* might have swung the 2008 election. Candidate appearances on soft news had substantial influence not only on voters´ evaluations of presidential candidates (Moy et al., 2005b); but also on the voting behavior of the audience who had watched those shows, especially among the less politically motivated (Baum and Jamison, 2006).

In addition, these programs can function as a sort of doorway to traditional news source and spark interest among the audience in political matters (Young, Feldman, 2008). In fact, Young and Feldman (2008) have found that viewers of late-night comedy programs, *The Tonight Show* with Jay Leno and *The Late Show* with David Letterman in particular, became more interested in national network and cable news than non-viewers.

It is interesting to note that there is some interesting literature – for instance, Zemke (1991), Wells (2002) and Truett (2011) – on the positive effects humor has on learning that can be applied similarly and extended to learning and acquiring knowledge in the field of politics.

Diversion and disconnection

The second point-of-view, "entertainment media as a distraction or a source of disengagement" (Delli Carpini, 2012), maintains that political comedy does not meet the needs and requirements of any democratic system, since public information is discredited; and political events and facts turned into spectacle and parody. Some studies agree the starting point of this line of reasoning is the audience loss of interest in traditional news over the last few decades (Pew Research Center for the People and the Press, 2008; Project for Excellence in Journalism, 2009).

Blumler and Gurevitz (1995) refer to a "crisis of public communication," arguing those shows deprive citizens of the most relevant instrument to exercise democracy: legitimate news sources.

Putnan (1995a,b, 2000) is convinced that television entertainment is a significant factor in the deterioration of social capital and democratic engagement, especially among young people.

Shah, Kwak and Holbert (2001) distinguish between informational and communicative uses of the media *versus* recreational and entertainment ones. The former is positive for an active, participatory society; whereas the latter may erode civic engagement.

Middle position: alternative outlet for opinion formation and learning

The third position, "Entertainment Media as an Alternative Source of Political Engagement" (Delli Carpini, 2012), considers that, under particular conditions and for certain people—especially those who do not follow traditional news outlets—entertainment media can have an impact on citizen's behavior, perceptions, views and knowledge similar to the impact and effects caused by traditional news. The reasoning behind this position is that many TV viewers prefer soft, entertainment programs to traditional news sources. Since the humor and satire genres have increasingly introduced political content, the audience can, thus, benefit from it and increase their political knowledge.

A variation of this school adopts a complementary or combination approach between traditional news sources and entertainment news. Studies have found that higher education students not only watch the news on television but also satire shows and the Internet (Diddi & LaRose, 2006). Moreover, Young and Tisinger' research (2006) illustrates that programs such as *The Daily Show* do not replace traditional news; on the contrary, these entertainment formats complement and reinforce traditional news.

The 2016 U.S. Presidential Election

Entertainment Media has today become the norm for candidates, "a staple of the presidential campaign" (Weprin, 2016), in an effort to present a more human side of themselves before the eyes of the electorate, and gain their sympathy and votes. Late-night viewers during 2016 for *The Tonight Show* with Jimmy Fallon amounted to 3.5 M; *The Late Show* with Stephen Colbert was followed by an audience of 2.5 M.; *Jimmy Kimmel Live*, by 2.0 M.; *Late Night* with Seth Meyers, by 1.5 M., etc. (Nededog & Gould, 2017). These figures show the high number of potential voters candidates can potentially reach out to and why their presence in those shows is required. Another substantial argument is the opportunity to influence young electors, who may disregard TV news (Weprin, 2016).

During the 2016 Presidential Campaign, Hillary Clinton and Donald Trump did not underestimate the value of late night and made noteworthy appearances in some of the most popular shows. Hillary Clinton attended *The Tonight Show* in September 2015[1]. She had a fake conversation with Donald Trump, performed by Jimmy Fallon. While they talk, Hillary offers views and insights on issues and policies relevant to the campaign with a great sense of humor, joking about Trump´s hair, etc. In January 2016, again at *The Tonight Show*, Fallon poses "crucial" questions to her in a "Mock Job Interview for President"[2]. In September 2016, Clinton appears once again in Fallon´s show.[3] On this occasion, Fallon reads and comments with Clinton on letters written to her by children. In addition to Clinton´s presence in *The Tonight Show*, she appeared in *The Saturday Night Life*, in October 2015, and played the role of a bartender who has a comic exchange of views with a fake Hillary Clinton personified by Kate McKinnon.[4]

Donald Trump attended late night shows in fewer occasions than Hillary Clinton. He showed his sense of humor but not as vividly as Clinton. He appeared three times on *The Tonight Show*. In September 2015, he "interviews himself in the mirror." The moderator, Jimmy Fallon, on the other side of the mirror, imitates him and leads the interview.[5] In January, again on the show, he accepts the "mock interview for President" and answers Fallon´s questions in a good mood, trying to be entertaining.[6]

---

[1] Phone Conversation with fake Donald Trump. *The Tonight Show*, September 2015. Retrieved from https://www.youtube.com/watch?v=ONRQZshyrPI

[2] Mock Job Interview for President. *The Tonight Show,* January 2016. Retrieved from https://www.youtube.com/watch?v=PiDFL8tgn0Q

[3] Kids Letter with Hillary Clinton. *The Tonight Show,* September 2016. Retrieved from https://www.youtube.com/watch?v=K818ZgIcoWE

[4] Hillary Clinton Bar Talk. *The Saturday Night Life*, October 2015. Retrieved from https://www.youtube.com/watch?v=6Jh2n5ki0KE

[5] Interview in the mirror. *The Tonight Show*, September 2015. Retrieved from https://www.youtube.com/watch?v=c2DgwPG7mAA

[6] Mock Interview for President. *The Tonight Show*, January 2016. Retrieved from https://www.youtube.com/watch?v=Xb7jWw5lft4

In September 2016 we see him in another "mock interview," this time more oriented toward campaign issues considering Election Day is closer. This appearance is one of the most acclaimed and commented.[7]

The 2016 Presidential Election has set new trends for political satire, since Trump and Clinton performed more the role of comedians or entertainers than interviewees (Manoliu, 2017). The "comedian or clown strategy" represents a new element in the history of campaigning and late night that the candidates have taken to create empathy and appeal to potential voters.

Both Trump and Clinton had a very intense media presence and proved their sense of humor, "attacking or impersonating the opponent, making fun of his statements or physical aspects, talking about their own policies proposals in a simplistic way, and ultimately being able to make fun of themselves" (Manoliu, 2017, p. 88).

Conclusion

Nowadays, it is important to recognize the importance of political entertainment. Viewership reports reinforce this reflection with the most popular late-night shows attracting audiences in the millions (Nededog & Gould, 2017).

In this chapter, we have discussed the work of scholars who think that a considerable amount of people get informed and acquire political knowledge through entertainment talk shows, including during major political moments such as elections campaigns. From a critical point of view, considering talk shows repercussions and influence, these programs need to transmit high-quality information, no matter if it is combined or "seasoned" with satire and humor. They should also avoid "fake news."

Scholars have supported the crucial role political comedy plays in strengthening, and even "saving" democracies by engaging citizens with politics (McClennen & Maisel, 2014). From this perspective, it is interesting to mention a media initiative launched in Nigeria, where entertainment shows have been produced to spread democratic principles and civic values (Chen, 2018).

The unavoidable question is whether it is best for citizens to be informed through traditional media outlets and news programs format; and, if so, in what

---

[7] Trump allows Fallon to mess his hair. *The Tonight Show*, September 2016. Retrieved from https://www.youtube.com/watch?v=u0BYqzdiuJc

ways the consumption of such "classic" formats can be enhanced in an age where entertainment politics together with online news and platforms have reached such a formidable success (Pew Research, 2009).

Finally, some researchers advocate for a more integrative theory of political communication and argue for the futility of making genre distinctions such as news versus entertainment, comedy versus drama, print versus image, and television versus internet. According to this perspective, the essential aspect lies in understanding how the current media environment influences citizens in different ways with "various mediated messages" (Delli Carpini, 2012).

Acknowledgments

I want to express my gratitude to The Centre for Media and Celebrity Studies (CMCS), CUNY School of Journalism, and to other friends and colleagues involved in this publication, for the chance to develop this enriching research project and work and learn together.

References

Baum, M. (2002). Sex, Lies and War: How Soft News Brings Foreign Policy to the Inattentive Public. *American Political Science Review*, 96(1): pp. 91–109.

Baum, M. (2003a). Soft News and Political Knowledge: Evidence of Absence or Absence of Evidence. *Political Communication*, 20(2): pp. 173–90.

Baum, M. (2003b). *Soft News Goes to War: Public Opinion and American Foreign Policy in the New Media Age*. Princeton, NJ: Princeton University Press.

Baum, M. (2005). Talking the Vote: Why Presidential Candidates Hit the Talk Show Circuit. *American Journal of Political Science*, 49(2): pp. 213–34.

Baum, M. & Jamison, A. S. (2006). The Oprah Effect: How Soft News Helps Inattentive Citizens Vote Consistently. *Journal of Politics*, 68(4): pp. 946–59.

Baym, G. (2008). Infotainment. *The International Encyclopedia of Communication*. Edited by Wolfgang Donsbach. Blackwell: 2008.

Blumler, J. G., & Gurevitch, M. (1995). *The crisis of public communication* . London: Routledge.

Chen, A. (2018) Mockery and Democracy. *The New Yorker*, January 22, 2018.

Delli Carpini, M.X. (2012). Entertainment Media and the Political Engagement of Citizens. *The SAGE Handbook of Political Communication*. SAGE: 2012.

Delli Carpini, M. X., & Williams, B. A. (1994). Fictional and non-fictional television celebrates Earth Day. *Cultural Studies*, (8):74-98.

Dörner, A. (2001). *Politainment: Politics as part of the mediated event society*. Frankfurt: Suhrkamp.

Diddi, A. & LaRose, R. (2006). Getting Hooked on News: Uses and Gratifications and the Formation of News Habits Among College Students in an Internet Environment. *Journal of Broadcasting & Electronic Media*, 50(2): pp. 193–210.

Gerbner, G., Gross, L., Morgan, M., Signorielli, N. and Shanahan, J. (2002) Growing Up with Television: Cultivation Processes in J. Bryant, ed. and D. Zillmann (eds.), *Media Effects: Advances in Theory and Research. Mahwah*, NJ: Lawrence Erlbaum Associates. pp. 43–67.

Harris, K. (2014). *Mass Media Satire - the Modern Public Sphere: How Modern Satire Serves a Unique Purpose in Democratic Society*. University of Nebraska at Omaha.

Jackson, D. J. (2002). *Entertainment and Politics. The Influence of Pop Culture on Young Adult Political Socialization*. Peter Lang Inc.

Jones, J. & Baym, G. (2010). A dialogue on satire news and the crisis of truth in postmodern political televisión. *Journal of Communication Inquiry*, 34(3), 278-294.

McClennen, S. & Maisel, R. (2014). *Is Satire Saving Our Nation?: Mockery and American Politics*. New York: Palgrave Macmillan

Moy, P., Xenos, M. A., and Hess, V. K. (2005a). Communication and citizenship: Mapping the political effects of infotainment. *Mass Communication and Society*, (8), 111-131.

Moy, P., Xenos, M. A. and Hess, V. K. (2005b) Priming Effects of Late-Night Comedy. *International Journal of Public Opinion Research*, 18(2): pp. 198–210.

Nededog, J. & Gould, S. (2017). Who's winning and losing late-night TV under Trump. *Business Insider*. Retrieved from http://www.businessinsider.com/late-night-show-tv-ratings-under-trump-2017-3

Nieland, J. (2008), Politainment. *The International Encyclopedia of Communication*, Edited by: Wolfgang Donsbach.

Pew Research Center for the People and the Press (2008). Key News Audiences Now Blend Online and Traditional Sources Audience Segments in a Changing News Environment http://people-press.org/report/444/news-media

Pollio, H.R. (2002). Humor and college teaching. In S. F. Davis and W. Buskist (Eds.), *The teaching of psychology: Essays in honor of Wilbert J. McKeachie and Charles L. Brewer* (pp. 60-80). Mahwah, NJ: Lawrence Erlbaum.

Project for Excellence in Journalism (2009) State of the News Media: An Annual Report on American Journalism. http://www.stateofthenewsmedia.com/2009/index.htm

Putnam, R. (1995a). 'Bowling Alone: America's Declining Social Capital', *The Journal of Democracy*, 6(1): pp. 65–78.

Putnam, R. (1995b). Tuning in, Tuning Out: The Strange Disappearance of Social Capital in America. *PS: Political Science and Politics*, 28(4): pp. 664–83.

Putnam, R. (2000) *Bowling Alone*. New York: Simon and Schuster.

Reilly, I. (2010). *Satirical fake news and the politics of the fifth estate*. The University of Guelph. Retrieved from http://www.academia.edu/670662/Satirical_ fake_ news_and_the_politics_of_ the_fifth_estate

Shah, D. V., Kwak, N. and Holbert, R. L. (2001). 'Connecting' and 'Disconnecting' with Civic Life: Patterns of Internet Use and the Production of Social Capital. *Political Communication*, 18(2): pp. 141–62.

Timberg, B. M. (2002) *Television Talk. A History of the TV Talk Show,* University of Texas Press.

Truett, K. (2011). Humor and Students' Perceptions of Learning. (Doctoral Dissertation, Texas Tech University).

Waldman, A. J. (2009). 'SNL' Political Satire. *TelevisionWeek*, 28(13), Retrieved from http://ezproxy.lib.calpoly.edu/login?url=http://search.proquest.com/ docview/2038 34666?accountid=10362

Weprin, A. (2016). Hillary Clinton and Donald Trump take the campaign back to late night TV. *Politico*. Retrieved from https://www.politico.com/blogs/on-media/2016/09/hillary-clinton-and-donald-trump-take-the-campaign-back-to-late-night-tv-228027

Williams, B. A. & Delli Carpini, M. X. (2009), *The Eroding Boundaries between News and Entertainment and What They Mean for Democratic Politics*, New York: Routledge.

Young, D. G., Tisinger, R. M. (2006). Dispelling Late-Night Myths: News Consumptionamong Late-Night Comedy Viewers and the Predictors of Exposure to Various Late-Night Shows. *The Harvard International Journal of Press/ Politics*, 11(3), pp. 113–34.

Young, D. & Feldman, L. (2008). Late-night comedy as a gateway to traditional news: An analysis of time trends in news attention among late-night comedy viewers during the 2004 presidential primaries. *Political Communication*, 25(4), 401-422.

Zemke, R. (1991). Humor in training. *Training* 28(8), 26. Retrieved from http://ezproxy.lib.calpoly.edu/login?url=http://search.proquest.com/docview/2033 77471?accountid=10362

Ziv, A. (1988). Teaching and learning with humor: Experiment and replication. *The Journal of Experimental Education, 57*, 5-15.

Learning from Young Mothers and Dr. Drew: MTV's *Teen Mom* as Public Pedagogy

Colin Ackerman

Abstract. This chapter seeks to critically analyze select contemporary episodes of MTV's *Teen Mom* to determine whether criticisms lodged against the text are warranted if the show's presenters and cast members can be considered intellectuals, and to what extent the show serves as public pedagogy. The study found that while many of the criticisms of the show continue to be prevalent, they provide an arena to discuss, describe and dissent against problematic dynamics such as stereotypes or hegemonic discourses. The presence of Dr. Drew Pinsky, in addition to personal accounts of the four main cast members, enhances the text's framing as public pedagogy with these people serving a public intellectual role. This work draws from the theoretical work of Antonio Gramsci and H.A. Giroux as well as other scholars who have examined the *Teen Mom* text.

Keywords: Public Pedagogy, *Teen Mom,* Traditional Intellectual, Organic Intellectual, Gramsci.

Introduction

The current popular culture landscape cannot be ignored. I do not believe there is ignorance in terms of viewership or awareness of content, but rather an ignorance of the various roles popular culture texts can hold in our society. Reality television, or 'docudrama' as they are sometimes called, is a form of popular culture which is frequently derided in the public discourse for lacking substantive content and pushing problematic representation (among other criticisms). While these criticisms may be warranted, to define reality television only by its negative attributes misses an opportunity to uncover the full scope of influence these kinds of texts hold in our society and culture.

Teen Mom is one such show which has primarily been relegated to being seen as inconsequential entertainment; however, I argue that this is not the case. *Teen Mom* holds excellent potential for cultural analysis because the show addresses wide-reaching societal concerns (e.g., drug use, mental health, birth control) with a blend of expert discussion along with realistic portrayals of struggles. This study intends to critically analyze selected contemporary episodes from MTV's *Teen Mom* to judge whether criticisms of the show are resonating if the presenters and cast members of the show can be labeled as intellectuals, and to what extent the text can be defined as public pedagogy.

Before exploring these question, I will provide a brief description of the history of the show for context and a broad framing of the arguments I will be making. This will be followed by a review of academic literature examining the show.

History of the Show

MTV's *Teen Mom* franchise began in June 2009 with the show *16 and Pregnant*. Facing declining ratings as network, *16 and Pregnant* was created out of a desire to make shows that, as MTV's president of entertainment put it, "focus less on silly hooks and more on young people proving themselves," because "these are the themes that are consistent with the Obama generation" (Seldon, 2016, n.p.). It was reminiscent of other docudrama series airing on MTV (and elsewhere) at the time such as "True Life" in that there was no recurring cast. Each episode followed the journey of a different pregnant teenage girl facing tensions between their pregnancy and high school, relationships, and family. The show featured expectant mothers came from all parts of the country and different socioeconomic backgrounds with each episode presenting the hardships and tough decisions a pregnant teenager must face.

Teen Mom premiered in December 2009 and followed four of the teenagers (Farrah Abraham, Maci McKinney, Amber Portwood, and Catelynn Baltierra) featured on the first season of *16 and Pregnant* through their first year of motherhood and placed a greater emphasis on how teenage motherhood impacts interpersonal relationships, both with their romantic partners and families. The show was another rating success for MTV, and two additional spin-offs were created (*Teen Mom 2* and *Teen Mom 3*). The original *Teen Mom* and *Teen Mom 2* are still on the air as of 2018 (having aired seven and eight seasons, respectively).

Dr. Drew joins the Teen Moms

At the end of the first season of *Teen Mom*, MTV introduced a unique episode format called "Check-Up with Dr. Drew." This is a talk show style follow-up special to catch the audience up on what has been happening in the lives of the cast members since the cameras stopped rolling as well as reflect on the occurrences from the previous season. This end of season special has become a mainstay of the series, with host Dr. Drew Pinsky offering very candid, sometimes brutally honest, advice to the cast members about their decisions. The special acts as a sort of public therapy session where Dr. Drew pokes and prods the cast members to encourage them to own up and accept the decisions they have made and hopefully work towards a more positive future.

Though a board-certified internist and addiction medicine specialist, Dr. Drew has been accused of being exploitative of patients in their rehabilitation and mental illness, with many feeling the public setting of shows such as *Teen Mom* makes it impossible for treatment to be truly effective (Allen, 2016). One of his most prominent criticisms centers around five celebrities who participated in his show "Celebrity Rehab with Dr. Drew" later committing suicide, though medical experts have come to his defense claiming causation between participating and committing suicide years later is unlikely (Farrell, 2013). Regardless of the criticism waged against him, he has become a critical part of the *Teen Mom* storytelling structure as well as the show's popularity.

Why is this show worth discussing?

While *Teen Mom* (and similar reality docudrama series) have faced criticism and analysis on whether they actually mirror social reality (Stiernstedt and Jakobsson, 2017), *Teen Mom* provides a fertile environment for discussion about the ability for a television series to educate the public and provide an arena to discuss and resist against dominant stereotypical narratives. This study aims to analyze the text of *Teen Mom* (specifically, the show's most recent "Check-Up with Dr. Drew") to see if it warrants being viewed as an educational resource for the public rather than being of no consequence.

The crux of my argument is that *Teen Mom* is representative of public pedagogy or space for learning outside the traditional classroom environment (this concept will be explored further in the next section). *Teen Mom* warrants the label of public pedagogy not only because of the ethos brought by Dr. Drew Pinsky, but also the frank and candid participation by its four central cast member, who first started the show while in high school and are now all in their mid-20s. This diachronic account of the struggles of young motherhood combined with the show's viewership position the four cast members as what uniquely qualified and impactful in speaking on their experiences of motherhood.

Literature Review

Upon the premieres *16 and Pregnant* and *Teen Mom* in 2009, both shows garnered attention from academic researchers. The lines of inquiry into mediated representations of young motherhood were mostly critical. While researchers saw the *potential* for these texts to serve an educational or advocacy function, there was an almost uniform critique at the dominant cultural discourses represented as well as the show's ability to reproduce these discourses. The criticisms of *16 and Pregnant* and *Teen Mom* can be broadly placed into three categories: 1) creating and augmenting stereotypical narratives, 2) pushing hegemonic discourses, and 3) lacking diverse representations of young fatherhood.

There was a flurry of academic attention paid to *16 and Pregnant* and *Teen Mom* in the years immediately following its premiere. Since then there has been little work done examining the texts. While *16 and Pregnant* ended its run in 2014 after five seasons, *Teen Mom* and *Teen Mom 2* are still on the air as of 2018. It is necessary to revisit these original critiques of the show as they provide a bar to compare its current incarnation against. Upon viewing recent episodes of *Teen Mom,* particularly the Dr. Drew hosted reunion special, it is observed some of the criticisms are still appropriate while others have been addressed.

Creating and Augmenting Stereotypical Narratives

A fundamental criticism lodged against *16 and Pregnant* and *Teen Mom* is its tendency to provide messages of feminism and empowerment on the surface but upon closer examination directly serve to push and create stereotypical social narratives of young mothers. For example, Murphy (2013) argues the shows present their subjects as "postfeminist neoliberal subjects" (p. 4). This means the cast members exhibit postfeminist sensibilities, in which "women [are] autonomous agents no longer constrained by any inequalities or power imbalances" (Gill, 2007, p. 153), yet their worth is measured by their ability to "reconstitute their identity around motherhood" while still adhering to neoliberal capitalist values (Murphy, 2013, p. 4). This creates a standardized narrative for young motherhood which gives fodder to judge a young mother's actions as a valuative success or failure.

Similarly, other critique focused on the already existing stereotypes *16 and Pregnant* and *Teen Mom* reinforce. Guglielmo and Stewart (2013) claim the programs "simply reinforce stereotypes common in the rhetoric of teen pregnancy and sex education in the United States and facilitates the co-opting of the young women's narratives" (p. 20). The fear is that the struggle and journey of the young females are overshadowed by the needs of other players in her story (e.g., boyfriend, family, friends). By de-centering the young mother from the story the show potentially can warp a viewer's idea of the agency of a young mother, producing an image where the young mother must be concerned with those around her over her own needs. This is mainly seen in the representation of romantic relationships on the show, where the worth of young females is dependent on their attractiveness and desirability to males in spite of their newly found label as a 'young mother.' (Fallas, 2013). This creates an 'ideal teenage mother' stereotype who must forgo all selfish desire to be seen as a 'good mom' (Todd, 2013).

Pushing Hegemonic Discourses

The creation and reinforcement of stereotypes and narratives in shows such as these are problematic because it not only essentializes what it means and looks like to be a young mother, but also that pushes hegemonic discourses around class and race. The vast majority of subjects on *16 and Pregnant* and all of the four cast members on *Teen Mom* are white. Fallas (2013) argues that young white females are presented as an ideal type. According to Fallas, "The *Teen Mom* series relies on pre-existing dominant forms of white femininity to frame its portrayals of young women who have become 'other' by their pregnancies and subsequent motherhood's clear violations of normative social structures guiding white female youth" (Fallas, 2013; p. 50). Not only does the show serve to 'other' the young mother, but it predominantly creates a frame for the white mother and neglects to show the viewing public diverse characterizations of young motherhood. This is problematic because, despite a marked difference in pregnancy rates between young women of color and young white woman, the show mostly shows a singular construction of young motherhood characterized by class and race exclusion (Fallas, 2013).

Like the hegemonic discourse of whiteness purportedly pushed by this show, there is equal concern about the representation of class within the texts. Friedman (2013) finds the show presents poverty as the "logical conclusions to the perceived moral failings of the show's protagonists" (p. 68). There is a message that unplanned pregnancy necessarily leads to social turmoil which inevitably leads to poverty of financial strain. Aspects such as this are observed to pathologize teenage pregnancy (Thomas, 2013). According to the representations and discourses within the show, a young girl becoming pregnant is less likely to be a blessing and more likely to be a curse. While these accusations are quite alarming if true, it is admittedly difficult to deduce the direct effects of the hegemonic discourses present within the show on teenage viewers (Daniel, 2013).

Representations of Young Fatherhood

Depictions of young fathers is one of the few areas of the series which have engendered a certain level of praise; albeit very measured praise. McLanahan (2013) argues the heterosexual imaginary for young men, "or the belief that to achieve a sense of well-being in life one must be involved in a heterosexual romantic relationship" (pp. 142-143) is both supported *and* disrupted by these shows. The shows provide examples of how young fathers can be successful without being romantically involved with the mother of their child. However, McLanahan (2013) also argues certain norms around young fatherhood recur across the series which also have the adverse effects of stereotyping what young fatherhood *should* or *ideally* look like. Beggs and Schatz (2013) found the format of the show to be constrictive of the young men portrayed to find their own parenting style organically but claims the young fathers on the shows overall convey "their desire to be there for their children, even if they cannot financially provide for them" (p. 125).

Other researchers have taken a more negative stance towards the representations of young fatherhood on the *16 and Pregnant* and *Teen Mom*. Tropp (2013) claims the programs "represent ambivalent views of fatherhood: girlfriends and family members constrain the power of the men to be in their children's lives, the drama of television emphasizes dysfunctional fathers. And the program frames the primary role of the fatherhood as serving, first and most important, an economic function" (p. 161). Similar to the young mothers, there is also an overall concern about racial representation of the young fathers across the shows (McLanahan, 2013; Beggs and Schatz, 2013; Tropp, 2013).

Another aspect of this analysis is a discussion of whether or not *Teen Mom* can be labeled as public pedagogy. Before beginning the analysis, a brief conversation about the concept of public pedagogy will provide context to how this term is being used.

Public Pedagogy and the Intellectual

Defining Public Pedagogy

Inquiry and research into the way in which people learn are broadly placed under the umbrella of "educational research." While this is not an inaccurate classification, it tends to limit the research to look at how students and teachers interact in a school/classroom environment. A subgenre of educational research has emerged focusing on educational activity occurring outside the traditional schooling setting, referring to these alternate sites of learning as *public pedagogy*.

The reason for this newfound perspective on educational research was the underlying notion that mainstream educational research was not doing enough to identify and analyze alternate sites of learning and this omission could have consequences on increasing understanding about how children learn. Mainstream education research tends to operate under the assumption that schools are the most salient and therefore most substantive site of learning.

Operating under this false assumption of schools being a closed system results in incomplete accounts of how and where learning takes place (Giroux, 2000).

Since the term's proliferation in the mid-1990s, the use of public pedagogy has engendered widespread use. Unfortunately, frequently the term is used without explicating its exact definition or how it is being used concerning other uses of the phrase. This has led to a cheapening of the term public pedagogy which in turn has stunted the development of research. Sandlin, O'Malley and Burdick (2011) sought to remedy this by conducting a meta-analysis of 420 articles which use the term public pedagogy and were able to derive five broad categories of public pedagogy research in order to "...provide a preliminary but needed methodologically rigorous organizing schema for reviewing and theorizing public pedagogy and welcome alternate perspectives" (p. 341). The five categories are (a) citizenship within and beyond schools, (b) popular culture and everyday life, (c) informal institutions and public spaces, (d) dominant cultural discourses, and (e) public intellectualism and social activism. Of these categories, popular culture and everyday life, as well as public intellectualism and social activism, are most prevalent for the current discussion of *Teen Mom*.

Public Pedagogy and Popular Culture

Gramsci's (1982) often quoted idea that "every relationship of hegemony is an educational one" (p. 350) can serve as a broad framing of where much of the work looking into where popular culture related inquiry into public pedagogy resides. Public pedagogy theorists see popular culture as a site where children can learn dominant social/cultural norms. H.A. Giroux (2000, 2001) is a leading scholar looking at popular culture as public pedagogy. Giroux draws from the theoretical frameworks of Hall (1997), Gramsci (1982), and Freire (1973) to demonstrate that popular culture does not automatically reproduce dominant cultural norms, but rather provides an arena for people to struggle against hegemonic forces - sometimes succumbing and sometimes transcending. Giroux's work in this area shows that popular culture texts are a critical aspect of culture which needs to be examined due to its implications with cultural norms (socially and economically).

Public pedagogy scholarship involving popular culture is overwhelmingly concerned with the negative implications of learning taking place outside the traditional schooling environment. I argue that while a show like *Teen Mom* could potentially contain fodder for pushing destructive cultural norms (a claim to be to be explored further in proceeding sections) but it is worth examining the potentially positive aspects of learning outside the classroom environment with this popular culture text.

Public Pedagogy and Public Intellectualism

Within theorization of public pedagogy, the issue of the role of the public intellectual is a recurring element. Sandlin, O'Malley and Burdick (2011) claim public intellectuals do not necessarily need to be institutionally located and can be impactful outside of traditional academic or research environments. An extension of this is to say public pedagogy and the public intellectuals connected to it share expert knowledge to the general public for a particular purpose (Fulcher, 1999).

Gramsci (1982) provides a useful categorical frame for different kinds of intellectuals: traditional and organic. He defines the traditional as professional intellectuals from academic backgrounds "whose position in the interstices of society has a certain inter-class aura about it but derives ultimately from past and present class relations and conceals an attachment to various historical class formations" (p. 131). Conversely, organic intellectuals are defined "by their function in directing the ideas and aspirations of the class to which they organically belong" (p. 131).

Both kinds of intellectuals are present in mediated texts including, as I will argue, *Teen Mom*. Obviously, Gramsci could not have anticipated the proliferation of mediated forms which have led to a surfeit of widely heard voices claiming to be an 'authority' or 'expert' on particular subjects, but nevertheless, these categories are still useful. *Teen Mom* potentially demonstrates utilization of both traditional (Dr. Drew) and organic (the four cast members) intellectuals as a means to relay both expert and pragmatic information on issues including teenage pregnancy, drug addiction, mental health, and interpersonal effectiveness.

Research Questions

The discussed literature has led to the creation of the following three research questions:

RQ1: Has *Teen Mom* contemporarily addressed or ignored the problematics previously raised by researchers?

RQ2: Can the cast members of *Teen Mom* and Dr. Drew be considered intellectuals?

RQ3: If the cast members of *Teen Mom* and Dr. Drew are public intellectuals, to what degree can *Teen Mom* be construed as a public pedagogy?

Method and Object of Analysis

To explore the stated research questions, I performed a textual analysis on the season six two-part finale titled "Check-in with Dr. Drew" (originally aired June 3, 2017 and June 10, 2017). While there are six previous seasons providing arenas for analysis, I chose these episodes because of the inclusion of Dr. Drew and its magazine format which facilitates the discussion of a wide array of topics. Dr. Drew's presence in the reunion specials provides the best opportunity to analyze *Teen Mom* from a public intellectual perspective as he and the four main cast members being in the same space (the only time this occurs in the series) best demonstrates the dichotomy between traditional and organic intellectuals.

The areas of interest gleaned from the watching the program can be organized into four categories of subject matter: relationships, mental health, substance abuse, and birth control. The episode does address topics outside of these categories, however the majority of the discussion involves at least one of these subjects. These four categories are used to describe the kinds of content discussed in the special. After this descriptive account, this study will close with an analysis and discussion of the special concerning the research questions.

Description of Special

Relationships

The two kinds of interpersonal relationships explored in the special are co-parenting and romantic. Of the four cast members, only Catelynn is still in a committed relationship with the father of her child; however, the fathers of the other cast members' children (other than Farrah, whose former partner has passed away) are still actively involved with the show and their child's life leading to different accounts of what co-parenting can look like.

Amber co-parents her daughter with her former partner Gary and his wife, Christina. While Amber has issues in her personal life, her co-parenting relationship with Gary and Christina is very stable. Amber and Christina consider themselves to be close friends and confidants and Amber and Gary consistently reiterate that they are entirely on the same page when it comes to their daughter. Dr. Drew affirms the positivity in their co-parenting arrangement and describes it as "a model example for young separated parents everywhere." He also commends Amber, Gary, and Christina for persevering through some instability in the early years of their shared child's life.

Amber and Gary's co-parenting dynamic is juxtaposed with that of Maci and her ex-partner, Ryan. Maci has struggled to co-parent with Ryan ever since their son was born effectively. Ryan's new wife McKenzie and Maci have a contentious relationship, with McKenzie claiming Maci has always been unfair to Ryan when it comes to visitation and custody arrangements. Dr. Drew points to the differences in the co-parenting of Maci and Ryan to that of Amber and Gary. These two segments provide alternative examples of co-parenting giving Dr. Drew plenty of material to present the importance of effective co-parenting to the audience.

In addition to examples of co-parenting, each of the four cast members provides a different kind of romantic relationships for Dr. Drew and the audience to compare against one another. Catelynn and Tyler are married and have been together since they were 16; Maci has not been with Ryan for years and is now in a stable marriage with a man named Taylor; Amber is in a long-term relationship which at the time of filming was extremely strained; Farrah recently left a long-term relationship and is casually dating. Each of these young women started on the journey of parenthood around the same time with respective romantic partners. The continued focus on romantic relationships on *Teen Mom* presents diverse examples of how those young relationships can flourish or falter without it being necessarily tied to stability within the family.

Mental Health

Mental health is a recurring topic throughout all of *Teen Mom*. Depression, anxiety, and personality disorders are among the issues throughout the entire series. This makes mental health a primary area of exploration in the finale reunion special. Amber has struggled with mental health her whole life and was recently diagnosed with borderline personality disorder, leading to a fruitful conversation with Dr. Drew about the journey of someone with mental illness. Dr. Drew frequently affirms when Amber constructively speaks about her mental health and commends her for her work as a mental health peer-counselor in prison. Catelynn similarly speaks of her experience with depression, saying she is on medications but taking a break from talk-therapy and experimenting with equine therapy and other alternative forms of counseling. Dr. Drew brings attention to Amber and Catelynn's different approaches to mental health to illuminate mental health concerns being a very personalized journey.

A dichotomy is presented between the accounts of Catelynn and Amber against that of Deb, Farrah's mother. Dr. Drew interviews Deb with her fiancé but without Farrah and is clearly probing her to come to terms with her denial of some of her mental health issues. Deb very clearly has exhibited symptoms of a potential personality disorder (a fact which Amber comments on later in the broadcast). This has included violent outbursts and sudden shifts in moods. Because this is not a proper therapy session, Dr. Drew does not question Deb very aggressively but in his questioning demonstrates a textbook example of denial with Deb's fiancé being an enabling presence. Shining a light on mental health journeys is Dr. Drew's career hallmark. In this special, he is able to frame successful and in process journeys for the audience.

Substance Abuse

Substance abuse stories recur throughout the *Teen Mom* franchise and this special, much like the other categories discussed in this description, presents different stories of addiction and provides insight into not just how addiction affects the individual, but also the people around them. One substance abuse story involves Maci and the father of her child, Ryan, who recently entering rehab for opioid addiction. Ryan is not present for the taping of the show, but his wife McKenna chastises Maci for not speaking out about her suspicions of Ryan's drug abuse sooner. Dr. Drew mediates the tense confrontation and repeatedly says, "You both need to get on the same team." At the end of the conversation, Dr. Drew pivots to a direct appeal to the audience about the ferocity of the opioid epidemic and lists resources for people to get help.

An alternate story of addiction comes from Tyler, Catelynn's husband. His father, Butch, has struggled with drug addiction throughout all of Tyler's life. In spite of getting clean and relapsing multiple times, Tyler has stayed supportive and loving towards his father. He not only is accepting of his father's mistake but also proud of his father's continued dedication to striving for sobriety, even through relapses. Tyler, his father, and his wife are much further along in the recovery process than Maci and Ryan (and their families) which again presents alternate accounts of the same struggle thousands of families go through.

Birth Control

Advocating for smart birth control practices and general birth control education has always been a focus of the *Teen Mom* and *16 and Pregnant* franchises. Even though the young teenage mothers originally featured are now adults, Dr. Drew checks-in consistently and facilitates an honest conversation about birth control. In each of the cast member's segments, Dr. Drew asks what methods of birth control they are currently using. Each of the cast members utilizes a different method of birth control and acknowledge their preferred method has changed frequently over the years. The normalcy and frankness of the discussion of birth control make a sometimes taboo subject approachable.

In addition to the cast members sharing their personal habits and stories regarding birth control, Dr. Drew also makes more direct appeals to the audience to strongly and thoughtfully consider what form of birth control works best for them. He plugs a website called "bed-sider.org" which provides free resources and information for learning about birth control, saying, "Women using birth control account for only 5% of unplanned pregnancies in American, so be proactive and use protection." Dr. Drew's endorsement is seconded by the cast members, who all wish they had more resources when they became young mothers almost ten years ago.

Analysis

RQ1: Has Teen Mom contemporarily addressed or ignored the problematics previously raised by researchers?

As noted in the literature review, academic discussion of *Teen Mom* has raised issues of the show's tendency to create and augment stereotypical narratives, push hegemonic discourses, and lack diverse representations of young fatherhood. While evident efforts have been made to address the common criticisms against the text, the format of the show itself makes it nearly impossible to wholly devoid itself of criticism. For example, in the description of the show I referenced how a given topic discussed covers at least two separate narratives to underscore the uniqueness and difference in each individual's circumstances (a practice which has increased as the show progressed). This certainly helps defend against the claim of creating and augmenting stereotypical narratives, however; in focusing on the same cast members season after season, the impact of the diverse experiences diminishes as the audience hears the experiences of same people season after season.

The observed show was more effective in pushing against the claim that *Teen Mom* pushes against hegemonic narratives, particularly the claim that the show presents poverty as the "logical conclusions to the perceived moral failings of the show's protagonists" (Friedman, 2013, p. 68). The special does shed light on various turmoil in each cast member's current life, but it also very much highlights their successes and ongoing stability. All four cast members' own their own homes and three out of the four have parlayed their level of fame into successful small business ventures. The show no longer serves to, as was claimed, pathologize young pregnancy.

Unfortunately, the claim of the show pushing white motherhood as an 'ideal type' is not addressed. All four cast members are of Caucasian descent, and their extended networks tend to lack people of color. The series spin-off *Teen Mom 2* does feature people of color as central to the show (one cast member and four former partners of cast members), but the lack of diversity in this flagship edition is still an issue.

While some criticized *Teen Mom* for displaying limited representations of fatherhood, others found the show's portrayal of fatherhood to be one of its few positive traits. After viewing this special, I tend to agree with the latter. Are their shortcomings in the representation of fatherhood? Of course, there are; however, this show does give a platform to young fathers to discuss their unique trials and tribulations, and present different cases of what being an active father can look like. For example, Tyler's experience with his father's addiction is discussed concerning how it impacts his parenting of his own daughter. Gary's steadfast commitment to his daughter seeing her mother as much as possible, despite Amber's personal turmoil, shows a proactive, committed version of fatherhood which earlier versions of the show did not capture.

RQ2: Can the cast members of Teen Mom and Dr. Drew be considered intellectuals?

Returning to Gramsci's definition, a traditional intellectual is defined as an individual whose ethos and notoriety is derived from their professional accomplishments and that profession's stature in society. Organic intellectuals are individuals whose knowledge and expertise is derived from their upbringing and personal experiences. In my opinion, *Teen Mom*, and more specifically its season end reunion show, present compelling examples of both. Dr. Drew presents the traditional intellectual; his education and profession posture him as a voice of authority on the topics discussed on the show. Navigating the turmoil within co-parenting situations or other familial dynamics, addiction, recovery, and birth control are well within Dr. Drew's professional skill set and his credibility is enhanced for the audience due to his lengthy broadcasting résumé.

Complementary to Dr. Drew's traditional intellectual framing, the four main cast members function as organic intellectuals. According to Gramsci (1982), "...every social group [has] its own particular specialized category of intellectuals" (p. 113). In this instance, the cast member can be accurately defined as organic intellectuals because the intersection of social groups they come from (e.g., socioeconomic background, geographic location, age in which they first became pregnant, etc.) give them specific insights and knowledge which can be imparted onto the viewing audience.

In speaking of the role intellectuals play in society, Gramsci (1982) states, "The relationship between the intellectuals and the world of production is not as direct as it is with the fundamental social groups but is, in varying degrees, 'mediated' by the whole fabric of society and by the complex of superstructures" (p. 118). The strength of having both versions of intellectuals present in the same text is that the traditional intellectual (Dr. Drew) is able to 'mediate' the experiences of each cast member unique backgrounds to the audience. For example, Farrah at one point becomes flustered because she does not wish to discuss her relationship with her mother's fiancé. Dr. Drew is able to use probing questions, reminiscent of a therapist, to guide Farrah to realize and name the emotions she is feeling. Farrah is then able to give an eloquent account of her struggle, enhancing her role as an organic intellectual. The main cast members possess a wealth of experiential knowledge which Dr. Drew is able to operationalize for the broader population, leading to this text to be a fascinating conversation starter and wealth of experience within popular culture.

RQ3: If the cast members of Teen Mom and Dr. Drew are public intellectuals, to what degree can Teen Mom be construed as a public pedagogy?

As I have just argued, I do consider the *Teen Mom* cast members and Dr. Drew as public intellectuals. This claim is not meant to sanctify *Teen Mom* or its related show as beacons of essential knowledge, but rather show that the text is a potential site of learning outside traditional classroom or school settings. As noted in the literature, popular culture, within the context of public pedagogy, does not automatically reproduce dominant cultural norms but instead provides an arena for people to struggle against dominant cultural discourses. As demonstrated in the discussed *Teen Mom* reunion episode, the show offers representation and discussion of omnipresent social issues (addiction, mental health, money concerns, birth control, etc.) and gives an arena for a person to observe, learn, and pass judgment about the public discourse presented to them.

Criticisms about the show (as covered within RQ1) are entirely warranted and should not be ignored; however, these problematics being present do not preclude it from being considered public pedagogy; they enhance its standing as public pedagogy. The lack of non-white representation or diverse representations of fatherhood provides potential starting points for discussions about the issues which would serve to resist against the hegemonic narrative. For example, these episodes could be shown to a group of high school students as a starting point for a wide-ranging discussion on social issues as well as what can be learned by omissions of diverse representations about the contemporary media landscape. I believe *Teen Mom*, through further analysis and discussion, has the potential to elucidate private narratives and how they connect with ideas of social reproduction and hegemony.

Conclusion

Teen Mom is not perfect. Its strengths are just as apparent as is its flaws; however, the show's shortcomings have dominated the conversation. The reason this text is worth revisiting (both for the current research and future projects) is the presence of socially positive messages along with socially problematic ones. As public pedagogy, *Teen Mom* contains many essential examples of issues which *need* to be discussed even if the presence of these examples is problematic. *Teen Mom* could help facilitate conversations around opioid addiction as well as the importance of diverse representations on television. The crux of this feature of the show is the strength of the cast members' ability to reflect on their experiences (which is facilitated by them having been featured on the show for close to 10 years) as well as Dr. Drew's expertise being available to fill in knowledge gaps in the cast members' accounts.

The present research only examined a small sample of the show, and there is a myriad of other areas which warrant further consideration. How masculinity is presented and coped with by the male cast members has fascinating implications. Also, the cast members long-term presence on the show provokes questions about their identity formation and construction in light of maturing to adulthood on camera. If popular culture is to be taken up and examined as public pedagogy, texts such as *Teen Mom* are critical. Identifying intellectuals within these kinds of shows and the kinds of messages and values they are purporting (purposefully or incidentally) is key to continuing to chart popular culture's impact on society.

References

Allen, E. (2016). The Last Days of WWE's Chyna and the Unraveling of Dr. Drew's Celebrity Alumni. *The Daily Beast*. Retrieved August 3, 2017, from http://www.thedailybeast.com/the-last-days-of-wwes-chyna-and-the-unraveling-of-dr-drews-celebrity-alumni

Daniel, C. (2013). Teen Sex: An Equal Opportunity Menace: Multicultural Politics in *16 and Pregnant* (L. Guglielmo, Ed.). In MTV and Teen Pregnancy (pp. 79-93). Lanham, MD: Scarecrow Press.

Fallas, J. (2013). Othering the Mothering: Postfeminist Constructs in *Teen Mom* (L. Guglielmo, Ed.). In MTV and Teen Pregnancy (pp. 3-19). Lanham, MD: Scarecrow Press.

Farrell, H. (2013). In Defense of Dr. Drew. Retrieved August 3, 2017, from http://www.psychologytoday.com/blog/frontpage-forensics/201302/in-defense-dr-drew

Friedman, M. (2013). 100% Preventable: Teen Motherhood, Morality, and the Myth of Choice (L. Guglielmo, Ed.). In MTV and Teen Pregnancy (pp. 67-78). Lanham, MD: Scarecrow Press.

Guglielmo, L. and Stewart, K.W. (2013). *16 and Pregnant* and the "Unvarnished" truth about Teen Pregnancy. (L. Guglielmo, Ed.). In MTV and Teen Pregnancy (pp. 19-34). Lanham, MD: Scarecrow Press.

Gill, Rosalind (2007) Postfeminist media culture: elements of a sensibility. *European Journal of Cultural Studies*, 10 (2). pp. 147-166.

Giroux, H. A. (2000). Public pedagogy as cultural politics: Stuart Hall and the "crisis" of culture. *Cultural Studies*, 14, 341–360

Giroux, H. A. (2001). Stealing innocence: Corporate culture's war on children. New York, NY: Palgrave Macmillan.

Gramsci, A. (1982). Selections from the Prison Notebooks of Antonio Gramsci. Lawrence and Wishart.

Hall, S. (1997). The centrality of culture: Notes on the cultural revolutions of our times. In K. Thompson (Ed.), Media and cultural regulation (pp. 208–238). Thousand Oaks, CA: Sage.

Murphy, C. (2013). Teen Momism on MTV: Postfeminist Subjectivities in 16 and Pregnant (L. Guglielmo, Ed.). In MTV and Teen Pregnancy (pp. 3-19). Lanham, MD: Scarecrow Press.

Sandlin, J. A., O'Malley, M. P., and Burdick, J. (2011). Mapping the Complexity of Public Pedagogy Scholarship 1894–2010. *Review of Educational Research*, *81*(3), 338–375.

Seldon, W. (2016, September 6). Let's Talk about Sex (Baby): Pushing The Decline In Unintended Pregnancy Even Further. Retrieved from http://www.huffingtonpost.com/willa-seldon/lets-talk-about-sex-baby-_b_11876338.html

Stewart, M.A. (2013). Sensationalizing the Sentimental: National Culture and Futurity (L. Guglielmo, Ed.). In MTV and Teen Pregnancy (pp. 93-108). Lanham, MD: Scarecrow Press.

Stiernstedt, F., and Jakobsson, P. (2017). Watching reality from a distance: class, genre and reality television. *Media, Culture & Society*, *39*(5), 697–714.

Murphy, C. (2013). Pathological Motherhood, Parental Relationships, Expert Counseling, and Heteronormativity: A Framework of Anxiety and Reassurance through MTV's *Teen Mom* (L. Guglielmo, Ed.). In MTV and Teen Pregnancy (pp. 3-19). Lanham, MD: Scarecrow Press.

Todd, A. (2013). Teen Moms Negotiate Desire: The (Re)production of Patriarchal Motherhood. (L. Guglielmo, Ed.). In MTV and Teen Pregnancy (pp. 35-48). Lanham, MD: Scarecrow Press.

Talking of Terror: British Television Intellectuals and Bridging the Gap between Celebrity and Intellectual Culture

John Tulloch and Belinda Middleweek

Abstract. This paper explores the theme of 'bridging the gap' between celebrity and intellectual culture through a parallel analysis of terrorism reportage across television genres. Drawing on the British television series *Atheism*, the documentary series *I Survived* and a selection of British and Dutch television news interviews we illustrate the varying ways in which public scholars negotiate the institutional constraints underpinning national and international approaches to terrorism reportage. The final section of this paper offers a personal and professional example of 'bridging the gap'.

Keywords: British Television Intellectuals, Celebrity, Elaborated Discourse, Terrorism Reportage, Iconic Images.

Introduction

This paper takes as its starting point the theme of 'bridging gaps' between celebrity and intellectual culture. By adopting a parallel analysis across television genres, we illustrate the varying ways in which public scholars negotiate the institutional constraints underpinning national and international approaches to terrorism reportage. One of the authors, John Tulloch, a media academic with extensive experience of television studios via his ethnography of production books, and also a survivor of the London terrorist bombings on 7 July 2005, was catapulted into the public spotlight when British newspaper outlets used his photograph as a symbol of the attack. In that instant, Tulloch became an unwilling celebrity whose status was reaffirmed via numerous international requests for interviews at each anniversary of the explosions, while his photograph stood as an iconic image repurposed in newspapers for political expediency. Through his television appearances for British and international broadcasters, Tulloch gained insight into this short-grab genre of television production and, much like British public intellectual Jonathan Miller before him, was able to use, at times, his conceptual and editorial control of the narrative to explore several presentational identities in an elaborated discourse that signaled the gradation of possibilities available to both Miller and Tulloch as contemporary television intellectuals. The other author of this paper, Belinda Middleweek, has the advantage of being an academic *and* television producer who interviewed Tulloch about his survival for the series *I*

Survived...Stories of Australians and thus provides a production perspective on the institutional constraints governing their television interview.

British Television Intellectuals

Britain does not seem to cherish public intellectuals. Timothy Garton Ash, an Oxford professor and respected journalist, has commented about this in *The Guardian*.

> Is the person sitting next to you [on the tube] an intellectual? Are you? Or would you run a mile from the label? The other night I asked a commentator I consider to be obviously a British intellectual whether he is an intellectual, and he replied, with a flicker of alarm behind his spectacles, 'Oh no!' Why not? 'Because I'm afraid of suffering from Imposter Syndrome' (Ash, 27 April 2006).

Jonathan Miller, whose series *Atheism* we will be analysing here, has said something similar. He argues that a 'life of the mind' interest is deeply suspect in England, where you tend to be seen as a 'pretentious pseud' if involved in it. Moreover, he complains that the kinds of television histories of ideas which he produced in the past are becoming increasingly hard to do unless, he says 'they are presented by what is now called a celebrity' (2010) – and at the beginning of his three-part series he explains why he does not like that.

However, Stefan Collini argues in his book *Absent Minds: Intellectuals in Britain* that we should not *over*-emphasize the recent growth of 'celebrity culture.' Nor should we link this with the so-called 'decline' of intellectuals, which has been blamed on two forces: (i) the increasing sub-division of inward-looking academic disciplines; and (ii) 'the rise of celebrity culture, with the dynamics of the popular media increasingly governing the public sphere of modern societies, leading to the displacement of the intellectual by the media personality' (Collini 2006, p.451).

Collini refutes the view "that the kind of public presence once enjoyed by intellectuals is in the process of being *replaced* by the glitzy superficiality of celebrity culture" (2006, p.473, 474). He argues that when we look historically from the early 19th century onwards, we see "a plurality of overlapping publics reached by a plurality of overlapping media," always offering 'intellectuals new opportunities' (2006, p.488).

So Collini concludes that intellectuals today "can make use of existing media to reach those publics who, being neither doped nor dumbed down as fashionable commentary suggests, *do* want to see issues of common interest considered in ways that are less instrumental or less opportunistic, more reflexive or more analytical, better informed or better expressed" (2006, pp.495-6).

So what are these media outlets? Between them, Garton Ash's and Collini's list of British media outlets for intellectuals is both wide and embracing. It includes BBC Radio, the *Times Literary Supplement*, *The London Review of Books*, the internet and the blogosphere. But – here's our point – *neither* Ash *nor* Collini include television. In this medium, Collini argues, the visual dominates. In contrast, radio is good for 'the oral exposition of ideas'; while the sheer length of newspapers does allow for nuance and complexity. But in television, he says, a "speaker's appearance and manner" is what counts. Discussion, says Collini, "is brutally abbreviated; liveliness, conflict, and sound-bites are over-valued" (Collini 2006, p.490).

Now, this may be true of shorter television forms, like news and documentary interviews, but even there Tulloch experienced some very positive collaboration as his co-author Middleweek will later address. However, the early British television intellectuals did found a new television genre as public intellectuals. They include Professor AJP Taylor, Sir Kenneth Clark, Dr Jacob Bronowski, Dr Jonathan Miller, Professor David Starkey, Dr Simon Schama, and Professor Marcus du Sautoy. They are all men, and they are mostly middle-aged – which is why Tulloch held back the completion of his book *British Television Intellectuals* for five years, allowing for the emergence of many strong female presenters (like Mary Beard) and also younger men (like Brian Cox). Still, those early patriarchal pathfinders did reach enormous audiences through television. They created models for television emulation elsewhere in the world. They were *not* starved of length, having as many as 13 one-hour episodes to develop nuanced and complex arguments. Their discussion was *not* brutally abbreviated.

Collini says that "when a future historian is writing the history of Britain's intellectuals at the beginning of the 21st century, appearance on television will not be a significant criterion for inclusion" (2006, p.493). We disagree. Tulloch himself is an historian educated in history at Cambridge University, at the same time as Simon Schama who has done rather well for himself as a public intellectual. We are not challenging Collini's point that 'Editors and sub-editors will cut, re-write, and headline according to the prevailing wisdom of their guild' – though we would use the term 'tacit' or 'intuitive' knowledge' rather than Collini's apparently dismissive 'wisdom of their guild' (see Middleweek and Tulloch, 2018). And, yes, producers will have an eye on their time-slot and their audience ratings. But we do not agree that, in this developing television genre, they are always "quick on both counts to cut contributions they consider too long or too boring'; with presenters and interviewers always pressed," Collini says, "to extract the memorable over the judicious, the partisan over the even-handed, the accessible over the daunting, the short over the long" (2006, p.494). This can be demonstrated by looking briefly at Miller's TV series, *Atheism: A Rough History of Disbelief*. In particular, we will look at a few sequences from his discussion of 9/11. This is near the beginning of episode 1 (which is available on YouTube). We hope to show some ways that good intellect and good television *can* work together.

A Rough History of Disbelief

Jonathan Miller's *Atheism* is, as he says at the start of episode one, a narrative of the historical disappearance of something: and that something is belief. Yet Miller's emphasis is as much about current religious *resurgence* as about the past loss of faith, linked, among other things, to terrorism.

Miller, writing and recording the series in 2003, deliberately begins his narrative in the present, in New York City. We edit to a clear blue sky. It is the same clear blue sky that those planes flew out of on September 11, 2001, just two years before. Miller is on the Staten Island ferry, and as the camera tilts, like those planes, down to the Manhattan skyline, we see Miller, with one New York icon, the Statue of Liberty in the background, noting the absence of another icon, the Twin Towers. This reminds him, he says, "of the religious implications of what one saw on television on that hideous day." We see Miller among young passengers on the ferry, as he continues: "although when it happened many people said it was a cowardly act – atrocious it certainly was – it's really hard to see it as *cowardly* exactly, since it was perpetrated by people who sacrificed themselves in the certain knowledge of their forthcoming death." Miller is at the rail of the ferry staring at the *new* Manhattan skyline without the Twin Towers, and we may be reminded of those opening words of the episode: "This series is about the disappearance of something," as Miller, in close focus ponders these difficult words about terrorism.

We then edit to shots inside Manhattan. The camera looks up to the *remaining* skyscrapers, mixed with downward shots to the ubiquitous yellow taxis below in the streets, and then to near pavement-level views of unassuming people walking in the sunlit city as they had done on that fatal day. We see Miller walking among those crowds in a long shot. His voiceover talks about how it was only in the name of absolute assurance of a permanent life after death that anyone would be willing to undertake such an act against a society whose lack of religion they deplored. "It is these people-in-the-street," Miller adds, whose supposed "support for Jewish claims in what is called the

Holy Land [the terrorists] were implacably opposed to." Miller is already elaborating his nuanced discourse, as he continues:

> Therefore the conspicuous absence of the Twin Towers, involving as it does the conspicuous *conflicts* between Christianity, Islam and Judaism, is I think one of the most powerful expressions of religious fanaticism in the late twentieth and early twenty-first centuries.

This is a strong statement; which he develops further, saying,

> But it is important to remember that you only have to travel a few miles from New York City to find yourself in the middle of a country which, far from being the *secular* world which was deplored and attacked by the Islamic fundamentalists is, in fact, *intensely Christian*, and therefore in its own way of course just as religious as the Moslem world that attacked it.

We now see Miller at home watching on his television screen the grainy TV images of Ground Zero, with firemen and George W. Bush coordinating operations as mechanical diggers destroy what remains of the hideous site. In voiceover Miller comments: "But for someone like myself, who has nothing you could possibly call religious belief...the spectacle of September 11 is a forceful reminder of the potentially destructive power of the three great monotheistic religions which have dominated the world in one way or another for nearly 2000 years." These words, emblematized by visual destruction on and after the day of 9/11 convey the central narrative theme of the series *Atheism*, as on-camera Miller walks on, in long-end of the lens close-up through the streets of New York.

However, the television visuals are telling their *own* story as Miller takes the Staten ferry and walks through the strong sun and shadow of New York streets talking of terrorism. Even as he speaks of the suicide bombers' beliefs, it is hard not to notice that Miller is surrounded in New York's streets by people who could well be Muslim, and, early in this sequence, the camera image of him is momentarily, almost subliminally, blurred and obscured by one of them getting in the way. Yet the next shot, his point-of-view, follows with positive, *non*-threatening images. It is a multicultural pavement of New Yorkers: Latinos, African-Americans, Asians, an elegant young Hispanic woman with sunglasses perched fashionably in her long hair, an older bearded man, possibly a street person, with brimmed hat squashed down on his head. They are all walking towards us. Maybe our response watching it lay in the image itself, or in what Miller goes on to describe as the viewer's intuitive memory, but it was hard not to feel strengthened by this visual moment of melting-pot democracy.

Yet this tacit belief is then threatened visually. These shots of an active democratic people walking to work or shopping are systematically obliterated by quick, harsh lateral shots of traffic and water jets obscuring this New York public. This is followed, cued by Miller's words "what is called the Holy Land," by huge words on a truck emblazoned with the Stars and Stripes: "Gone, But Not Forgotten September 11." The *ideological* drama of combat is already expressed by this conjuncture of image and words. This image is displaced by the shots looking up skyscrapers we mentioned earlier, as Miller gradually elaborates his overall *conflictual* theme; and his strong statement about the potentially destructive power of the world's three great monotheistic religions is matched instantly by a zip-pan to a Christian cross fashioned out of the wrecked girders at Ground Zero. We see shots of young Americans looking at firemen and at display boards from Ground Zero, with the words scrawled over the images, "Never Forgive Never Forget (God Bless America)." But the word 'Never' has been rubbed out by another hand; and the camera focuses on this, and on the graffiti words, "Ave Maria Holy Queen!"

What immediately follows this Ground Zero sequence is interesting visually and audibly. 'Vox-pop' interviews – the voice of the people – are standard television fare in most genres. But in the earlier histories of television intellectuals vox-pop interviews hardly occur. Yet they do occur *twice* in Miller's three-part series, and the first is in this terrorism sequence. This vox-pop begins immediately after Miller talks the elaborated clauses and sub-clauses of academic qualification as 'a thinker.' "I wouldn't want to say, and I think it would be entirely inaccurate to say, that my interest in, or my objections to these religions were actually *provoked* by the events of the last two years" – not exactly the quick sound bite Collini predicts. And appropriately to this intellectualized discourse, there is now a camera edit from an over-the-shoulder shot of Miller watching 9/11 images on his television to a zoom-in to his own study. Miller sits on his large, comfortable sofa, his full bookshelves behind him. This shot reveals the familiar Miller hand gestures, and, in close-up, his lined, expressive face, as he speaks another elaborated sentence: "All the same, these events do bring one face to face with the consequences, both social and political, of beliefs in the divine, the supernatural, the holy, the sacred and the transcendent, ideas which I like *many* others find alien, uncongenial and, to be frank, almost *unintelligible.*"

By now Miller is shaking his head in puzzlement. Jonathan Miller has, from the start of this episode, presented himself as the wise, thoughtful, ironic, but somewhat distanced intellectual; and this scene ends with Miller's face, his mouth a little disdainful, leaning into the camera as he gets up from his sofa. But, in immediate contrast to this world-weary shot, the production team juxtaposes a cluster of four visually dynamic vox-pop television interviews in *support* of Miller's position. We see a young man of mixed ethnicity with a northern English working-class accent saying, "I don't believe in God. I don't think there's enough evidence to prove that there's a guy up there in the sky...There's people starving all over the world, there's wars...Why would he stand by and let that happen?"

Technically, this vox-pop shot is *internally* dramatic in three ways. It shifts back and forward between the grainy image and slightly muffled sound of this young man on Miller's TV, and the clearer original camera recording by the production team. It also uses rapid focus-pulls within the short ECU sequence to generate within-frame movement. Furthermore, the vox-pop head of the young man slams forward towards the viewer (and Miller watching the sequence). This is even more apparent in the third vox pop interview, where an angry grandmother who has not believed in god since the death of her three-year-old grand-daughter visually seems to slam into the face of Miller himself watching her on his television. Why is it shot and edited this way? What does it *do* in the narrative? We think this vox-pop sequence is important to Miller's series in four ways.

First, it gives cross-age, class, gender, ethnicity support to Miller's carefully intellectualized words, academic posture, and *books*-dominated mise-en-scène. It adds an everyday-ordinary drama to the otherwise very 'BBC Four' self-presentation of Miller. One thing that TV professionals particularly dislike is static intellectual talking heads pontificating in abstract words to the camera. But this vox-pop camera style establishes a talking-head *dynamic.*

Second, it acts as non-academic support for the very *similar* discussion Miller has with the arts and sciences 'experts' who are a structural, dialogical and ideational motif of this series. For example, a blond vox-pop woman replicates in her words author Henry Miller's more elaborated comments about his period of belief during childhood.

Third, it replicates, but also varies another key ideational and stylistic strand of the series. This is the insertion of actor Bernard Hill – who was famous in Britain for his iconic black-humor lead as Yosser in *Boys from the Blackstuff,* mockingly serious in its depiction of Thatcher's Britain. Here Hill, always in chiaroscuro, and looking exactly like Yosser, appears in ECU throughout the series, speaking the same disbelief as the young multi-ethnic vox-pop man, with the same "if God exists and is omnipotent, why then?" formulation. But, in the Hill/Yosser sequences it is voiced in the *elaborated* and nuanced words of philosophers from Miller's brief history of disbelief: people like Epicurus, Democritus, Aristotle, Cicero and Seneca.

Fourth, these stylistically different actants in the series narrative – the academic and literary experts talking with Miller in the relaxed comfort of their book-lined homes, lit naturalistically; the inter-textual Yosser persona of actor Bernard Hill lit expressionistically; the age-, gender-, and ethnicity-differentiated vox-pop participants, in dynamic movement and represented visually as both 'on TV' and 'live in the street' – are all augmented by the multiple *presences* of Miller himself. In this series, Miller switches seamlessly (and certainly not boringly) from the elaborated discourse spoken to camera from his study, to the silent watcher-ethnographer moving through the crowded streets of New York; to the celebrity ironist seen in several moments of the series. There are also the many Millers seen on his laptop by the bookish Miller in his study as he summarizes and speaks back to his figure on the laptop, as though in a university tutorial. And then, finally in the *other* vox-pop sequence in episode 3, we see a different Miller again. Here Miller, speaking at length about his own nearness to death, becomes the secular comforter to a dying old lady in the most moving sequence of the series.

So, through the series we see many different self-representations of Miller *himself*, as he switches across several presentational identities: as medical scientist, as young Cambridge Footlights comic, as academic tutor, and as sharer of secular termination with other old people. Miller and his production team combine all these identities within this particular mediated role of the television intellectual; and, in our argument, fuse the intellectual with the popular at many different levels.

Talking Terror

Our second approach in this paper about 'talking terrorism' will proceed along two axes: an *institutional/generic* axis, on one hand, and a *personal/subjective*, on the other. We illustrate these axes via four very different kinds of television institution and different performance subjectivities that impact on the way in which we 'bridge the gap' between academic and celebrity culture. At the centre of this discussion is co-author John Tulloch, whose photograph became one of the iconic images of the 7/7 attack, and Mohammad Sidique Khan, the terrorist who exploded the bomb in Tulloch's London Underground carriage. In a selection of interviews for English, Welsh and Dutch broadcasters Tulloch explores his and Khan's mediated constructions as 'victim' and 'terrorist', and confronts the hijacking of his image by the popular press for political purposes. By being part of the conversation, Tulloch is accorded more airtime, more creative and editorial control and further opportunities for the sharing of his intellectual expertise. Both axes are crucial because being a public intellectual will vary according to the institutional positioning of the program (prestige or popular), the subjective positioning of the academic (their 'role') and the way the media shapes and frames that dialogic exchange.

BBC 2 'Newsnight'

The earliest of Tulloch's TV interviews took place some five months after the London terrorist attack for BBC2 Newsnight – one of Britain's most prestigious current affairs programs – as part of their end of year broadcast. The authoritative self-presentation of Britain's famous television host, Jeremy Paxman establishes a prestige institutional frame from the outset. He opens by responding directly to the misuse of Tulloch's bloodied and bandaged image on the front page of Britain's most popular tabloid *The Sun*.

The producer had initially phoned proposing Tulloch would talk as a media academic about 7/7 images of his own choosing. He responded by offering interview cues he hoped producers would adopt in editing. By repeating the word 'image' Tulloch attempts to steer the segment, in the absence of having any program control.

> TULLOCH: It's like an image. I have an image of it. It's like being pulled like a rubber photo. That bar that goes down the end of the seat…my head smashed it. It was all in images you see, just little images.

That cueing of images enabled Tulloch to establish his media academic competence in a longer, two-minute exchange with interviewer Liz McKeen. Each chosen image is analysed in turn, with prominence given to the rescue of bombing victim Davinia Turrell and a still of British Prime Minister Tony Blair reflecting on the bombing aftermath.

> TULLOCH: I was in a lot of pain and…I saw this photograph of Tony Blair…and the first feeling I had was, what a performative act…He's standing like this *(Tulloch bends over)*, head down, hands down. Given that he told us countless times, 'it's not if it's going to happen, it's when it's going to happen', if you were Tony Blair wouldn't *you* be ready for how you performed the day it happened? Of course you would!

> McKEEN *[V/O iconic image of Tulloch]:* Given his skepticism, it's ironic that last month John became an unwitting agent for the Prime Minister in his bid to get controversial anti-terror legislation past reluctant MPs.

> TULLOCH: It's interesting if you compare [my image] with the other iconic image that came out of Edgware Road of Davinia Turrell who was shown everywhere…in the first few days, with the mask. But of

course, by the time you get terror laws the mask becomes an impediment. Now what *The Sun* wants is 'the victim'. This is me, in my view, reduced to a category. I am a victim, I have no voice. Well then, let's use his voice – without ever asking me of course – 'Tell Tony he's right' *[this headline's positioning beside Tulloch's mouth appeared as though they were his words]*.

McKEEN: And of course that wasn't your voice, that doesn't reflect what you were thinking at all.

TULLOCH: No...if I'd put my words on there it would've been, 'Not in my name Tony'.

The dialogue here conveys the pitch of this 'prestige' Newsnight program in which Tulloch was positioned as 'the media professor interpreting images' – a *non*-victim identity that contrasts with flashes of his vulnerable persona in the interview. These three identities – survivor, celebrity and intellectual – exist simultaneously in Tulloch's critique of a photograph of terrorist Khan. In voiceover Tulloch describes his commitment to better understand the motivations of the bomber while on screen a photograph of Khan appears sitting among colleagues at a primary school in Beeston where he worked as a teaching assistant.

TULLOCH: Suddenly these aren't terrorists as 'Other', shady people from outside. There's the man who bombed my carriage Mohammad Sidique Khan and he's got this expression of listening and there's me in hospital thinking...How can these people do this?

McKEEN: You're talking about the bombers with understanding. Do you feel any anger over what they did?

TULLOCH: ...We must, if we're going to make our country better and more secure and more democratic and more multicultural, understand this better.

ITN UK

Tulloch elaborated the need to 'understand this better' in his subsequent appearances on ITN News, London in July 2006 to commemorate the first anniversary of the 7/7 bombings. Instead of an interview about 'images' as in the Newsnight program, Tulloch was accorded the unusual privilege of conceptual and editorial control over a three-minute television segment, a result of the mutual professional respect developed in his earlier interviews with the network. Tulloch reverses Khan's journey to the London Underground on the morning of 7/7 by interviewing residents from Khan's hometown of Beeston as well as students from Leeds University. After viewing the rushes at the end of a nine-hour edit, ITN doubled the initial offer of a three-minute segment, extending Tulloch's story to a two-part special running over two nights prime-time. In the first part we see the television academic steering the narrative in a more institutionally-embedded role as *interviewer*.

> TULLOCH *[V/O]*: I know all about the Khan who devastated people's lives on 7/7. But I've heard about another Khan: the teacher's aide who tracked kids' education, the guy who helped teenagers with other social problems in the community. I wanted to hear about both Khans and what life's been like in Beeston since 7/7. In a local park where Khan played football I met some Beeston residents.
>
> TULLOCH: What was your impression of him?
>
> WOMAN: That he was a very nice young man, very well spoken, very pleasant, always polite and actually quite a nice lad.
>
> TULLOCH: And was that a general view as far as you knew?
>
> WOMAN: Yes, I've never heard anybody say a bad word about him.

In the role of professional interviewer Tulloch 'gives voice' to those who knew the 'nice lad' and challenges Khan's mediated construction as 'paranoid killer', especially via the words of a school governor who emphasized that it was British foreign policy which led to this terrorist act, and a woman who spoke angrily about the exploitative behaviour of media who came to interview in Beeston.

In the second part of 'John's Journey' Tulloch's editing control was especially evident in his choice of statements from the four young Muslim students he interviewed, and in his deliberately mono-tonal voiceover, the latter intended to focus audience attention on the *interviewees'* knowledge and experience. Unlike the forthright Paxman of Newsnight, the 'chatty' ITN newsreader conveys the 'popular' institutional positioning of a national commercial broadcaster.

> NEWSREADER: John Tulloch stood three feet from Khan as he exploded his bomb at Edgware Road. Yesterday we followed John as he visited Beeston to see how 7/7 has changed the community Khan grew up in. Tonight he meets young Muslims to hear what they think of the bombing one year on. Here is part 2 of John's story.
>
> TULLOCH *[V/O]*: I've come to Leeds to speak to young Muslims in the area about Mohammad Sidique Khan and what 7/7 meant to them. Like Khan, they're university educated and their local mosque was at

the centre of investigations the week after 7/7. They strongly feel the bombers were motivated by foreign policy.

TULLOCH: These Muslim students are *living* their studies. Hamza is a master's law student.

HAMZA: Tony Blair…went…into an illegal war, got it justified through an international lawyer which every international lawyer knew was illegal. We were all misled and he has no responsibility for it. Why does he not have any responsibility for it or when will he have responsibility?

TULLOCH: And Barro is a medical student studying dentistry.

BARRO: The reality of the matter is… Iraq has the highest rate of children death in the whole world and let me tell you about simple medical equipment in Iraq. Simple drips…lying around in a hospital…in England…yet in Iraq these simple things that save lives are not there.

These Muslim students reveal different takes on the 'foreign policy' theme of the 7/7 bombings, and in the remainder of the interview, discuss the threats to their civil liberties in the aftermath of the attack. In voiceover, Tulloch steers the narrative with reflections such as 'I was learning all the time here' and attempts to 'understand this better' in the role of interviewer. Importantly Tulloch learned about the Arabic term 'Umma', representing the supra-national Islamic 'community', which led to all four students saying that, though they didn't agree with what Mohammad Sidique Khan did, they agreed with what he *said* – a point of sufficient surprise to Tulloch to end the interview talking about it in ECU. The ITN special enabled Tulloch also to develop his multiple identities (this time his 'learner' and professional-organizational identities, not simply that of 'a survivor') within a popular institutional media frame.

VARA

In a much longer interview sequence for the Dutch television program *De Leugen Regeert* on Netherlands' VARA public broadcaster, Tulloch is provided a lengthy to-air platform to draw on his academic expertise. In one three-and-a-half minute interview excerpt, Tulloch's argument about multiple subjectivity is stated clearly and intellectually as he recounts *The Sun* newspaper's use of his photograph to represent the voice of the people, his own retort in *The Guardian* newspaper two days later with the headline 'They stole my voice', the issue of consent to the use of his bleeding and bandaged head on the front page of *The Sun,* and the one-dimensionality of victim and perpetrator narratives. As with Jonathan Miller's elaborated discourse in the British TV series *Atheism*, in this Dutch interview Tulloch is also afforded elaborate sentences, philosophical musings and multiple subjectivities. The opportunity for elaborated discourse on Dutch television can be explained, in part, by the program's journalism-specific focus. The program title, '*The Lie Rules*' was inspired by a famous statement made by the former Queen Beatrix of the Netherlands about the country's declining journalistic standards in a post-privatization climate. The program format involved a liberal-left panel of journalists debating the issues of the day in front of a live audience. This group-institutional setting combined with a commitment to the publicizing of 'alternative voices' not only signaled the program's journalistic values but also enabled Tulloch to perform his multiple identities.

ITV Wales

Our final interview excerpt was a Welsh regional ITV news special to mark the first anniversary of the 7/7 bombings. In this interview, Tulloch's argument about the multiple subjectivities of himself and Khan are visualized in 'three-way boxes' or split screens in which Tulloch affirms, "I'm a bit more than just victim and he's a bit more than just paranoid killer" (ITV Wales, July 2006). Without the opportunity for elaborated discourse as in the Dutch Vara program, we see the importance of having the visual equivalent of one-liners such as "I'm not just a victim and he's not just a paranoid killer" when being a public intellectual on a popular visual medium.

Our argument is that 'bridging the gap' between celebrity and intellectual culture will vary according to subjective and institutional factors. Subjectively, by offering professional cues, steering the creative and editorial direction of his television appearances, engaging in productive and collaborative dialogue and showing an understanding of, and appreciation for the industry, Tulloch was able to procure more air-time and share his academic expertise. But, 'bridging the gap' will vary according to the institutional framing of the particular television program – be it prestigious or popular – and the conventions, expectations and structural imperatives of news-making.

Conclusion: Tulloch/Middleweek – Bridging Dialogues

In 2012, Middleweek's camera crew and executive producer flew to Wales to interview Tulloch for the Australian version of the U.S documentary series *I Survived...* which catalogued the twists and turns of fate of survivors of traumatic events such as natural disasters and terrorist attacks. Though Tulloch was pleased with the interview he was disappointed that the final cut did not retain any of the elaborated discussion that Middleweek accorded as interviewer, and Tulloch himself had accorded the Muslim university students. However, Middleweek was producing a local version of an international franchise and was bound by institutional constraints, one of the axes that affects the 'bridging of gaps' between celebrity and intellectual culture. For instance, each episode was structured by three interwoven survivor narratives, interview grabs in the place of voiceovers or dramatisations, strict durations for sound grabs and templates for each graphic to set the scene and unfolding action. The remit was to celebrate the triumph of the human spirit and survival against the odds and was in keeping with Tulloch's desire to elaborate on dimensions of his survival: the physical, psychological and intellectual.

From aspects of Tulloch's survival the script moved to the media's appropriation of his image which, in Tulloch's view, was yet another emotional obstacle he had to overcome and 'survive.' The graphic, 'Pictures of John's bloodied face appeared in media around the world,' was used to introduce the topic and enable Tulloch to elaborate on the circulation of his photograph in the proceeding interview excerpts:

> …it became one of the iconic images everywhere. And they were using me as a bit of a political football – I kept appearing on front pages of different newspapers, each one with a different politics... And I felt I didn't have a human life, I was being used…So I thought positive…'I've got time off work, I'm going to start looking into iconic images'.

Though Tulloch's reference to 'iconic images' remains intact in this script, the remainder of the sentence was cut because of commercial time constraints. Thus, Tulloch was denied the opportunity to elaborate further on his research of iconic images for a book (Tulloch and Blood 2012). Nevertheless, out of this initial disagreement Tulloch and Middleweek were able to generate positive collaboration in a publication that bridged another gap, this time between ethnographic methods, textual analysis, psychoanalytical and risk sociological analysis (Tulloch and Middleweek 2017), as well as the finalizing of Tulloch's book, *British Television Intellectuals*, the Afterword for *Screen Production Research* (2018), and this current chapter.

As authors we still do not agree on some things, but do agree about reflexivity and mutual, inter-personal, inter-disciplinary and stimulating exchange. We think that is how 'bridging the gap' should always be – a galvanizing experience between academia and industry.

References

Ash, Timothy Garton. (27 April 2006). Are there British intellectuals? Yes, and they've never had it so good, *The Guardian,* Retrieved from https://www.theguardian.com/commentisfree/2006/apr/27/comment.mainsection

BBC News, (December 2005), *Newsnight*, London, UK, BBC2.

Collini, S. (2006). *Absent Minds: Intellectuals in Britain*, New York, NY: Oxford University Press.

Denton, R. (October 2004), *Atheism: A Rough History of Disbelief,* PBS.

Graham McNeice Productions (January 2012), *I Survived...Stories of Australians*, Sydney, Australia, Foxtel.

ITN Productions, (July 2006), *John's Journey, part 1*, London, UK.

ITV Wales, (July 2006), *One Year On*, Cardiff, Wales.

Middleweek, B and Tulloch, J. (2018) Afterword: Tacit Knowledge and Affect – Soft Ethnography and Shared Domains. In C. Batty and S. Kerrigan, *Screen Production Research: Creative Practice as a Mode of Enquiry*, pp.233-248. Switzerland: Palgrave Macmillan.

Tulloch, J and Blood, W (2012). *Iconic Images of War and Terror: Media Images in an Age of International Risk*, New York: Routledge.

Tulloch, J. and Middleweek, B. (2017). *Real Sex Films: The New Intimacy and Risk in Cinema*, New York, NY: Oxford University Press.

VARA Broadcasting Association, (n.d.) *De Leugen Regeert*, The Netherlands.

Expert Crisis or Journalistic Laziness: Bridging the Gaps between Academics and TV Journalists in Serbia

Aleksandra Krstić

Abstract. This chapter examines the key aspects of the existing gap between academics and journalists in Serbia. Based on interviews with full-time academics at the University of Belgrade and full-time TV journalists, this research tries to add to the existing knowledge about the main constraints in communication between media and academia. The main research questions of this study are: how do journalists of national TV stations in Serbia perceive the role of university professors in the media and how do academics perceive their own roles in TV programs.

Keywords: Academics, Journalists, Media Appearance, Television, Serbia.

Introduction

There is a popular joke in Serbia saying: "A university professor enters a taxi and the driver asks him: 'Which TV station?'" This joke illustrates the fact that some academics have become well recognized by the public as regular commentators on television. It also gives the impression that Serbian people really like to watch TV. The latest research (Media Ownership Monitor Serbia, 2017) shows that television has been the most popular medium in Serbia and the main source of information for Serbian citizens, with the highest consumption frequency for years. Therefore, when university professors get invited by journalists to provide interpretations of what has been happening in the country and the world, it can be expected that they achieve greater public influence when they appear on TV rather than in print or online media.

However, only a limited number of academics appear on national Serbian TV stations to discuss politics, economy or other aspects of social life. There is an impression that the public is watching the same university professors all the time, regardless of what the subject is, with the only difference being the suits and ties which they change from one TV talk show to another. Is this resulting from an already established practice of creating the 'usual suspects' contact lists of academics whom journalists in Australia, the UK and the USA use to call to comment (Rowe, 2005)? Or, has there been an expert crisis in the Serbian national TV stations, since a significant number of academics refuses to speak for TV channels because they want to keep their public image as 'gatekeepers of knowledge' (Cvetković, 2003)? Have TV journalists been too lazy to look for fresh faces at the university? This study will try to answer these and other questions in this regard, as it will try to propose concrete solutions and try to add to the existing knowledge about the key aspects of the gap between academics and journalists by focusing on Serbia.

Theoretical Background

The relationship between academia and the media has been mostly addressed as an existing gap between theory and practice that needs to be bridged (Barkho & Saleh 2013, Niblock 2015). It has been researched in national and comparative perspectives and dominantly Western settings. Although universities around the world have invested more money and efforts to secure media coverage (Rowe, 2005, p. 273), academia has usually been seen as "far removed from the mission of the media" (Orr, 2010, p. 25) and often criticized as an 'ivory tower' (Rowe, 2005).

Leaving the ivory tower and going more public is often addressed in studies examining academic activities in the media and the relationship between university professors and journalists. Making academic work more public is perceived as a political responsibility and "an important category of ethical action" (Steiner Editor & Rosen, 1994, p. 368). Niblock (2015, p. 231) addresses the need to make both journalism and academic work more public, while Steiner Editor and Rosen (1994) suggest that journalists should start thinking about the public more seriously, and scholars need to change the way they think about the public, in a way "that will allow journalists to join the search for better truths as equal partners" (p. 370).

Studies that examine writing practices or academic blogging have shown that blogging, as "do-it-yourself public intellectualism" (Orr, 2010, p. 26), is a useful tool which can contribute to a better relationship between the academia and the broader public (Kirkup, 2010). However, a qualitative analysis of one hundred academic blogs conducted by Mewburn and Thomson (2013) reveals that academic blogging is usually intended for academics and that blogs are most often written about self-help, academic practices and technical or career advice: "most academic bloggers were actually writing for themselves – or people like themselves – rather than explicitly trying to reach a group of people differently circumstanced" (Mewburn & Thomson, 2013, p. 1113).

Besides blogging, academics use social media, professional online networks and academy-specific platforms to connect to the public and peers. As Barbour and Marshall (2012) have noticed, academic research has migrated online as universities and academics have become "highly digitized and interconnected through online sources." For example, some core offline academic activities, such as publishing journals, conference organization, papers' reviewing, administering students, have moved online (Barbour and Marshall, 2012). For Marshall (2015), an online academic persona is "absolutely essential to their sense of professional and public self" (p. 131) and social media in general and even smaller social media networks are important in building academic selves and measuring prestige (Marshall, 2016, p. 44). Looking into how academics connect to the world through their online academic activities, Barbour and Marshall (2012) have mapped five clusters identified as "particular selfs" or personas: formal or static self resembling to earlier online generations; public self focused on networking; comprehensive self as a strong private persona trying to keep up with friends and family; teaching self focused on students and new generations, and uncontainable self not engaged with new media.

Unlike the growing field of studies about the role of Internet, social media and other online platforms in building academic persona, the role of broadcast media in the debate about public intellectuals' connection to the real world has been neglected. This field of academic research has mostly been focused on prominent public figures from print media and lately from the Internet, while TV and radio have rarely been examined (Park, 2006). Therefore, Park (2006) suggested that all media should be considered as "potential carriers of public intellectual messages" (p. 122). Rowe (2005) conducted an interesting comparative qualitative research and interviewed 32 full-time academics and journalists working in both print and broadcast media in Australia, the UK and the USA. The study revealed the main constraints in communication between academics and journalists, such as tight deadlines, "media time" enforced on the academic (Rowe, 2005, p. 276), risk of being misinterpreted, sanctions by peers and various negative consequences for academics "being too visible in the media" (Rowe, 2005, p. 284).

Interestingly, studies which investigate existing journalistic practices and media communication with academics observe their relationship in terms of power constellations and constant struggle to influence public opinion. For some authors (Orr, 2010) academics are believed to have "little direct power to shape debates" in comparison to editors who "through selection and inflection... have a significant, even constructional influence over the public agenda" (p. 24). Others address "mediaphobia" and skepticism as legitimate academic positions driven from so-called "three media traits," which represent, for example, media's short attention span, media's preference for the scandalous, and the media's elevation of opinion into analysis (Orr, 2010, p. 29). Former journalists now working at universities address more practical issues of the existing gap between academics and journalists and suggest that the foundation of that fruitful partnership must be "mutually relevant, practical and useful – for both journalists and for academics" (Eltringham, 2010, p. 391).

Although academic interest in researching the relationship between media and academia has produced a wealth of literature in western countries, Serbia has rarely been considered in comparative research or included as a specific case in academic collections (Trkulja, 2002). National qualitative studies are also limited in number and scope. The role of university professors in public life and their media appearance has mostly been examined in studies which, for example, investigate broader understanding of intellectual elites in post-Yugoslav settings and their connections to mass media. Rosić (2014, p. 98) argues that mass media in Serbia contributed to the shift of core intellectual activities, moving them from creative and critical thinking towards frequent political engagement and distribution of political power. This kind of shift has been especially acknowledged in social sciences and humanities in Serbia. Academics' relation with mainstream politics is sometimes criticized by scholars who insist that intellectuals should be the 'gatekeepers of knowledge,' even if they make their public appearance as defenders or critics of those in power (Cvetković, 2003). Furthermore, academics frequently appearing in Serbian media, especially in highly rated national TV programs, have been criticized by their peers in scientific journals. For example, a few sociology professors regularly speaking for the media have been accused of becoming ordinary media "commentators" or "analysts," thus betraying their discipline. They have been criticized for talking more about things relevant to the media instead of keeping up with their field of expertise and acting like true experts and sociologists (Bolčić, 2011, p. 492). At the same time, Serbian media have been accused of constantly ignoring important national scientific conferences they are invited to and for focusing on irrelevant "entertaining bizarre events with celebrities and criminals" (Bolčić, 2011, p. 490). However, the belief that intellectuals in the Serbian society have to be apolitical and kept away from any kind of social engagement is also argued to be deeply wrong, because they can become real societal actors through mass media and other public activities, like individual initiatives, social protests and movements (Golubović, 2005).

Along the lines of the presented theoretical background, the two main research questions of this study are:

1) How do journalists of national TV stations in Serbia perceive the role of university professors in the media?

2) Why academics appear on television and how do they see their own role in TV programs?

Taking into account that qualitative research of the relationship between academics and journalists in Serbia has been scarce, this study will try to provide new insights into the key aspects of the existing gap between media and academia and propose solutions for bridging that gap.

Method

For the purpose of this study, ten semi-structured expert interviews were conducted with five full-time academics from social sciences and humanities at the University of Belgrade and with five full-time journalists working in national private and public TV stations in Serbia.

Experts interviewing was applied as a qualitative research method because "interviewees are of less interest as a (whole) person than their capacities as experts for a certain field of activity" (Flick, 2009, p. 165). Experts interviewed for the purpose of this study are competent persons and authorities in their field of expertise. The first set of interviews was conducted with academics working at various social sciences and humanities faculties at the University of Belgrade (e.g. Faculty of Philosophy, Faculty of Political Sciences, Faculty of Dramatic Arts and Law Faculty) and who frequently appear in the media. The University of Belgrade has been chosen as the university with the highest rank in the country and the one with the longest tradition, compared to other state universities in the country. The interviews with academics explored their communication with the media and journalists, their practices of media appearance, academics' views on the interplay between media, university and political influences, their media roles, as well as ethical considerations regarding their public visibility.

The second set of interviews was conducted with professional journalists working in central news programs or talk shows at public and private TV stations, journalists who have had experience in interviewing academics. Journalists vary in age, experience, and newsroom roles, but they all cover actual politics, economy and social topics. There were three interviewed journalists from private national TV stations and two journalists from the two public broadcasting services. The interviews with journalists explored journalistic work practices, roles and ethics regarding interviewing academics and their communication with the University in general.

Interviews were conducted face-to-face between March and May 2017, recorded and transcribed afterwards. The average length of the interviews was 45 minutes. The interpretation of the interviews was based on qualitative content analysis (Bernard & Ryan, 2010; Lindlof &Taylor, 2011). The responses to the interview questions were categorized alongside the main theoretical concepts of this article. All interviewees remain anonymous and are referred to by their profession and the interview number (e.g. academic/interview 3, journalist/interview 4).

Findings

In the following section, findings from the analysis of interviews with academics and journalists are presented with regard to the main issues identified throughout the interviews. Core explanations about academics' media role, understanding of topics, criteria for TV appearance, professional risks, political views and influences, and the main flaws in communication between academics and journalists will be presented and compared.

Perception of academics' media role

Academics see that it is their public duty to appear on television. They think their role is to provide new data, facts and thorough interpretations of ongoing events. Some interviewees think they are more informed than other people and therefore feel obliged to articulate their knowledge in public. Mostly, academics think their role in the media is to provide knowledge-based, well argued and well-measured answers and possible solutions to the ongoing problems in society. The TV camera is perceived as the tool which can bring academics more social power and a great opportunity to become more visible and recognizable in the academic community. Interestingly, one interviewee (academic/interview 4) makes a clear distinction between his university and media role: "As a university professor, I cannot and I do not express my personal attitudes in front of my students, but on TV I often talk about my personal impressions or comment about unverified information. Therefore, I make a distinction between the two public roles." (Academic/interview 4)

Similarly to academics, journalists think that academics have a moral obligation to participate in TV programs and talk shows. Journalists mostly understand that the academics' role in the media is to answer questions and contribute to the discussion. For all interviewed journalists, academics are perceived as important public figures, able to make greater influence when they appear on TV than in other media types. One journalist said her daily TV show scores higher ratings when "an educated academic appears than when a popular politician is invited" (journalist/interview 5). Also, journalists make a difference between political analysts or commentators and university academics. The former are distinguished as "fake intellectuals" (journalist/interview 2), "talking heads" (journalist/interview 3), "so-called experts talking too much and saying nothing" (journalist/interview 1). Journalists share negative views about experts who desperately want to appear on TV, but actually know nothing about the topic. One quote is illustrative: "University professors are not just well-informed citizens, they are so much more than that. Well informed citizens are for example those political commentators we see a lot on TV. However, we always try to call academics first, and use analysts only as the last option." (Journalist/interview 4)

Understanding of topic

Academics believe that journalists always expect broader interpretations of specific events and most of them are familiar with providing answers beyond their field of expertise. However, this practice is seen to be imposed on academics by the media because they think journalists want to "talk about everything that is going on in the country and the world around us" (academic/interview 5). One political science professor said that going beyond the field of expertise is actually „me doing the journalistic work" (academic/interview 5). For example, professors are very often invited by the media to provide all sorts of background explanations about specific events which are later used in journalists' voiceovers. Analysis of the interviews shows that academics want to have control over the topics discussed in the media, but sometimes feel out of control. For example, some try to approach the topic from an academic angle, but they know if they slip into teaching on TV like they do at their faculties, they might "lose the audience as well as the next invitation to the show" (academic/interview 4).

Journalists, on the other hand, think academics have broader knowledge than what their field of expertise is and expect academics to share the knowledge with the audience. However, journalists see it is not their task to provide explanations to academics before and during TV talk shows or TV bulletins, but they expect from academics to know the subject completely: "If we cover the war in the Middle East, I cannot explain the details to the professor or tell him what the conflict is about. I expect him to know all about it." (Journalist/interview 1)

Criteria for TV appearance

Academics think they have been invited by journalists because of their academic background, relevance, credibility and expertise. For academics, it is particularly important to know the journalist in person, to know what the TV show is about and what the background of the media outlet is – that builds academics' trust in the media. Some academics said they usually refuse to talk for tabloids and "suspicious" TV shows because their sentences might get misinterpreted and taken out of context. Sometimes the most important condition for a professor to establish a professional relationship with the journalist or certain media outlet is to be clearly interpreted within the TV program (academic/interview 4). Interestingly, the analysis reveals a difference between early career and senior scholars when they talk about criteria for TV appearance: early career scholars never refuse a call from journalists, as they always tend to appear on TV and use every opportunity to advance their academic careers.

Journalists have built somewhat idealized picture of academics appearing in the media. Academics are expected to give quality answers, explain current trends and make valid prognosis about future events: "It is important that we get an academic we can trust, someone who can explain why is something going on and what might happen next." (Journalist/interview 2) Academics are also expected to have a firm attitude, high personal and professional integrity and 'the sense' for TV and media in general, to be able to explain complicated things in simple, non-academic discourse. Academics rejecting to speak for television are usually perceived as people who "gave up" on the belief that their media appearance could contribute to the societal progress or make positive changes.

Professional risks

One of the frequently mentioned professional risks for academics who regularly appear on TV is "betrayal of science" (academic/interview 3). Academics are also afraid of negative peer comments and celebritization of their academic personalities. Some interviewees are quite aware of their frequent presence in the media and therefore choose to take a break to be able to teach or do research properly. Academics appear not to have understood the media logic as they often talk about time constraints and not having enough time to prepare for TV as current topics need quick media reactions: "We invest a lot of time to research and write, and journalists only want something instant and attractive for TV or a headline" (academic/interview 1). On the other side, others who have adapted to this media logic and always respond to media invitations positively risk of becoming TV celebrities instead of being celebrities in their own academic community.

For journalists, program structures are severely influenced with the lack of competent experts. One of the major problems is the availability of credible sources from the academic community: "Sometimes it is harder to reach the University rector than to get the deputy prime minister to my TV talk show. I still cannot understand why." (Journalist/interview 3) Having problems to find new "faces" from academia or being rejected by scholars who know a lot but consider television "a dirty thing" (journalist/interview 5), journalists and TV producers are often forced to invite the same group of experts for specific topic. The lack of experts is especially notable in the issues of country's security, US politics, relations with Russia and China: "There are only four to five academics at Belgrade University who know a lot about the issues of the country's security and who are ready to react when we call them" (journalist/interview 2); or „If you want to make a program about Russia, as a journalist you are limited to couple of propagandists. Or if you cover China, for example, which is being established as a global power and an important partner of Serbia, there are just a few people at the University who can explain what the Chinese economic boom is about or what the New Silk Road actually means" (journalist/interview 3). Lack of relevant experts in TV programs is seen as a journalistic fault too. One journalist admitted that she has often invited academics who have already appeared on another TV station the day before because she often does not have time to search for other interviewees: "I know we invite the same people all the time, but it is what it is. Sometimes I invite the same academic who appeared in another TV program the night before on my TV. It happens, but I cannot really follow everything." (Journalist/interview 4). New faces from academia are more than welcome, but very rare: "They are hidden in anonymity, but when they accept invitation, we regard them as a 'revelation'" (Journalist/interview 3)

Political Views and Influences

Some interviewees think academics should express their political views clearly and that they should not pretend to be impartial on TV or to try to disguise their political views. Interviewees who had been politically active or members of political parties during their academic career say they have never allowed their two roles, political and academic, to get mixed on TV. But, it is interesting to observe how they perceive the complicated interplay between media and politics in Serbia. One university professor at the Faculty of Philosophy thinks that the frequent media appearance is guaranteed only if an academic talks positively about parties in power or if academic thoughts and forecasts correspond with the mainstream politics – otherwise, an academic risks to never get invited to the media. The following quote is illustrative: "I used to appear in the media in 2004, but as soon as I started to talk about things which did not coincide with mainstream politics, journalists stopped inviting me to their programs." (Academic/interview 4) Academics, however, agree that even if political views are articulated publically, they must not only be supportive, but also critical. "I do mind when I see colleagues saying 'bandit government' or 'the opposition is like this or like that' in the media. Having said something like that, an academic is actually cheering for certain political option or just repeating the party mantra, which can be dangerous." (Academic/interview 5)

Journalists usually like when academics show their political preference, because they are believed to articulate politics better than some political party officials. The interview analysis has shown that journalists distinguish between true and disguised political views expressed by academics. Genuine political position of an academic is very important for journalists: "If we talk about politics, I expect the academic to have a clear and a firm political opinion. I also think it is impossible to make a valid analysis of daily politics in Serbia without having political opinion. Moreover, our viewers like to watch academics who have a political attitude." (Journalist/interview 4) However, journalists also believe that political preferences expressed by some academics are not genuine but actually curled in the interests of a certain political group that might be secretly financing the academic sitting in the TV studio. This is considered a dangerous practice: "Academics express certain attitude as their own, but actually we know their job is to promote a certain political narrative. Such practice can distort public opinion and destroy political journalism." (Journalist/interview 2).

Flaws

In general, TV journalists are criticized for not being interested in reporting about the University events, issues of higher education, new research results or even a book launch. Academics think journalists do not pay attention to what academics say during the broadcast, but read the questions from the list instead. Interestingly, one interviewee holds other scholars responsible for being too arrogant when communicating with the media and for wrongly believing that academic work is more appreciated than any other profession. However, even if they talk about being available for everyone, interviewed academics actually do not pay much attention to online communication with the media or with the public. Only one out of five interviewed academics has Facebook, Twitter and LinkedIn accounts and uses them regularly to promote their research, new books and journal articles. Other interviewees do not have accounts on social media and do not write blogs. Journalists have addressed this lack of online communication with academics as one of the largest problems. Journalists complain about academics sticking to traditional ways of communication and deliberately avoiding social media or blogging. Also, journalists criticize the lack of university staff and special PR departments which would help them in production of stories. Journalists face problems in their everyday communication with the university because there is no staff appointed at faculties to communicate with media, the kind of staff that would tell journalists whom to call or who could be relevant for the topic. Most of the time journalists call professors directly and get rejected.

Discussion and Conclusions

The presented findings reveal where the existing gaps between academics and journalists in Serbia stem from and where one can look for possible solutions to fix the broken relationship. In sum, both academics and journalists have built their ideas of one another on wrong and often prejudiced assumptions (see Table 1). Both camps have completely different perceptions of what the true role of academics the media is and should be.

Table 1. Perceptions of academics and journalists in Serbia about what each group thinks of the other

Academics	Journalists
What do we think you want from us?	**What do we want from you?**
Explanations based on knowledge	
Spectacular sentences, bombastic headlines	Quality answers
Clear but clever language	Simple language
More time, not instant reactions	To understand "media time," to react quickly
Clear, not masked political views	Clear, not hidden political attitude/or not any
You do not need new faces, we can talk about everything	New faces hidden within walls of academia
Don't call us all the time, we have work to do	Don't call us, we will call you

Academics in Serbia see engagement with journalists as their public duty, just as their colleagues in countries of the West (Rowe, 2005). However, they have problems to understand media logic and quite often think that journalists only look for sensational sentences. At the same time, they want to have control over their media appearance and usually expect to give lectures on TV, refusing to speak in soundbites and approaching journalists in a somewhat elitist way. The "ivory tower" of the University of Belgrade is becoming even higher through wrong academics' assumptions about what journalists want and through absolute ignorance of possibilities offered by new media. Television journalists, on the other side, have been trapped between time constraints, problems in communication with the university and failure to find new experts who would contribute to societal debates.

The broken relationship between media and academia, recognized in academic literature and presented in the theoretical part of this article, has been driven by a mutual misunderstanding of journalists and university professors in Serbia. The only bridge between the two camps revealed in this research exists in terms of knowledge (see Table 1). Perhaps solutions can be found around this commonality. The need for explanations based on knowledge is insistently expressed by both academics and journalists throughout our interviews. It means that journalists and academics only need to leave their comfort zones and know more about each other. Journalists should try searching harder within universities and inform themselves more about academics' activities. Academics should make their knowledge more public, not avoiding TV appearance or media in general. They should try to ask questions and initiate new debates on TV rather than merely provide answers. Moreover, both academics and journalists should try to collaborate more, working together on projects and initiatives that would contribute to their visibility and the overall democratic progress in Serbia.

References

Barbour, K. & Marshall, D. (2012). The academic online: Constructing persona through the World Wide Web. *First Monday, 17*, Retrieved December 12, 2017, from http://journals.uic.edu/ojs/index.php/fm/article/view/3969/3292

Barkho, L. & Saleh, I. (2013). Towards a praxis-based media research. *Journal of Applied Journalism & Media Studies, 2*, 3-18.

Bernard, R. & Ryan, G. (2010). *Analyzing Qualitative Data: Systematic Approaches.* London: SAGE.

Bolčić, S. (2011). O skorašnjoj „skrajnutosti" sociologije i sociološke profesije/On recent 'neglect' of sociology and the profession of sociology. *Sociologija, 53*, 489-496.

Cvetković, V. (2003). Kad sveci mešetare/When saints mix. In Trkulja, J. (Ed.), *Intelektualci u tranziciji/Intellectuals in transition* (237-252). Kikinda: SO Kikinda.

Eltringham, M. (2013). Towards a new relevance: Why the new media landscape requires journalists and media scholars to forge a genuine partnership for the first time. *Journal of Applied Journalism & Media Studies, 2,* 387-396.

Flick, U. (2009). *An introduction to qualitative research*. 4th edition. London: SAGE.

Golubović, Z. (2005). Intelektualci u epohi pomerenih vrednosti/Intellectuals in the era of changed values. Retrieved December 6, 2018, from http://www.republika.co.rs/350-351/19. html

Kirkup, G. (2010). Academic blogging: academic practice and academic identity. *London Review of Education*, *8*, 75–84.

Lindlof, T. & Taylor, B (2011). *Qualitative Communication Research Methods*. 3rd edition. London: SAGE.

Marshall, P. D. (2015). Understanding the emerging contemporary public intellectual: Online academic persona and The Conversation. *Media International Australia, 156*, 123-132.

Marshall, P. D. (2016). *The celebrity persona pandemic*. Minneapolis: University of Minnesota Press.

Media Ownership Monitor Serbia. (2017). Media consumption. Retrieved January 14, 2018, from https://serbia.mom-rsf.org/en/context/media-consumption/

Mewburn, I. & Thomson, P. (2013). Why do academics blog? An analysis of audiences, purposes and challenges. *Studies in Higher Education*, *38*, 1105-1119.

Niblock, S. (2015). From the high ground to the swamp: A model for immersive journalism research. *Journal of Applied Journalism & Media Studies, 4,* 223-237.

Orr, G. (2010). Academics and the media in Australia. *Australian Universities' Review, 52*, 23-31.

Park, D.W. (2006). Public intellectuals and the media: integrating media theory into a stalled debate. *International Journal of Media and Cultural Politics*, *2*, 115–129.

Rosić, T. (2014). Ugled na ponudu: intelektualci, građani i revolucionari/Reputation for Sale: Intellectuals, Citizens and Revolutionaries. In Roksandić, D. & Cvijović Javorina, I. (Eds.), *Intelektualac danas/An Intellectual today* (91-105). Zagreb: Univerzitet u Zagrebu

Rowe, D. (2005). Working Knowledge Encounters: Academics, Journalists and the Conditions of Cultural Labour. *Social Semiotics, 15,* 269-288.

Steiner, L. & Rosen, J. (eds.) (1994). Scholars in the public sphere. *Critical Studies in Mass Communication, 11,* 362-388.

Trkulja, J. (ed.) (2003). *Intelektualci u tranziciji/Intellectuals in Transition*. Kikinda: SO Kikinda.

Curatorial Culture's Challenge to the Television Critic as Public Intellectual

MJ Robinson

Abstract. Since the late 1980s, the democratization of production has enabled academics to create videos that occasionally made it to "television" outlets. Most recently the democratization of distribution and consumption has transformed "television" into a form that is consumed across multiple mobile, streaming, broadcast, cable and web-based platforms. The resulting "curatorial culture" is a media environment in which academics, public scholars and intellectuals can create and distribute television programming that makes important and crucial interventions in our polis. Making that programming known to a demassified and vastly fragmented audience and encouraging its consumption is now the challenge. Professionally trained television critics (i.e., curators) should be more popular than ever. However, algorithms based upon big data, social media PR campaigns guided by bots and the ungatekept world of the digital commons have resulted in a loss of gravitas, authority and audience for even the most accomplished and academically trained of television journalists (e.g. David Bianculli, Neil Genzlingler, the members of the Television Critics Association). This paper interrogates the profession and professionalization of television critics as public intellectuals in our current curatorial media environment, examines the roles that celebrity and social media play in the contemporary practice of television criticism, considers television criticism as a specialized form of knowledge-based journalism and investigates television criticism as a cultural practice increasingly under fire from the rise of non-academic thought leaders and citizen "influencers" even as it seeks to guide viewers to the crucial conversations that can now be had "on TV" by today's engaged academics.

Keywords: Television Criticism, Curatorial Culture.

Introduction

Television criticism sits in a Venn diagram in which circles representing journalism, consumer advice, film criticism, popular culture criticism, theatrical criticism, printed television guides and the commercial television industry overlap.

A tectonic change in the media ecosystem caused by the explosion of networked digital technologies and the increased ubiquity of high-speed internet connections has transformed both journalism and television. It is the democratization of the *distribution* of media forms which has/is or will ultimately reconfigure all fiduciary relationships within all media industries due to the decontexualization of content, elimination or eliding of gatekeepers and the ascendance of the reader/consumer/viewer/user/viewser to a position of unprecedented power. We have already seen this happen in music as Napster first created a free peer-to-peer platform for the exchange of music, iTunes then recommodified music in its own ecosystem and according to its own valuations, and music bloggers and musicians themselves began offering a hybrid of free/freemium/paid content on their websites and social media pages. In journalism, the aggregation of decontextualized news on platforms such as Huffington Post replaced the original ads with those whose revenue went directly to HuffPo at the same time that other advertising revenue streams such as classifieds and full-page display dried up in favor of Craig's List and branded website content.

Video production began to be democratized in the late 1980s with low-cost prosumer video equipment – which made it much easier for "anyone" to make media of a variety of different forms. The advent of low-cost digital video cameras (and now the ubiquity of their inclusion in all smartphones) has resulted in 4K video quality and, most importantly, the ability to endlessly duplicate a video without a loss of quality. However, the promise of these technologies – that "anyone" could make a film or television show could not truly be fulfilled until distribution became democratized – until these short films or videos could be made discoverable by a wider, infinite and undifferentiated audience. This happened with the debut of YouTube in 2005 – an international distribution platform and social network whose clarion call is "Broadcast Yourself." YouTube also demonstrated to legacy broadcasters and distributors that there was a vibrant, engaged and actively seeking and consuming web-viewing audience which spurred the creation of internet television sites such as Hulu and licensing deals with Amazon and Netflix. The same smartphones and tablets that democratized 4K production also made viewing mobile. Space- as well as time-shifting freed viewers from the tyranny of television as a push media and reconfigured it, just like music and journalism before it – into a "pull medium" – one that puts viewers in control of their own viewing choices. Lastly, the growth of social networks such as Facebook, Twitter, Instagram and whatever was invented while I was writing this paper has provided citizen viewers with platforms in which to display, discuss and engage with the television that they watch – as commentators, curators and critics. This new media environment is "curatorial culture" in which the scarcity of viewer attention, not the scarcity of viewing options, is the driving economic force (Robinson, 2017).

The main challenge of a curatorial culture inheres in the curatorial act itself – more labor and time intensive than choosing from among limited options, curating requires attention and winnowing of search results that can number in the millions in milliseconds and are presented in a way that does not differentiate based on provenance. Thus, as the definition of "television" has expanded to include everything from the legacy broadcast and cable networks and production companies to HBO to Amazon and Netflix original series to everything and anything on YouTube – the viewing choices are infinite. One would think this is exactly the moment when television critics – those professionals whose specialized knowledge should uniquely position them to guide viewers to the "best" content would be heralded as oracles. However, because the media ecosystem in which they publish has also had its distribution pipelines democratized, this has not happened. Curatorial culture turns everyone into a curator, and, because curating is NOT just another way of saying "choosing" – it turns everyone into a potential or actual critic. Today, however, a curatorial culture created by tectonic changes in media ecosystems and industrial practices has impacted and altered the cultural authority of these professionals as well as the television forms upon which they cast their critical eyes.

A Brief History of Popular Culture Criticism and Television Criticism

Professional television critics are prime examples of what Bourdieu (1993) calls cultural intermediaries. These experts, historically our 'first' television curators have acquired cultural capital, through employment by and regular publication in a newspaper or magazine and an amassed quantity of column inches devoted to the discussion and analysis of televisual texts. This gives them the authority to adjudicate matters of art and taste and thus to play a significant defining role in what is or isn't considered an acceptable object of criticism – in this case, what is or isn't television.

Seldes' *The Seven Lively Arts*, first published in 1924 and reissued in 1957 made what was first called 'popular culture' and later 'mass culture' an object of scholarly inquiry and debate. Rather than arguing about distinctions between the "great" and "lively" arts, Seldes "made an impassioned pitch that highbrow critics should be less myopic and expand their vision of artistic creativity as well as suitable subjects for assessment." (Kammen, 1996, p. 87). Seldes actively lived this pitch, and by 1955 was well established as a professional radio and television critic (Kammen, 1996). Later in the 1950s he wrote about television for the *Saturday Review of Literature,* contributed to *TV Guide*, was a program consultant for CBS and National Education Television (NET), the precursor to the Public Broadcasting Service, and in 1959 served as the founding Dean of the Annenberg School of Communications at the University of Pennsylvania.

In addition to *The Seven Lively Arts*, Seldes also published *The Great Audience* (1950) and *The Public Arts* (1956), both of which examined television and the relationships between public opinion and television and critic and broadcaster. *The Great Audience* took a rather pessimistic view of the impact of film, radio and television on the mass audience and the conflict between a commercial imperative and expressions of culture. In *The Public Arts* Seldes reported on the results of a viewer study he conducted which revealed that "only a fragment of the total audience cares *much* for what the broadcasters transmit." (Seldes, 1956, p. 205). This same audience preferred what was on to no television whatsoever but one quarter of them indicated that they would be willing to pay for programming they liked. In many ways, this foreshadowed the contemporary conundrum facing content producers and distributors – how much are viewers willing to pay for programming, especially when it is spread across multiple platforms and behind multiple paywalls?

Seldes also foreshadowed the democratization of cultural (and therefore television) criticism, particularly in the last ten years of his life. In March 1963 he received the Alfred I. Du Pont Award in Radio and Television and concluded his speech with an "eloquent appeal for Americans to exercise the power required to shape and control their own cultural institutions, however complex, that had emerged." (Kammen, 1996, p. 372). He seemed to advocate for what we now recognize as citizen criticism, noting that the critic in a democratic society faced a dilemma: "how to justify telling millions of people that according to some cerebral or perhaps idiosyncratic criteria, programs that they were prepared to like really did not deserve their attention." (Kammen, 1996, p. 375). The solution was for the "great audience," as he called it, to be more discerning "in a very practical sense..." writes Seldes biographer, "he yearned for Everyman to be his own critic." (Kammen, 1996, p. 375). Which, of course, is exactly what has come to pass.

Lotz (2008) identified three distinct phases of television criticism: the origin of television (the 1940s to the 1960s); the late 1960s to 1980; 1980 to the present. These phases are determined and defined by various technological, industrial and cultural factors and the relation of television to its viewers as well as television to the journalism industry.

During phase one, the late 1940s-late 1960s, television criticism "pursued the twin goals of commenting on the emergence of the medium and developing an appropriate language to discuss its visual and narrative forms." (Lotz, 2008, p. 25). In the period just after World War II, television was very ephemeral – most of it was broadcast live and, like the daily news, it had a small window of chronological influence. As a result, writing about television was differentiated from other types of criticism – the critic writing about a newly released film, or newly opened play or art exhibition would know that his or her reading audience had at minimum several weeks in which to go see the performance, film or exhibition. While comparisons to film criticism may be apt, particularly in the age of aggregated citizen journalism and the blogosphere, the immediate predecessor to television criticism and the origin of its first critics was the radio criticism that appeared in newspapers and magazines from the 1920s through the 1950s and which reported on the popular entertainment available on the radio networks. Specialized journalists such as Jack Gould of *The New York Times* and John Crosby of the *New York Herald Tribune* began publishing analysis, critiques and encomia of the previous evenings offerings and readers of daily newspapers counted on professional critics to inform them of what was on, what would be on, what was quality and what was frivolous. The work of early critics defined the medium, commented on its development and in many cases, pled for its improvement while shaping the public perception and understanding of what was and was not "good" television.

Gould began his journalism career at the *Tribune* and moved to the *Times* in 1937 as a "reporter city desk – drama" (L. Gould, 2002, p. 6). When the television industry began to emerge in New York City in the post-war era, Gould was perfectly positioned to begin reviewing television shows broadcast live from the NBC and CBS studios. Gould's viewing routine acknowledged the consumption venues of the new media form: believing that it was crucial that he, like his readers, watched shows at home, he had three television sets (one for each network), installed in one room of his house in Connecticut. Since he had a deadline of 11:20 p.m. by which to file his review for the next day's paper, he had to work quickly to prepare his 300 to 750-word reviews for primetime shows aired from 7:00-11:00 p.m. (L. Gould, 2002).

As a critic working in the nascent period of broadcast television, Gould was well aware of critics of the utility of his work. "Most criticism," Gould wrote in 1972, "is useless and wasteful in a mass medium distributed for free." (J. Gould, 2002, p. 11). Nonetheless, he also believed that "a medium which daily pre-empts the attention of millions of adults and children surely cannot be ignored." (J. Gould, 2002, p. 11). He knew that there were those who found television (and indeed any broadcast) criticism to be an adventure of dilettantes since television was a mass-produced mass-media whose central purpose was to carry the advertisements of companies who funded its mass-production. As Gould summarized it, "the cultural conceit of the television critic is unparalleled in its fundamental arrogance" (J. Gould, 2002, p. 12). At the same time, he also asked: "Is there any difference between a critic who judges all kinds of programs and a network executive who thinks he can select all kinds of programs?" (J. Gould, 2002, p. 12). Gould sought to assess programming within its cultural context and wrote criticism that aimed to "understand what the program is trying to accomplish" (L. Gould, 2002, p. 12) rather than to weigh in on whether those goals were achieved. What is clear is that Gould was very aware of the power and importance of this new medium. Gould took seriously his duty to his readers, even as his placement within the paper worked against him – "the radio and television columns had their place at the back of the daily paper, interspersed with advertisements and notices about shipping news and other drab matters…. [his] columns and reviews competed for space in an obscure section of the paper, so readers had to make a special effort to find his criticism every day." (L. Gould, 2002, p. 15).

Beyond his daily column, Gould also contributed essays to the Sunday *Times*. This long-form journalism was reported the same way any story would be – Gould spent time at the office and in the city, chasing leads, interviewing television industry insiders and working with sources. These essays took a much deeper dive into a contemporary episode or series, or explored a larger issue facing the television medium and broadcast industry (L. Gould 2002). Gould's impact echoes through the history of television and media journalism. David Bianculli of NPR called Jack Gould "one of the first and best TV critics to serve on an influential newspaper." (Bianculli, 2000, p. 59). Fifty years later, Brian Stelter landed a job at *The New York Times* for similar long-form television writing that he published on his *TVNewswer* blog while in college.

At the end of this first phase of criticism and beginning of the second phase, more scholarly studies of television and collections of television criticism began to appear. Stan Opotowsky's *TV: The Big Picture*, the result of a year-long investigation of the creative operations, economics, labor relations, technology and operation of the television industry was published by Dutton in 1961. *The Eighth Art*, a collection of twenty-three essays on the contemporary nature of television by twenty public intellectuals/cultural critics and three professional television critics, appeared in 1962 from Holt, Rinehart and Winston (and clearly owed a substantial debt to Seldes' *The Seven Lively Arts*.) These books were published for consumption by the general reading audience to signal that interest in television in a medium, in the ways in which shows were made and produced, and in the nature of what television "should" be or provide were part of the public discourse much earlier than Neil Postman's revolutionary *Amusing Ourselves to Death* (1985) and long before the focus on the economics of the television industry sparked and by entertainment newsmagazine shows of the 1980s. The importance of these books to a viewing public and to the rise of citizen television critics should not be underestimated. From a very early point in the development of television, viewers were invited to think critically about the medium, its role in their lives, its relationship to the society in which they lived and its responsibility as a mass medium that almost every American watched on a daily basis.

The second historical phase of television criticism coincides with the mature period of the network system (1960s-late 1970s) – at least one television could be found in almost every American home and viewing choices were limited to the schedules of one of three national networks. Television networks (who were also the producers of their shows) battled for audience through the creation of programming that spoke to the largest undifferentiated group. This LOP (least objectionable programming) was designed for mass distribution and mass consumption but also relied on the opinions of the television critics of major papers to help set a national agenda of prized consumption. The increased use of filmed or pre-taped shows and series, rather than live broadcasts and specials also changed both the critics' accessibility to programming and the ways in which they wrote about programming. In the early 1970s, television networks began offering closed-circuit "preview" screenings to screenings at their local affiliates in major markets. Not surprisingly, television critics were among the earliest adopters of home videocassette technology and networks began sending preview tapes directly to critics in the mid-1970s making them the first time-shifters.

These changes in distribution made it possible for the public to read critics' reviews of shows prior to their airdates and to use these assessments in making their viewing decisions. Networks realized the positive potential providing advance access to shows might have, but also understood a possible downside to early screenings – bad reviews could drive viewers away from their network to competitors. The industry sought to remedy this by wooing critics through the sponsorship of all-expenses-paid "junkets" – tours and trips designed provide them access to the creative staffs of television programs but also a chance for the lining of critics' pockets with additional money for "cab fare" or "laundry" in exchange for positive coverage (Lotz, 2008, p. 27). Contemporary critiques of the critics exposed what were clearly questionable practices such as allowing autograph-seeking star-struck critics access to major television stars during work-related events and pressuring papers that owned television stations to refrain from criticizing shows produced by the network affiliate of the locally-owned station. Additionally, since these network-sponsored events were "by invitation only," the networks decided who was and wasn't a professional television critic by deciding who did and didn't get all-important advance access to their new slates of shows. Being too honest or disparaging of a network's offerings one year could result in one's exclusion from the event the next. This would cost critics wanting to engage in objective analysis and interpretation readership since it ensured that their competitors would "scoop" him or her on the all-important stories leading up to the new season premieres. What ultimately emerged from this period was a situation in which there was a close (and possibly too close) connection between critics and the industry they covered even as television became a "legitimate news beat." (Lotz, 2008, p. 27).

A major development of this period (and attempt to counter the critiques of the critics) was the formation of the Television Critics Association, a professional organization formed in 1977. Working television critics wanted to increase their perception as "professional journalists" which was impossible in an environment that only provided them advance access through network-controlled events. The TCA worked steadily during the late 1970s and early 1980s to disrupt network control and influence over their membership and its work. This, according to Lotz (2008) resulted in the replacement of junkets with two annual press tours organized by the TCA. Timed to coincide and support the traditional September-May 26-28 week broadcast television season the main tour takes place during three weeks every July and a shorter, two-week tour commences in January. Journalists pay their travel expenses to come to and stay in Los Angeles, while whatever network is presenting material each day pays for meals and the costs of the presentation space (Lotz, 2008). Per the TCA website, membership in the Television Critics' Association is limited to "full-time TV writers at newspapers, magazines, trade publications, news wire services, news syndicates, and text-based Internet [which it defines as "advertiser-supported online sites] organizations," in other words, no amateurs. Since the TCA determines membership, it also arbitrates the list of attendees at the two press tours and thus access to new shows. This has contributed to the professionalization of the television critic by allowing for substantially more objectivity in reporting and assessing network output. At the same time, with the rise of blogging, citizen journalists and fan sites, it also has created an interesting distinction between who 'is' and 'isn't' a television critic. While the TCA was formed substantially before the World Wide Web made everyone a publisher (or producer), it has had the unforeseen effect of legitimizing certain journalists' labor to the exclusion of others.

The third period of television (which extends to the present day) saw a transition in the type of reporter who became a television critic. If the critics of the first two phases were writers or journalists "primarily interested and trained in the arts," according to Lotz (2008), in the third period, which not surprisingly begins in the immediate post-Watergate era, television critics came from those "trained in journalism for whom reporting rather than writing criticism was perceived as a central task." (p. 27). Trained in investigative techniques that viewed Woodward and Bernstein as heroes; steeped in the personalized approaches of Tom Wolfe and Joan Didion's "New Journalism;" and energized perhaps by viewings of *Lou Grant*, many of these new critics saw their duty anew, as journalists to speak truth to power and advocate for social change. Their experience of the ecology of popular culture was different from that of their predecessors because this was the first generation of television critics who had grown up with television, rather than experienced the transition from radio to television. A significant parallel may soon arise, in the next ten years, an entire generation of critics who are "digital natives" will begin work and, of course, their perception of television and "what is television?" will have been substantially shaped by being raised in a time shifting/space shifting, over the top, off the box viewing environment.

The Rise of Curatorial Culture and the Citizen Critic

The availability of innovative new content across broadcast networks, digital subchannels, cable networks, subscription cable, original streaming (Amazon, Netflix), paywalled apps (Hulu, CBS AllAccess) and free internet video (YouTube) has created the same problem for the critic as for the viewer – there are just too many shows for any one critic to successfully stay current. Viewers are discovering these shows through more mechanisms than ever before, many of them automated and aggregative – which, in a world where the scarcity is now that of the viewer's time and not of the network's offerings means that curation it is more important than ever. "When people are frustrated with search, they go searching for human curation" wrote Shirky (2008, p. 67). In this case, they go searching for critics. The cacophony of critical voices made possible by the democratization of online journalism and the creation of fan sites, critical aggregators and social media communities serves the very needed purpose of adding critical voices and curators to the mix. At the same time it substantially complicates our ability to assess the legitimacy of the cultural capital that, per Bourdieu, we expect our cultural intermediaries to have. This is a dilemma: by what criteria does one curate one's curators?

In the 1950s, sociologists Lazarfeld and Katz (1955/2005) theorized the concept of opinion leaders. Countering the media manipulation hysteria that was popular at the time, they stated that a two-step flow of information (from person to person) was more influential on public opinion that a larger undifferentiated media message. Certain people, however, were considered more influential within groups of friends than others and therefore, information that flowed from the media to one of these opinion leaders and then to their friends would have a bigger impact than information that flowed to a less influential friend in a friend group or directly to the friends without intermediation from the opinion leader. Thus the type of curation that occurs when search fails to do everything that people want or need it to do "isn't just about information seeking, it's also about synchronizing a community."

(Shirky, 2008 p. 67). We cannot personally watch everything that's on, but we can personally interact with our friends to see what they are watching, what their friends are watching, what show's hashtags are trending and how many "likes" they are getting on a social media site (and then, perhaps, we could even check the Nielsen ratings). Since two-thirds of American adults now report that they get some of their news via social media (2017) it is considerably more likely that they are being driven to television criticism through the recommendations of opinion leaders within their social networks. It is, to be sure, quite possible that some of those influencers are retweeting, posting, or touting the work of professional television critics, all of whom must now maintain web and social media presences (more on this later); but it is equally as possible that these persons have found citizen curators and critics whose work they admire – or, that they themselves are engaged in television commentary. In this case, everything old is new again as historically television, one of the major mass media (and thus creators and agenda-setters of mass culture) could traditionally count on "water cooler" moments among groups of co-workers and friends to encourage viewership. Ultimately, what we're talking about here is how to make an intervention in the word of mouth in the digital world – the 'digital commons' is a place where discussions that used to take place among people in close geographical proximity are amplified and publicized, but, in many ways, retain their intimacy and influence.

McConnell and Huba (2007) identify four 'types' of social media users whose activities provide a way to categorize the impact of these digital opinion leaders. In order from most to least curatorial they are: filters, facilitators, fanatics and firecrackers. Filters "collect media stories, bloggers' rants and raves, podcasts, or fan creations about a specific company or brand and then package this information into a daily or near-daily stream of links, story summaries and observations." (p. 5). Websites or blogs maintained by these people become curated destinations for other webizens who have an affinity for the topic and the curatorial style of the filter. Facilitators create fan sites or moderate discussion boards. As the owners or managers of these boards they may also establish or institute guidelines for participants and thus shape the presentation of content of their site. Fanatics are filters who weigh in with their opinions – they may or may not provide filtering (curatorial) functions, but mainly, they are the active ones on the message boards – they have distinct ideas about the products they use or the shows they watch and they take full advantage of the interactivity of blogs and websites to voice them. Firecrackers (2007) are "one hit wonders" (p. 19) who do not regularly engage in curatorial activity nor have an ongoing interest in organizing and presenting information to others.

While the individual social media activities of the filters, facilitators and fanatics might be the most influential in spreading opinions about shows to those in their individual networks, the actions of those individuals spread to other filters, facilitators and fanatics through their individual networks. All of that activity will generate website hits, Facebook likes, hashtags, retweets, mentions, tags, and of course all of that activity is captured to alter the SEO ranking, popularity, and trendiness of the shows and/or critics that are mentioned. The impact of all of this activity and, indeed the perceived relevancy of the concept of trending is driven by what Surowiecki (2005) refers to as "social proof." (p. 43). Social proof is based on metrics, not conformity – the idea that if a great number of people are doing something – Suroweicki uses the example of a crowd looking up at the sky – others will look up based on the assumption that the people in the crowd wouldn't be doing that if there wasn't something to see. Therefore, social proof is "the tendency to assume that if lots of people are doing something or believe something, there must be a good reason why." (p. 43). So – while certain critics, 'influencers' or 'bloggers' may be particularly key in steering audience toward shows or premieres (as they have always been), the sheer numbers of participants in the online world, and the scale of "likes" possible, have an effect because "the crowd becomes more influential as it becomes bigger: every additional person is proof that something important is happening." (Surowiecki, 2005, p. 43). This erodes the traditional cultural authority of the professional critic as gatekeeper and cultural intermediary because it places them and their work in the same media ecology as bloggers, fans and citizen critics and shifts the markers of legitimacy and cultural capital in ways that are in conflict with the publication deadline driven practices of professional journalism. The authority of citizen critics, write McConnell and Huba (2007) is dynamic because of its ceaseless and ubiquitous interactivity and is maintained by "continuous, productive activity." (p. 29).

Critics Strike Back

The response of traditional television and film critics to the rise of more fan-based or citizen-critic-centered public sphere echoes larger concerns about the professionalization of journalism, the production of knowledge and the circulation (and competition) of new, diverse and informed voices. A "Film Criticism in the Age of the Internet" (2008) symposium sponsored by *Cineaste* magazine asked a range of film critics about their experience of the growing presence of online distribution on their craft and the possible future heralded by print/internet hybridity. Opinions are varied, as may be expected. Some, such as Armond White of *The New York Press,* echo the fears of the loss of status and authority that Andrew Keen wrote about in *Cult of the Amateur*. White ("Film Criticism in the Age of the Internet," 2008) stated "the joke inherent in the Internet horde is that they chip away at the professionalism they envy, all the time diminishing critical discourse." (p. 30). Others, such as Sicinski ("Film Criticism in the Age of the Internet," 2008), saw online criticism as the savior of critical integrity – freeing critics from editorial interference by corporate-owned and produced media: "Given the present environment of enforced journalistic mediocrity and corporate line-toeing, I suspect that if Kael, Sarris and Farber were producing their most influential work today, they would have had to start blogs to do it." (p. 38).

The participants in *Cineaste's* symposium were asked to respond to four general concerns or questions regarding the effect of the internet on the practice of film criticism: first, had 'internet criticism' "made a significant contribution to film culture?"; next did the participants read blogs and if so, how did they compare those by known print critics to those of "amateur cinephiles?"; third, does the participatory and interactive possibilities of the internet positively contribute to the growth of a new "cinematic community"; and last, if the explosion of blogs and film commentary and criticism of the web was contributing to a loss of "status and authority" by the traditional [presumably meaning print-based] film critic ("Film Criticism in the Age of the Internet," 2008, p. 30).

The opinions of the twenty-two participants ran the gamut and many depended on whether they were coming to the questions in the middle or end of a long career of successful and lucrative film criticism (Jay Hoberman, Amy Taubin), or were just embarking into the new world of film blogging with some success (Zach Campbell, Karina Longworth.) Most agreed that it is now and will become harder in the future to make one's living as a "professional" film (or television) critic. J Hoberman of the *Village Voice* said it is because film and television critics are "hostage[s] to the fortunes of two declining cultural forms, popular cinema and the print media." ("Film Criticism in the Age of the Internet," 2008, p. 34). Amy Taubin of *Film Comment* says it is because "the century in which history was written as cinema is over and film itself no longer has the cultural, social, and political importance it once did. The internet has marginalized traditional film culture." ("Film Criticism in the Age of the Internet," 2008, p. 44). Ultimately, all agreed that a new film culture, as well as new film criticism, was created by Web2.0. While in this period streaming video was still in its infancy, one can see how what began as the internationalization of film culture made possible by the multi-region DVD player and the availability of popular genres such as Hong Kong action, anime and Bollywood, was substantially expanded by the online distribution of cinema across international boundaries (and alas, without concern as to intellectual property.) The same situation developed with television – with the internationalization of series through licensing deals with Netflix (now in 130 countries) or the international (and illegal) redistribution of television in real time via the posting of episodes to YouTube by McConnell and Hubers' "fanatics."

It is also important to note that the print venues for film criticism have always provided considerably more variety for readers and options for writers than those available to television. In addition to national and local newspapers, mass-market magazines such as *Time* (and in an earlier age *Life* and *Look*); specialized publications devoted to film criticism have always been published. Semi-academic journals such as *Film Quarterly, Film Comment, Cineaste* and *Sight & Sound*; publications aimed at filmmakers (or would- or wanna-be filmmakers) *Moviemaker, The Independent, Filmmaker, Creative Screenwriting*; genre-oriented or specialty magazines *Fangoria* have all provided publication outlets (and paychecks to film critics.) Television critics, by and large, have few print outlets beyond those of some mass-market magazines, and newspapers. Even then, as David Carr observed in 2008, critics are often among the first to be laid off when print newspapers attempt to cut corners

Writing in *The New York Times* in 2006, film critic A.O. Scott addressed "the perceptions that print-based film criticism was being challenged by a populist rebellion." (quoted. in Tryon, 2009, p. 125). This spawned its own news cycle of columns and coverage on the "endangered film critic" and, of course amplifies Keen's warnings about the rise of the amateur; Clay Shirky's statement that now, "everyone is a media outlet;" and Chris Anderson's conclusion that in the world of the undifferentiated and never-ending long tail, "the new tastemakers are us." Despite this, many professional television critics have joined the citizen bloggers online: David Bianculli, Maureen Ryan, Mary McNamara and Emily Nussbaum maintain blogs separate from the news organizations for which they write. And McNamara and Nussbaum won Pulitzer prizes for their television criticism in 2015 and 2016 respectively. Still, in a media ecosystem dependent upon circulation, it seems that traditional television critics could learn something from considering the curatorial culture in which their work now circulates. In Alyssa Rosenberg's "Why Everyone is freaking out over Emily Nussbaum's Pulitzer Prize for Criticism" op-ed in the *Washington Post*, the "everyone" freaking out would appear to be Rosenberg (who discloses she is a friend of Nussbaum), Maureen Ryan of *Variety* who tweeted about the win and… the seven people who commented on the article after its publication.

Conclusion

The challenges facing professional television critics are the same as those facing legacy news organization reporters: how to keep their audience content, how to become a destination, how to enter and stay engaged in the ceaseless flow of tweets, hashtags and other social proof of their work's relevancy, and how to attract influencers and move readers from "search" to "seek"?

Throughout most of television's seventy-year history, a particular segment of expert journalists – the professional television critics – have analyzed televisual texts and shared their opinions and interpretations with a reading public that turned to their columns to find answers to the question "What is good television?" Today, a curatorial culture of nicheified media formerly known as "mass" has resulted in new forms of television that are created outside of the traditional industry and circulate independently from network and cable distribution platforms. This has led professional television critics to grapple with the question: "What is television?" As these cultural intermediaries attempt to articulate the characteristics of this redefined cultural form, they have found that their readers, who journalism Professor Jay Rosen (2006) famously referred to as "people formerly known as the audience," have joined the conversation asking: "What is a television critic?"

References

Anderson, C. (2008) *The Long Tail: Why the Future of Business is Selling Less of More*. New York: Hyperion.

Bianculli, D. (2000) *Teleliteracy: Taking Television Seriously*. New York: Continuum/ Syracuse UP.

Bourdieu, P. (1993) *The Field of Cultural Production: Essays on Art and Literature*. New York: Columbia UP.

Carr, D. (2008) "Now on the Endangered Species List: Movie Critics in Print." NYT. 4-1-08

"Film Criticism in the Age of the Internet." (Fall, 2008) *Cineaste*. Volume XXXIII No. 4. Pg. 30-46.

Gould, J. (2002) *Watching Television Come of Age: The New York Times Reviews by Jack Gould* Austin, TX: U of Texas Press.

Gould, L. (2002) "Portrait of a Television Critic." In *Watching Television Come of Age: The New York Times Reviews by Jack Gould*, edited by Lewis Gould, 1-31. Austin, TX: U of Texas.

Kammen, M. (1996) *The Lively Arts: Gilbert Seldes and the Transformation of Cultural Criticism in the United States*. New York: Oxford UP.

Keen, A. (2007) *The Cult of the Amateur*. New York: Doubleday.

Lazarfeld, P. & Katz, E. (1955/2005). *Personal Influence: The Part Played by People in the Flow of Mass Communications.* New York: Routledge.

Lotz, A. (2008) On 'Television Criticism': The Pursuit of the Critical Examination of a Popular Art. *Popular Communication* 6:20-36.

Mc Connell, B. and J. Huba (2007) *Citizen Marketers: When People Are the Message*. Chicago, IL: Kaplan.

Robinson, MJ (2017). *TV on Demand: Curatorial Culture and the Transformation of Television.* London and New York: Bloomsbury Academic.

Seldes, G. (1950) *The Great Audience*. Westport, CT: Greenwood Press Publishers.

Seldes, G. (1924, reissue 1957) *The Seven Lively Arts*. New York: Harper & Brothers.

Seldes, G. (1956) *The Public Arts*. New York: Simon & Schuster.

Shearer, E. and J. Gottfried. (2017) *News Use Across Social Media Platforms 2017*. Pew Research Center. www.pewresearch.org.

Shirky, C. (2008). *Here Comes Everybody: The Power of Organizing without Organizations.* New York: Penguin.

Shirky, C. (2012) Gin, Television, and Social Surplus. In *The Social Media Reader*, edited by Michael Mandiberg, 236-241. New York: NYU Press.

Surowiecki, J. (2005) *The Wisdom of Crowds: Why the Many are Smarter Than the Few*. London: Abacus.

Television Critics Association. www.tvcritics.org/about. Accessed February 25, 2018.

Tryon, C. (2009) *Reinventing Cinema: Movies in the Age of Media Convergence*. New Brunswick, NY: Rutgers UP.

Zuckerman, E. (2013). *Rewire: Digital Cosmopolitans in the Age of Connection*. New York: W.W. Norton.

Towards an Aesthetic of Amateur Online Video

Bernardo Palau Cabrera

Abstract. Since the birth of sound movies, film language had been limited to certain aesthetic resources that television adopted without major changes within the extent of their formal possibilities. However, with the advent of online video, film language has grown considerably, expanding its expressive resources and even altering some aesthetic principles held since the beginning of cinema. The definitive consolidation of digital video as a recording format, the massification of smartphones, the use of applications that use the smartphone's video camera, and the multiple platforms that allow users to share their own creations, have been mainly responsible for the birth of a new visual language. That language breaks the traditional aspect ratios used in film and television, uses preset effects from apps and transforms the interaction with the viewer in a radical way through an interface that is interconnected with other content. In this chapter, I posit that understanding the elements of film language in online user-generated video is a necessary effort since this media could permeate film and television production in the near future, especially considering that the millennial generation, which is the main consumer of this kind of content, will lead the development of television and film in years to come.

Keywords: Amateur Video, Audiovisual Language, New Media Aesthetics.

Introduction

Online amateur video has become widespread up to the point that any of us can have a video camera, an editing system and an exhibition channel in our own pockets on our very own smartphone. Nevertheless, despite the huge levels of consumption of online video, especially among millennials (Palm & Pilkington, 2016), few scholars have studied and categorized the aesthetic that defines this media.

I believe that media studies have a pending debt to formal analysis of the audiovisual content made exclusively for the Web by amateur users, whether it is broadcasted through video-exclusive platforms (i.e., YouTube) or through social networks that display videos (such as Facebook). Although much has been written about the reach of online video from the consumers behavior point of view (Deloitte, 2017; Ericsson, 2017) and the revolution that user-generated content implies, very few have considered the formal characteristics and artistic conventions that this new media is using, and that could set future aesthetic trends for mass media (Dawson, 2007; McCreery & Krugman, 2015;

Ryan, 2017). Therefore, I believe it is important to look at user-generated video as a medium with its own aesthetics.

This chapter aims to define the main aesthetic characteristics of user-generated video content. Drawing upon recent bibliography and industrial reports such as 'The Perennial Millennial' (Palm & Pilkington, 2016), alongside the viewing of videos on online platforms and social networks, this article seeks to define new ways of communication and representation through video. The relevance of this analysis lies on the idea that both the millennial generation and the generation that follows them (generation Z), could transfer these aesthetic practices to both cinema and television in a not so distant future.

Film Language: Definitions

Since the dawn of the seventh art, cinema had been limited to reproducing the world just as the spectators watch a show in a stage box: the filmmakers used to set their camera and register the events that happened in front of the lens, with the sole purpose of reproducing these events later by projecting them on a screen. Still, they lacked the *mise-en-scene*, "the director's control over what appears in the shot" (Bordwell & Thompson, 2013, p. 112) and the editing (or *montage*) of the filmed material. Cinema was still making its first steps as a language and it would learn to walk in the following years thanks to pioneers such as David W. Griffith, Edwin S. Porter and the Russian formalists Sergei Einsenstein, Dziga Vertov and Lev Kuleshov. As a result of these filmmakers' work, cinema moved from being considered a fair invention capable of reproducing movement, to an art form in its own right.

As Metz established:

> If cinema is a language, it is because it works with the image of objects, not with the objects themselves. Photographic duplication [...] distances from the mutism of the world a piece of semi-reality in order to make a discourse out of it. The effigies of the world, set in a different way than life, plotted and restructured in the course of a narrative intention, turns into elements of enunciation (quoted in Martin, 2008, p. 27).

From then on, the development of this new language went forward as much as technology and creativity allowed it to. As director Martin Scorsese points out paraphrasing the French Jean Luc Godard: "We've had two important teachers in cinema history: D.W. Griffith, in silent cinema, and Orson Welles, in talking cinema. So, of course, there are basic rules" (Tirard, 2010, p. 77).

These 'basic rules' that Scorsese talks about are, in other words, film grammar and classic editing principles, which have allowed the moving image to evolve radically since its creation. The most dramatic evolution, however, may have come with the arrival of the digital age and the Internet, that forever changed our way of producing, consuming and sharing audiovisual content. As Stam argues "changing audiovisual technologies dramatically impact virtually all of the perennial issues engaged by film theory: specificity, auteurism, apparatus theory, spectatorship, realism, aesthetics" (2000, p. 319). Thus, in the following paragraphs, I describe the main aesthetic attributes that define the film language commonly observed in user-generated online video.

Online Video

Considering the fact that Youtube alone gets 500 hours of video per minute uploaded to its servers (Robertson, 2015) without taking into account other similar platforms, it is necessary to delimit our definition of online video, especially since media convergence has meant that cinema, television and other kinds of video content inhabit a homogeneous online video universe. Therefore, I want to posit three categories of internet video based on the origin of their content, namely, the transferred-to-the-Web video, the streaming platforms, and the native online video.

The first category, that I call transferred-to-the-Web video, includes the content that has not been created originally for the Internet, but instead uses it more as a repository. In this category, we can find:

- Live streaming of television content (Braun, 2013; Díaz-Arias, 2009, p. 66; Lotz, 2014, p. 15). In this case, television networks use their site as another distribution channel for their live signal.

- Content uploaded to the Web by television companies as a way to give access to the users and as a digital repository.

- Short films, medium-length films, and full-length feature films created to be projected in a cinema (or film festival) that end up on the Web, on video platforms such as Vimeo or YouTube. In other words, we can think of these films as part of a 'digital film repository'.

The second category includes streaming and VOD platforms, such as Netflix, Amazon or Hulu, where users can find TV series and other contents uploaded to the Web, mixing top quality content produced for film and already broadcasted television shows with content that has been produced specifically for their users. This content has been conceived to be seen from a computer or television screen, as directors of photography from series such as 'House of Cards' have mentioned (Consoli, 2014). The above is achieved thanks to systems that integrate internet content into television screens, like Apple TV, Chromecast and others.

As a third category, I want to propose the term 'online native video' as those audiovisual pieces that have been developed exclusively for watching through the World Wide Web and the devices that allow access to it (hardware). This implies that both in its contents and its aesthetic characteristics, whether they are voluntary (of style) or imposed by technological limitations, the creators have had in mind the distribution of its content through the Web.

Online Native Video: Between the Professional and the Amateur

Within the production of online native video, I posit two categories that should be differentiated by their production origin: the professional video (music videos, advertising, among others) and the amateur video created by average users.

In her remarkable work 'Reel Families: A Social History of Amateur Film', Zimmermann (1995) revises and analyses home-made movies looking to "retrieve amateur–film history from the garbage dump of film and cultural studies" (1995, p. 15), because for her it "is not simply an inert designation of inferior film practice and ideology but rather is a historical process of social control over representation" (Brownlee, 2016, p. XV). In this regard, Jenkins (2003) can help us contextualize the amateur video on the web:

> Prior to the Web, amateurs might write stories, compose music, or make movies but they had no venue where they could exhibit their works [...]. In many ways, the Web has become the digital refrigerator for the 'Do-It-Yourself' ('DIY') movement (2003, p. 287).

This digital refrigerator Jenkins talks about refers symbolically to the place of the house where family members put up their work for the rest of the family to see, like the drawings that children share at the center of the kitchen. For this very reason, the amateur video in the digital era is far from existing just to be watched inside our homes:

> No longer home movies, these films are public movies – public in that from the start, they are intended for audiences beyond the filmmaker's immediate circle of friends and acquaintances; public in their content, which involves the reworking of personal concerns into the shared cultural framework provided by popular mythologies (ibid).

Although authors Jean Burgess and Joshua Green focus on YouTube, I argue that their analysis is extendible to several video platforms since they mention that "YouTube is symptomatic of a changing media environment, but it is one where the practices and identities associated with cultural production and consumption, commercial and non-commercial enterprise, and professionalism and amateurism interact and converge in new ways" (Snickars & Vonderau, 2009, p. 90)

An example of this is the video blog of 'lonelygirl15' released in 2006, which starts with the on-camera confession of a young girl called Bree, who under the pseudonym of 'lonelygirl15' talks to a webcam about her problems. After its debut, the audience started following her and after a publication on the New York Times, her last video that week reached half a million views, a major increase compared to the figures between 50,000 and 100,000 she got weekly up to that moment (Burgess & Green, 2009, p. 27). Nonetheless, due to how well the plot developed and how well they were edited, an online debate (that later got to the offline world) soon arose about the veracity of Bree's story. Finally, the truth was revealed: 'lonelygirl15' was an experiment from directors Mesh Flinders and Miles Beckett (Burgess & Green, 2009, p. 28). Regardless, the developers had used the amateurism to present a fiction that is still considered one of the first fiction web series on the internet.

When making the distinction between professional and amateur video, there is a particular category that problematized the distinction, namely, the video essay. Defined as a "short analytical film about films or film culture" (Mcwhirter, 2015, p. 369), the video essay can't be considered as amateur video since many of these pieces make use of remixing practices (Mcwhirter, 2015, p. 372), which repurpose already existing intellectual property (i.e., films). Therefore, their aesthetic qualities are partly produced under industrial production regimes.

Characteristics of the Online Amateur Video

In this section, I posit five elements that radically define online amateur video, namely its amateur aesthetic, the liberation of the camera as the only device for recording movement, its short duration, its image-interface quality, and the use of close-ups and medium shots.

Amateur aesthetic

On an aesthetic level, spectators can distinguish a characteristic visuality, one that owes more to home-made video than to television or industrial cinema. On technical matters, amateurism is an audiovisual form which gives more priority to objects appearing in the shot, than how they look in terms of pictorial quality. As opposed to cinema or fiction television, in amateur online video, there is no attempt of generating an atmosphere through light or framing, but rather to allow the camera to capture the object in front of the lens.

Moreover, amateur aesthetic uses camera incorporated microphones to record sound, thus avoiding the use of more sophisticated equipment. The above translates in videos with a great amount of ambient sound, which creators usually try to avoid by adding music or recording in closed spaces.

In terms of its editing and post-production, amateur aesthetic usually translates into two distinctive elements: the use of non-linear editing systems and the use of the jump-cut. This kind of cut was popularized by the French *nouvelle vague* (Pinel, 2007), as we can see in the film '*À bout de souffle*' (Godard, 1960) and appears "when two shots of the same subject are cut together but are not sufficiently different in-camera distance and angle" (Bordwell & Thompson, 2013, p. 254), thus creating a rupture of the shot's continuity. While the French filmmakers used it with an expressive intention, in the case of amateur video creators the jump cut is usually a resource used to shorten the video. Some examples of this technique can be found mainly on video blogs (also known as vblogs), a "dominant form of user-created content, and it is fundamental to YouTube's sense of community. Typically structured primarily around a monologue delivered directly to camera, vlogs are characteristically produced with little more than a webcam and some witty editing" (Snickars & Vonderau, 2009, p. 94).

It is important not to confuse amateurism with sloppiness or lack of care during production. In this regard, an iconic case is the vloger Casey Neistat, a director and producer from New York. By watching his video blog, the spectator can understand that his *mise-en-scene* looks far more amateur than it really is. Neistat creates a piece of fast-paced, amateur-like content, while at the same time, brings "a decade of videographic experience to a subgenre that prizes amateur craft" (Puschak, 2016), which makes the "seemingly effortlessness of Neistat vblog an illusion" (Puschak, 2016).

Evidently, the aesthetic characteristics described in this section vary according to technology and the speed to which content creators teach themselves how to use these new technologies (through websites and online tutorials). Thus, amateur visuality is in constant change.

Liberation of the camera as the only device for recording movement.

As a part of this description of aesthetic resources that constitute the online amateur video, it is impossible to leave aside the presence of cellphones with the capacity to access the World Wide Web, also known as smartphones, which use applications that exploit the hardware in order to make the most out of it.

Thus, users can record, edit and upload videos on the spot, with just a smartphone and an internet connection.

Also, they have the advantage of not needing many skills in order to get a somewhat good video quality and get to places where it is not even allowed to record, whether it is for legal reasons or because of the size of a video camera (e.g., a museum). Astruc seemed to be right when he mentioned that "the history of cinematographic technic may be considered entirely as the history of the liberation of the camera" (Martin, 2008, p. 27).

Nowadays we can find film festivals dedicated to films recorded with this kind of phones, like the Mobile Motion Film Festival (MoMo Film Festival, n. d.) and several cases of feature films recorded with phones that even got to film festivals like Sundance (Kastrenakes, 2015). However, beyond this, smartphones have brought three interesting attributes to online native video:

- Changes in the aspect ratio of the image. By holding a phone vertically, it will record images whose height will be larger than its horizontal extension. If we consider that, on the one hand, the design of smartphones 'seems to encourage vertical video' (Ryan, 2017) and that 70% of consumers watch TV and video on a smartphone today (Ericsson, 2017), it makes sense that the production and consumption of vertical video would become an important trend in the last two years, to the point where different social media platforms seem to be adapting to this trend. In addition, another aspect ratio that has become popular in recent years thanks to applications like Instagram and Facebook is the 1:1 square proportion. These kinds of changes bring repercussions over how images are composed in a pictorial level, because they change the relation between the boundaries of the frame and the elements within it.

- Color correcting filters. Besides the already mentioned Instagram, the users of an average smartphone can add filters such as sepia, black and white, and others in an almost automatic way and even adjusting them according to the creators' necessities.

- Pre-set graphics. Both Snapchat and Instagram apps allow features such as adding masks over the recorded face, effects like snow and a long etcetera of pre-set animations. Moreover, in both apps, users can 'doodle' over the image using their finger as a pencil.

Short duration

"Forty years ago, Stanley Kubrick showed us 2001. The first 90 seconds are without dialogue and solid black. It's hard to imagine that working as the intro to a YouTube video today" (Godin, 2015). The duration of amateur online videos is usually short. Sometimes it is due to aspects of the platform where they are being shown on, and other times it is in order to reach the highest number of possible spectators and achieve being shared by other users.

In the first case mentioned, those platforms created with mobile access in mind tend to be stricter in this aspect: the late app Vine allowed a maximum of six seconds; Instagram allows to upload videos up to one minute of duration to a user's profile and videos within three and 60 seconds long in its Instagram Stories section (where videos are shown for 24 hours in vertical format); and Snapchat allows to upload videos between one and ten seconds long. Whereas in the second case, it is important to point out that while the platforms allow a longer duration, the creators of the videos that are uploaded to these platforms opt to make them short due to the 'watch time', defined by Youtube as the amount of time a spectator watches a video (Youtube, 2017). The relevance of this for a Youtuber lies on the fact that the algorithm that commands the platform gives recommendations to the user prioritizing the watch time of a video over its number of views (D'Onfro, 2015). This way, the recommendations we find on the right side of the Youtube screen are given according to the videos that keep their audiences for a longer time and not the ones with the highest number of views.

Wistia, a video hosting and statistics service, mentions in its tutorials the 'nose' of a video as the 2% of the time at the beginning. According to Fishman and Currier, the losing of viewers is closely linked to the duration of the video, up to the point that spectator loss in the 'nose' of videos between one and two minutes long would equal to 4,9% of the audience, while in videos between five and ten minutes long it would get up to 17,3% (Fishman & Currier, n. d.). This would explain why the first three seconds of successful Youtubers' videos start with an invitation to watch them: an appealing product, a premise, or a declaration of intentions. Like the video 'Make it Count' (Neistat, 2012) that begins with a product, or some of German Garmendia's (Garmendia, 2015) videos that begin with a joke.

All of the above lets us define online native video as a format where short duration rules.

Image-interface

The concept of *image-interface* was suggested by Manovich (2001), but its revision might be necessary considering the new technologies that have reinterpreted his vision seventeen years later.

> The term human-computer interface describes the ways in which the user interacts with a computer. [...] It also consists of metaphors used to conceptualize the organization of computing data. For instance, the Macintosh interface introduced by Apple in 1984 uses the metaphor of files and folders arranged on a desktop (Manovich, 2001, p. 69).

Not only computers and their operating systems have an interface, but also each site or app we use. The interface is nothing but the visible face of a computing code. Clips on platforms like YouTube and Facebook are integrated into interfaces bigger than them: the sites that contain them, making the videos compete with other suggested videos (in the case of YouTube) and other multimedia content (in the case of Facebook). Moreover, the new media that Manovich talks about has gone even further, transforming the representative image (i.e. the video itself) into an image-interface, where both uses of the image oppose each other (Manovich, 2001, p. 16). However, in the online native video and social networks era, these two functions complement themselves.

Consider, for example, the video players on YouTube and Facebook. In the first case, the author of a video can add notes to invite comments and buttons over the video to suggest that the spectator keeps on watching the same channel or to make him interact with the content. Furthermore, on Facebook Live, the interaction between the user, the image-representation (i.e., the video), and the image-interface that allows users to comment, happens all at the same time.

In the case of apps such as Instagram (in its Instagram Stories section) and in Snapchat (in its video section), the notion of image-interface is taken to a different level by letting us use the phone camera to record a video clip, play it and, then manipulate the image, adding text, animations or 'doodling' over it as if our finger were a pencil. Here the interface not only allows us to interact with the content, but also works as a very easy-to-use version of an image compositing software, such as Adobe After Effects. Once the content is published on the above-mentioned platforms, the image is reproduced and has a button that stops the video playing and lets us send a message to the video's owner.

Use of close-ups and medium shots

According to Ericsson's "TV and MEDIA 2017: A consumer-driven future of media," around 70 percent of consumers watch TV and video on a smartphone today, which is twice as many as in 2012 (Ericsson, 2017). Then, it should not be a surprise that the narrative of film language used in native online video content uses mainly close-up and medium shots.

The medium shot is that in which the human figure is shown from the waist up to the head (Sánchez, 2011). In online amateur video, it is hard to find a wide shot but for a few specific exceptions. It is worth mentioning that in the case of smartphones video apps, the character's distance is usually set by the length of the arm, or in some cases, by a 'selfie stick,' a cane that lets the creators record with the frontal camera available in most mobile phones. Although it seems like a minor detail, this self-portrait or selfie aesthetic, as we might call it, has meant that – unlike earlier audiovisual media like film or television – the 'environment' on the online video consists mostly of faces over specific locations.

Conclusion

As I have demonstrated in this chapter, online amateur video has its own aesthetic characteristics and should not be overlooked as a cinematic form. Instead, it should be seen as a new way of communication that obeys the possibility of having some "social control over representation" (Brownlee, 2016, p. XV). Created outside the limits of the more traditional industrial production regimes of film and television, amateur online video has its own film grammar born out of the changing audiovisual technologies that have appeared in recent years, first with the arrival of digital video cameras and, most recently, with the massification of the smartphone.

Whether amateur online video will permeate or not more traditional media like television and cinema is a question that only time will answer. However, it is a matter that media studies should not leave aside.

Acknowledgments

I am grateful to Macarena Palau for the translation of non-English references, comments, as well as the translation of earlier versions of this chapter.

References

Bordwell, D. & Thompson, K. (2013). *Film art: an introduction* (10th ed). New York, N.Y: McGraw-Hill.

Brownlee, S. (2016). Amateurism and the Aesthetics of Lego Stop-Motion on YouTube. *Film Criticism*, *40*(2). http://dx.doi.org/10.3998/fc.13761232.0040.204

Burgess, J. & Green, J. (2009). *YouTube: online video and participatory culture.* Cambridge ; Malden, MA: Polity.

Consoli, B. (2014, February 24). House of Cards (With Igor Martinovic) GCS025.

Retrieved January 17, 2018, from http://gocreativeshow.com/house-of-cards-with-igor-martinovic-gcs025/

Dawson, M. (2007). Little Players, Big Shows: Format, Narration, and Style on Television's New Smaller Screens. *Convergence, 13*(3), 231–250.

Deloitte. (2017). *2017 Global Mobile Consumer Survey - United States* (Statistic). United States: Deloitte.

D'Onfro, J. (2015, July 3). The "terrifying" moment in 2012 when YouTube changed its entire philosophy. Retrieved January 16, 2018, from http://www.businessinsider.com/youtube-watch-time-vs-views-2015-7

Ericsson. (2017). *TV and MEDIA 2017: A consumer-driven future of media* (No. 8). Stockholm: Ericsson. Retrieved from https://www.ericsson.com/en/networked-society/trends-and-insights/consumerlab/consumer-insights/reports/tv-and-media-2017

Fishman, E. & Currier, A. (n.d.). Understanding Audience Retention. Retrieved January 16, 2018, from https://wistia.com/library/understanding-audience-retention

Garmendia, G. (2015). *La Primera Vez | Hola Soy German* [YouTube video]. Retrieved from https://www.youtube.com/watch?v=oz0hdMkQ_9w

Godard, J.-L. (1960). *À bout de souffle.* Retrieved from http://www.imdb.com/title/tt0053472/

Godin, S. (2015, February 8). How we watch video now. Retrieved January 17, 2018, from http://sethgodin.typepad.com/seths_blog/2015/02/how-we-watch-a-video-now.html

Jenkins, H. (2003). Quentin Tarantino's Star Wars?: Digital Cinema, Media Convergence, and Participatory Culture. In D. Thorburn & B. Seawell (Eds.), *Rethinking media change: the aesthetics of transition.* Cambridge, Mass: MIT Press.

Kastrenakes, J. (2015, April 30). Watch the trailer for Tangerine, a Sundance favorite shot on an iPhone 5S - The Verge. Retrieved January 17, 2018, from https://www.theverge.com/2015/4/30/8523277/tangerine-trailer-movie-shot-on-iphone-5s

Manovich, L. (2001). *The language of new media.* Cambridge, Mass.: MIT Press.

Martin, M. (2008). *El lenguaje del cine.* Barcelona: Gedisa.

McCreery, S. P. & Krugman, D. M. (2015). TV and the iPad: How the Tablet is Redefining the Way We Watch. *Journal of Broadcasting & Electronic Media, 59*(4), 620–639. https://doi.org/10.1080/08838151.2015.1093483

Mcwhirter, A. (2015). Film criticism, film scholarship and the video essay. *Screen, 56*(3), 369–377. https://doi.org/10.1093/screen/hjv044

MoMo Film Festival. (n.d.). Mobile Motion - International Smartphone Film Festival. Retrieved January 18, 2018, from https://momofilmfest.com/

Neistat, C. (2012). *Make It Count - YouTube* [YouTube video]. Retrieved from https://www.youtube.com/watch?v=WxfZkMm3wcg&t=12s

Palm, M. & Pilkington, M. (2016). *The Perennial Millennial* (Executive Insights Spotlight on Media and Entertainment No. 1). London: L.E.K. Consulting LLC.

Pinel, V. (2007). *El montaje: el espacio y el tiempo del filme*. Barcelona: Paidós.

Puschak, E. (2016). *Casey Neistat: What you don't see* [YouTube video]. Retrieved from https://www.youtube.com/watch?v=JbiJqTBCQuw

Robertson, M. R. (2015, November 13). 500 Hours of Video Uploaded To YouTube Every Minute [Forecast]. Retrieved January 22, 2018, from http://tubularinsights.com/hours-minute-uploaded-youtube/

Ryan, K. M. (2017). Vertical video: rupturing the aesthetic paradigm. *Visual Communication*, 1470357217736660. https://doi.org/10.1177/1470357217736660

Sánchez, R. C. (2011). *Montaje cinematográfico arte de movimiento*. Buenos Aires: La Crujía.

Snickars, P., & Vonderau, P. (Eds.). (2009). The Entrepreneurial Vlogger: Participatory Culture Beyond the Professional- Amateur Divide. In *The YouTube reader*. Stockholm: National Library of Sweden.

Stam, R. (2000). *Film theory: an introduction*. Malden, Mass: Blackwell.

Tirard, L. (2010). *Lecciones de cine clases magistrales de grandes directores*. Barcelona: Paidós.

Youtube. (2017). Watch time report - YouTube Help. Retrieved January 17, 2018, from https://support.google.com/youtube/answer/1714329?hl=en

Zimmermann, P. R. (1995). *Reel families: a social history of amateur film*. Bloomington: Indiana University Press.

Guarding the Gates in Interactive Newsgathering

Jenny Hauser

Abstract. Social media have become an integral part of many journalists' toolkits, offering both opportunities and posing risks for the profession. This paper analyses the use of social media-sourced content in the news coverage of crisis reporting by the BBC, France 24 and Al Jazeera. Quantitative and qualitative data analysis of social media content examined sourcing routines in breaking news reporting of the migrant crisis in 2015. It seeks to contribute to the understanding of how journalists negotiate their roles as 'gatekeepers' and professionals in a potentially open, de-professionalized and inherently participatory news environment. Based on the findings, the paper discusses the emergence of journalist communities and networks on social media and their tendency to collectively set their own news agendas and amplify voices. The findings are consistent with existing research, showing often highly selective social media engagement. The paper contributes to the analysis of the practices and mechanisms by which networked journalists both compete and at times collaborate with media activists and other users to shape their own news environment on social media, maintaining oversight of what passes into the global news flow.

Keywords: Gatekeeping, Social Media, News Media, Professional Journalism.

Introduction

The Internet has thrown professional journalism into crisis not only by undermining its commercial business model with dwindling revenue plaguing much of the industry but through the contestation of professionalism in journalism. Described by Jay Rosen (2006) as "the people formerly known as the audience" and Dan Gilmore (2004) simply as the "former audience," news consumers are no longer the silent passive masses on the receiving end of a predominantly one-way mass media.

Since widespread access to the Internet radically lowered barriers to publishing and broadcasting, audiences both engage in news production and seek to influence and respond to the news coverage of professional news organizations. Two-way communication, typically facilitated by social media platforms, has given rise to interactivity in news production and distribution.

Hermida (2010) argued today's news environment is characterized by "ambient journalism," meaning audiences are able to dip in and out of participating in the production of news when it suits them. Here, ambience is understood as an awareness-system that switches between background and foreground in audience's consciousness. For example, the micro-blogging site Twitter, he argues, creates its own journalistic environment with its own logic that empowers non-professionals to engage in news production. "Micro-blogging can be seen as a form of participatory or citizen journalism, where citizens report without recourse to institutional journalism" (p. 300). This analysis separates Twitter users into a private citizenry category distinctly different from the mass media, and feeds into the early hypothesis that the Internet is leading the way towards the democratization of mass communication (Benkler 2006, Jenkins 2006, Shirky 2008).

As this alternative news environment driven by ordinary citizens, amateurs and grassroots journalists gained traction, other academics outlined the interactive nature of news production and distribution between users and their interdependence with mainstream news media. Both Bruns' (2006; 2012) description of "produsage" and Chadwick's (2011) "hybrid news system" consider collaboration, not only between news audiences but also between audiences and traditional news outlets as a hallmark of the digital news environment. As professional journalists continue to provide most of the available news content due to greater resources, Chadwick accepts that traditional news media remains dominant in this interdependence and also recognized how professional journalists compete on new media to outperform other actors and assert their dominance. Nevertheless, as journalists and ordinary people rubbed shoulders on social media platforms, he predicted the empowerment of non-elites to contest the mainstream news media's monopoly on dictating the news agenda.

Papacharissi (2015) echoes the collaborative spirit between citizens and journalists in her definition of "affective news streams" where "news [is] collaboratively constructed out of subjective experience, opinion, and emotion, all sustained by and sustaining ambient news environments." (p. 34) Everyone is invited to contribute, and established news production practices—such as neutrality—are called into question. Essentially, it is the ability to talk back and for subjectivity to shape part of the news stream that Papacharissi argues reconnects journalists with audiences.

With the radical changes in the relationship between newsrooms and their audiences, a new news discourse has been born where collaboration between professional journalists and amateurs has been integrated into the culture and ethics of news production, and where professional journalists are tasked with managing this interaction (Hujanen, 2016). This news discourse contains the perception of a dichotomy between professionalization in journalism and citizen debate. The former is characterized by a code of ethics and practices that are a requirement to inform the latter. Therefore, at its core it harbors a strong gatekeeping component.

Analysis of user-generated content (UGC) in news coverage explores how newsrooms have adopted social media to source news content. The purpose of the research is to investigate how newsrooms collaborate with social media users and how this has affected traditional power relations between sources and journalists in news production. Specifically, this research investigates the adoption of professional journalistic norms and routines in interactive newsgathering during the migrant crisis in Europe at three international news organization. It draws on Hall et al's (1978) seminal work on "primary and secondary definers" to analyses user identities among social media sources, and uses textual analysis to consider framing of social media-sourced content. Hall et al argue that professional ideology and routines "give rise to the practice of ensuring that media statements are, wherever possible, grounded in 'objective' and 'authoritative' statements from 'accredited' sources. "This means constantly turning to accredited representatives of major social institutions" (p. 58). These sources are referred to as primary definers. They are in a position to influence and frame the news agenda, whereas news media are secondary definers following their lead.

Aim

This research seeks to investigate the use of interactive newsgathering across three international news broadcasters for four weeks, straddling August and September 2015. The chosen timeframe both saw the migrant issue surge to the top of the news agenda among mainstream news media, and spark public debate, citizen initiatives and protests that were organized and discussed on social networks. Among western European governments it saw a turning point in rhetoric around the issue of asylum seekers. Social media played a multi-faceted role in how it facilitated public engagement around the topic, affected developments in the news events, and also served news organizations as a tool in their own news production. Online news texts containing social media-sourced content by the BBC World Service, France 24 English and Al Jazeera English and its offshoots AJPlus and AJStream were analyzed to identify the identities of social media sources, their source-power, and framing.

This chapter examines two research questions:

1. Who are the social media sources in the online news coverage of the migrant crisis?
2. How do newsrooms position journalists in interactive newsgathering?

Methodology

The websites of the news organizations, as well as their associated Twitter accounts, were searched for the keywords 'migrant', 'migrants', 'refugee' and 'refugees'. All of the relevant news texts were scanned for social media content. All news texts that did not contain any clearly identifiable social media content were disregarded, whereas those that did were analyzed using qualitative and quantitative methodologies.

A wide variety of news texts featured social media content across all three news organizations, ranging from hard news reports to opinion pieces, media reviews, live blogs and social media focused-sections. This reflects the diverse role that social media played throughout the crisis as it was used to communicate by the news media, government and social institutions, citizens and not least of all migrants.

The BBC sample consisted of 49 texts, comprising 40 news texts published on bbc.com and an additional 10 tweets published on one of four BBC Twitter accounts: @BBCWorld, @BBCTrending, @BBCMonitoring or @BBCOS. All of these texts, including the tweets, contained or referenced content that could be traced back to originating on social media. The social media-sourced content comprised text, images and audio-visual material. Overall, there were 47 news texts found on France 24's English language digital platforms that contained or referenced social media content. The texts were published both on france24.com/en and observers.france24.com/en. France 24 features both its own content as well as reports by Agence France-Presse (AFP). Both of these were considered in the sample. A total 18 AFP online texts distributed by France 24 form part of the sample. Al Jazeera featured 41 news texts. The main website aljazeera.com published 21 texts comprising or referencing content originating on social media. Four texts were published on the digital platforms of the AJStream web community. In addition, all tweets published on the @ajplus and @AJEnglish accounts containing the keywords were examined of which 16 contained content sourced through social media.

Quantitative Analysis

Twitter was the most commonly used social media platform for newsgathering across all three news organizations. A comparison between Twitter and Facebook sources shows differences in the type of users that were sought out. This was especially true for the news texts of the BBC and France 24, where collaborative newsgathering was found to be shaped by elite professional journalists and mainstream news organizations active on Twitter.

Twitter Source Identities

Twitter users were divided into nine groups: in-house journalists working at the respective news organization, other professional journalists, news organizations, politicians, state authorities, aid organizations, experts, citizens, and others. Humanitarian aid organizations, due to their activist nature, could not be considered 'expert' users, while their formalized and professional organizational structures also did not fit the citizen user group.

Table 1 Identities of Twitter sources

	in-house journalists	other journalists	news media	politicians	state bodies	aid	expert	citizen	other
BBC	26	24	3 (1)*	2	3	4	3	22	4
F24	5	5	0	3	3	0	2	11	3
AJ	2	13	3 (1)**	6	1	4	3	56	3

* News organization's own Twitter account
** Aggregator news source

The BBC had a total of 91 different Twitter sources with the use of content by in-house journalists in its coverage particularly prominent. BBC employees comprised the largest group of Twitter sources and in total more than half (52) originated in the mainstream news media, suggesting a mainstream media-centric approach to collaborative newsgathering on this platform. Moreover, the sample in Table 1 only comprises the BBC staff whose Twitter content was used in news texts. In addition, the BBC also directed readers to a Twitter list of 33 of its correspondents to follow for the latest news updates showing a push to distribute directly to news audiences through native content. Other professional journalists were typically similarly elite and English-speaking originating from international news organizations such as Channel 4, New York Times, ITV, The Guardian, German broadcaster RTL and Arabic Al Alan TV, as well as the newer online news outlet Buzzfeed. The third largest source group in the BBC sample were citizen users and had a strong international dimension with voices from across the world but an emphasis on Arabic users.

However, users from countries affected by conflict were very limited and showed that citizen users were talking about their perception of the migrant crisis as outsiders rather than those personally affected. France 24 stood out for its very limited use of Twitter for newsgathering with only 32 sources overall. Almost a third of them were journalists and another third were citizen users. Since the news event often played out in remote areas and involved people with very little opportunity to relay their experiences to a wider audience without the attention of mainstream news media, journalists arguably faced less competition from amateur sources in reporting from the field. The BBC's extensive use of Twitter as a source for news content primarily served to raise awareness of its reporters' social media activity. With a few exceptions, France 24 did not highlight its individual reporters but where it did, it also drew attention to their native news content. Al Jazeera had the largest number of Twitter sources (91) with the vast majority defined as citizen users. This was largely due to one AJ Stream webcast that involved many of the Twitter sources as contributors. The show format's aim is to facilitate a conversation between citizen users on social media and therefore it almost exclusively sourced such users.

The overlap in sources between the news organizations was limited, given the very different approaches to Twitter sourcing routines between the BBC and Al Jazeera. All three organizations shared only two Twitter sources; a cameraman for German broadcaster RTL (@RichterSteph) and the emergency director at Human Rights Watch (@bouckap). Despite France 24's extremely limited use of Twitter, it had more sources in common with the BBC (5) than Al Jazeera (3) did. France 24 and Al Jazeera had another three sources in common. Most overlaps were found among journalist sources, while there was also some overlap among citizen users. Although very limited, this showed that a small number of mostly professional journalists and expert sources had the highest source power, meaning their social media content was used in news texts by all news organizations. These sources can be understood as the biggest social media 'influencers' in the sample.

Twitter Source Weight

The quantitative analysis of source power or 'weight' was measured through the number of tweets by each user group in the news texts. Although a tweet may have been used more than once in different news texts by the same news organization, each was only counted once. However, some pieces of content were able to generate a considerable amount of coverage in the studied period.

Table 2 Source weight represented by the number of tweets by category

	in-house journalists	other journalists	news media	politicians	state bodies	aid	expert	citizen	other
BBC	80	46	3	3	5	5	3	24	4
F24	10	5	0	3	4	0	4	11	4
AJ	3	15	3	7	1	4	4	65	3

Among the 173 tweets used in the BBC coverage, nearly half originated from its own reporters tweeting from the field. On average a BBC reporter would see 3.1 of their tweets used in the BBC's coverage, while other journalist users would be featured with around two tweets on average. Citizen users, while being the third largest user group, would have comparatively little source power with just over one tweet per user.

France 24 featured 41 tweets. Albeit a much smaller sample group than that of the BBC, the outlet also gave the greatest platform to its own journalists with two tweets per user on average. Other journalists were only represented with one tweet each, the same as citizen users. The two expert users featured were represented with two tweets each.

Al Jazeera had the largest number of Twitter sources but only 107 tweets in its coverage due to the greater reliance on citizen users, a group with less source power overall. Citizen users were represented in the coverage with an average of 1.2 tweets. However, Al Jazeera did not give greater preference to media sources either with journalists also featured with only 1.2 tweet per user. The much more limited use of news media or journalist sources and the equal source weighting underlines Al Jazeera's more citizen-focused approach to Twitter, and social media overall, in as far as newsgathering is concerned.

Facebook Source Identities

This case study had a sizeable amount of Facebook-sourced content throughout the coverage, which permitted the distinction in sourcing routines between this social media platform and Twitter. As shown in Table 3, non-authoritative or

non-accredited users comprised the majority of the sources and were divided
into the first four groups in the table.

Table 3 Identities of Facebook sources

	BBC	F24	Al Jazeera
Syrian	10	2	2
Other individuals	8	5	4
Communities/Initiatives	8	7	6
Media activism/Citizen Journalism	0	2	0
Professional Journalists	0	0	3
News Media	1	2	0
Government/Pol	1	3	2

As already mentioned, the refugee crisis generated considerable civic
engagement—both in support and opposition to refugees—that also received
widespread news coverage. Often citizen groups and initiatives organized on
Facebook and the platform itself received media coverage amid a political
outcry about hate speech in Germany.

Syrians, the main focus of the migrant crisis coverage, were all but absent
from the sample of Twitter users. However, the BBC focused much of its
Facebook newsgathering on finding users that identified themselves as Syrian.
Common to all three organizations was their reference of Facebook users as a
gauge of public sentiment. Hence, Facebook groups, and community and
events pages represented the largest number of Facebook sources for France
24 and Al Jazeera. Where these pages were mentioned in the news coverage,
it was typically simply their existence and their purpose that was reported on,
while actual content posted to these pages by individual users was mostly

absent. The source power of Facebook users was also more limited than that of Twitter users. Users were referenced usually only once in the entire sample of the news texts, and groups and initiatives were reported on but not necessarily named or linked to. The overlap in sources again mirrored the trend found in the Twitter news sourcing, with BBC and France 24 having the most sources in common (three), while the three organizations only had one source in common.

While source power or 'influence' may be limited for citizen users, the wide range of different sources across the three news organizations suggests media diversity and plurality in sourcing practices. A closer look at the kind of sources sought out by the different news outlets shows the voices were also not originating from similar demographics. For example, Al Jazeera reported on a Turkish Facebook page that organized boat crossings to Greece and an Islamist Facebook community accused of providing a platform for extremists to divide Arab nations. France 24 focused both on European initiatives supportive of refugees as well as those strongly critical of the intake of refugees, including a Croatian Facebook community and the British incarnation of the German anti-immigrant PEGIDA movement. The BBC, on the other hand, did not mention any anti-refugee Facebook content, rather focusing on the different ways in which citizens were organizing their support across Europe. Another characteristic of the BBC Facebook sources was the use of illustrations, including satirical cartoons to convey a message. In general, Facebook content was used to contribute to a representation of public opinion. With a few exceptions, individual users were not the focus of the coverage rather than how their expressed views or actions represented the public mood. The one Facebook user comprised in the news coverage of all three outlets was an Icelandic initiative calling on Icelanders to open their homes to refugees. The page received 12,000 likes within days[1] and was treated in news coverage as representing public sentiment towards the refugee crisis. The other two users shared by the BBC and France 24 were a Syrian refugee and activist living in Vienna and a Hungarian TV station. The TV station attracted media attention due to footage tweeted by a German journalist, showing its camerawoman tripping up a man carrying a child as refugees broke through a police line. Hence, it was an extenuation of a news piece that originated on Twitter and did not fall into the trend of how Facebook was used as a newsgathering tool.

---

[1] Iceland has a population of 300,000.

Text analysis

Journalists as sources

As the quantitative analysis shows, tweets by journalists were sourced extensively. Analysis of some of the news texts shows how journalists reporting on the refugee crisis were given special coverage by news organizations based on the popularity of their social media content. With Twitter best understood as a many-to-many publishing platform (Kwak et al, 2010), news organizations were able to integrate it most easily into their traditional one-to-many broadcasting style. Essentially, journalists were able to report through Twitter, and their content was promoted by peers and news organizations that gave prominence to some of the most popular content they produced.

For example, photojournalist Daniel Etter, who was commissioned by the New York Times to cover the migrant crisis, was interviewed by the BBC Outside Sources show after one of his photographs attracted huge amounts of attention on Twitter. The photograph showed a father's tears of relief as he disembarked an inflatable boat after safely landing on the shores of the Greek island of Kos. Etter went on to win the Pulitzer Prize in Breaking News Photography in 2016 for his photo series of the refugee crisis. A tweet by @BBCOS on the 20th of August reads, "We speak to @DanielEtterFoto whose incredible photo of a refugee family has gone viral." The program could not be reviewed at a later date as it was no longer available online. However, a summary and other available information about it on social media showed that Etter was interviewed about his personal experience of witnessing and photographing refugees arriving in Greece, as well as his reaction to seeing his photo gain so much traction. The photo also received a special mention in a news piece titled "10 moving photos of Europe's migrant crisis" which was published by BBC Magazine two weeks later. A short text accompanying the photograph included a tweeted comment by an Irish journalist for Ireland's leading broadsheet Irish Times, saying, "An entire country's pain captured in one father's face."

The coverage of this photograph was framed as guided by its impact on social media. It was not simply a compelling photo by a professional photographer but a photo worthy of coverage thanks to it 'going viral.' The popularity on Twitter was taken to be an indicator of the image's ability to capture the public's interest.

The photo was first published by the New York Times on the 16th of August 2015 and some of the earliest mentions of the photograph on Twitter originate from New York Times staff accounts[2]. A look at all the tweets mentioning @DanielEtterFoto[3] in reference to the photo throughout the day showed many of them were journalists, including journalists working for Wall Street Journal, NPR and Vice. The photo was also tweeted by Barry Malone[4], producer of AJStream. Given that AJStream is plugged into social media communities, the tweet unsurprisingly received thousands of retweets. Etter tweeted the photo himself on 17th of August, captioned, "I am overwhelmed by the reaction to this family's tears of relief. This is why I do what I do." In the coming days, the photo went on to be featured by many international news organizations and their journalists. The reconstruction of the earliest users to share the image shows that professional journalists played a significant role in the distribution of the photograph on Twitter for several days. Effectively, the BBC's coverage simply contributed to building public awareness of the image and helping it 'go viral' further. The choice of a tweet by the Irish journalist to contextualize the photograph in the BBC Magazine news text underscored the weight given to journalist users in selecting what content makes the grade for news coverage. As perhaps expected, often this content is created by peers.

In a BBC Trending story published on 10th of September, a photo by BBC correspondent Manveen Rana was featured for 'going viral' on Twitter. The photo was described as showing a policeman hugging a Syrian toddler near a crossing in southern Serbia and the news text was framed as discussing why the photo attracted so much social media attention. The headline of the news text said, "Why this picture of a migrant child being hugged went viral." In the title the photo of a BBC journalist was contextualized as pertinent in the eyes of the public. The first six paragraphs of the news text described the scene and quoted Rana on what she witnessed at the border crossing putting the spotlight on her as the reporter. In the fifth paragraph, Rana was quoted on the Twitter reaction she received to the photo from Serbians. Only in the seventh and eight paragraph were tweets quoted from Serbians without identifying the users. In contrast to the headline's claim, the public debate was not given prominence in the news text. Rather the focus was on the BBC correspondent and her content. Rana was the main subject of the report, she was given voice through being named and cited over several paragraphs, while social media discussion independent of her was buried far down in the text. The fact of the social media

[2] Accessed at https://twitter.com/CeylanWrites/status/632945206862721024 and https://twitter.com/zeynep/status/632947936402501632
[3] Accessed at https://twitter.com/search?l=&q=%40DanielEtterFoto%20since%3A2015-08-16%20until%3A2015-08-20&src=typd&lang=en
[4] Access at https://twitter.com/malonebarry/status/633045091142254592

reaction itself was framed to give importance to her social media content and explain its worthiness of special coverage.

In the BBC coverage, creating a 'buzz' around the social media content created by professional journalists, and BBC reporters especially, was found to be a core element of their social media newsgathering routines. Social media was not only a reporting tool, or a newsgathering tool but also a promotion tool that has integrated interactive newsgathering. While publishing news content through social media platforms is a part of almost every news organization's distribution strategy, it was the reciprocal relationship between news organizations and individual reporters in distribution news content that stood out in the findings.

Although interactive newsgathering using Twitter was less prominent in the France 24 sample, it also placed one of its own reporter's Twitter activity at the center of several news reports. In a text headlined "The journey to exile notebook," three France 24 correspondents reported on joining refugees on their travels along the Balkan route to central and western Europe. The text featured a photo of the reporters at the top and presents a diary running from 31 August to 4 September that concludes with a feed to one of the reporter's Twitter account, @Fernande_VT, embedded at the bottom. However, already in the lead, the news text points to her Twitter activity and links to the account. Attention is drawn to the journalists reporting from the frontline and news audiences' ability to follow their latest updates in real-time on Twitter. Again Twitter was shown to serve mainly as a tool for diversifying news content distribution. Twitter is used primarily as a one-way broadcasting platform with the difference that journalists broadcast their content directly to audiences without the intermediary of the newsroom and its editors. The attraction to tune into one journalist is hinged on the appeal of their news content. The website serves as a preview to what this journalist might offer news audiences on Twitter. Calling attention to their own correspondents in this way is also prevalent in the BBC coverage, which highlights Twitter lists of their journalists to follow and incorporates their Twitter activity in its online news texts extensively. As audiences source their content from a huge selection of sources, news organizations push their own correspondents to the fore as becoming best-placed sources making social media engagement appear as a marketing ploy.

While the France 24 text also included some of the images shared on Van Tet's Twitter account, most of its content was reporting done exclusively for France 24's online website. In the most part the journalist's Twitter account featured content different from that presented on the website making the crossover between the two is less prominent than in the BBC's texts.

Al Jazeera English did not elaborate on journalists' role as social media sources, focusing mainly on interactive newsgathering as a way to foster participation by non-elite users. In one report, Al Jazeera journalist Barnaby Phillips described his week on a refugee rescue boat in the Mediterranean. The report featured a photo Phillips tweeted looking out over the sea from a cabin. While Phillips recorded his experiences on Twitter, the report did not mention his Twitter account nor cited the social media platform as the origin of the photo. So, while Al Jazeera correspondents were using Twitter in the same way to report and distribute native news content to audiences, the news organizations did not use its own proprietary platform as a feedback loop.

Conclusion

The findings in the case study of the migrant crisis have shown a reliance on professional news media and journalists as the most prominent and influential sources in interactive newsgathering. When looking at social media newsgathering in isolation, this suggests a shift in the hierarchy between primary and secondary definers whereby journalists are found to be influencers rather than just reporters. This is not only true inside the ecosystem of one news organization—for example, the BBC promoting its own reporters—but journalists interact and promote each other's work collectively. While the news environment on social media platforms may be open to widespread participation, the interaction between this sphere and the news organizations is tightly managed and often remains true to the hierarchy of traditional gatekeeping. The adoption of social media for newsgathering and distribution has created a loop between journalists and news organizations promoting one another. Oftentimes, professional journalist were sources that became primary definers of the news reports. Even in the news texts by Al Jazeera, which largely avoided sourcing social media content from journalists, non-elite users had a similar source power as in the BBC and France 24 texts. Therefore, professional journalists have benefited the most from social media engagement in terms of obtaining access to mainstream news media for their content. The collaborative news production that would foster a news media that reconnects with audiences through inviting widespread participation (Papacharissi, 2016) remains stunted as news organizations apply different formats of collaboration to non-elite users and elite users, with a strong hierarchy evident.

Acknowledgments

Special thanks to Dr Michael Foley, Dr Charlie Cullen, and Dr Harry Browne, and the Dublin Institute of Technology, where this research was carried out.

References

Benkler, Y. (2006). *The wealth of networks: how social production transforms markets and freedom*. New Haven: Yale University Press.

Bruns, A. (2006). (2006). Towards Produsage: Futures for User-Led Content Production. In F. Sudweeks, H. Hrachovec, & C. Ess (Eds.), *Cultural Attitudes towards Communication and Technology* (pp. 275–284). Tartu, Estonia.

Bruns, A., & Burgess, J. (2012). Researching News Discussion on Twitter: New methodologies. *Journalism Studies*, 13(5–6), 801–814.

Chadwick, A. (2011). The political information cycle in a hybrid news system: The British prime minister and the "Bullygate" affair. *International Journal of Press/Politics*, *16*(1), 3–29.

Gillmor, D. (2004). *We the Media*. Retrieved January 28, 2018, from http://www.authorama.com/we-the-media-8.html

Hall, S. M., Critcher, C., Jefferson, T., Clarke, J., & Roberts, B. (1978). *Policing the crisis: mugging, the state, and law and order*. New York: Palgrave Macmillan.

Hermida, A. (2010). From TV to Twitter: How Ambient News Became Ambient Journalism. *MC Journal*, 13(2), 1–10.

Hujanen, J. (2016). Participation and the Blurring Values of Journalism. *Journalism Studies*, *17*(7), 871–880.

Jenkins, H. (2006). *Convergence culture: where old and new media collide*. New York (NY): New York University Press.

Kwak, H., Lee, C., Park, H., & Moon, S. (2010). What is Twitter, a Social Network or a News Media ? Categories and Subject Descriptors. Www 2010, 591–600.

Papacharissi, Z. (2015). Toward New Journalism(s): Affective news, hybridity, and liminal spaces. *Journalism Studies*, *16*(1), 27–40.

Rosen, J. (2006, June 30). *The People Formerly Known as the Audience*. Retrieved January 28, 2018, from https://www.huffingtonpost.com/jay-rosen/the-people-formerly-known_1_b_24113.html

Shirky, C. (2009). *Here comes everybody: the power of organizing without organizations*. London: Penguin Books.

www.ingramcontent.com/pod-product-compliance
Lightning Source LLC
Chambersburg PA
CBHW070918270326
41927CB00011B/2632